Midge and Wayne
In The Middle East

By
Mildred Thompson Olson

World rights reserved. This book or any portion thereof may not be copied or reproduced in any form or manner whatever, except as provided by law, without the written permission of the publisher, except by a reviewer who may quote brief passages in a review.

The author assumes full responsibility for the accuracy of all facts and quotations as cited in this book. The opinions expressed in this book are the author's personal views and interpretations, and do not necessarily reflect those of the publisher.

This book is provided with the understanding that the publisher is not engaged in giving spiritual, legal, medical, or other professional advice. If authoritative advice is needed, the reader should seek the counsel of a competent professional.

Copyright © 1995 Mildred Thompson Olson
Copyright © 2008 TEACH Services, Inc.
ISBN-13: 978-1-57258-342-9 (Paperback)
Library of Congress Control Number: 2008926808

CONTENTS

1. Furlough Time 1
2. Getting Back To Business 12
3. Tragedy Strikes 23
4. The Best Of Times And The Worst Of Times 36
5. Beware The Ides Of March 48
6. Summers, Sea, Sand, And Surfing 52
7. Paul Never Had It This Good 55
8. Checking Out The Seven Churches And Patmos 69
9. Home Again 97
10. Medical Cadet Corps At Middle East College 102
11. New Year, New School, New Students 105
12. Living In Daniel's Land 116
13. Finding New Friends 127
14. God Works Overtime 144
15. Revolt And Revenge 155
16. Death Of A Hospital And The Aftermath 183
17. Iranian Odyssey 193
18. On The Damascus Road 206
19. Good Samaritans 217
20. The Unexpected 227
21. The Empty Nest 232
22. Goodbye, Middle East 242

Epilogue
A Review Of The Next Thirty Years 250

Appendix
Missionary Children 260

DEDICATION

I dedicate this book to:

All our friends in the Middle East. Fond memoreis will always be associated with that part of the world because of you and what you mean to us.

The children I taught in the elementary schools in Beirut, Lebanon, and Baghdad, Iraq, and their siblings and the missionary children in other Middle East countries whom I knew. In the appendix I have named you in my "Who's Who" list of special people.

My husband of almost 50 years, Wayne E. Olson, who left me a heritage of loving memories.

My daughter Ronnalee who critiqued my manuscript, my son-in-law Kermit Netteburg who put my manuscript into book form, and my friend Karen Cothren who helped wtih the finishing touches.

Until we meet again,

Mildred Thompson Olson

BLACK SEA
GREECE
Philippi
Istanbul
Thessaloniki
Neapolis
Berea
Troas
Pergamos
Thyatira
TURKEY
AEGEAN SEA
Sardis
Smyrna
Philadelphia
Athens
Ephesus
Corinth
Kasadasi
Laodecia
Tarsus
PATMOS
Antioch
RHODES
SYRIA
CRETE
CYPRUS
Damascus
Beirut
Sidon
Tyre
LEBANON
ISRAEL
JORDAN
Dead Sea
EGYPT
SINAI

CHAPTER 1
FURLOUGH TIME

Sweat glistened on the suntanned backs of the longshoremen as they loosened the hawsers of the S.S. Enotria and flung them free from the mooring. Italian crewmen deftly reeled the thick manilla ropes in through the hole in the ship's bow onto the winches. Then tugboats gently nudged our passenger liner out of the Beirut Harbor until it drifted into the open sea. The captain ordered the engine crew down in the steaming belly of the ship to rev up the motors. The ship vibrated as the engines took hold and powered the craft through the lapping waves of the Mediterranean Sea.

As I stood on the deck of the ship waving farewell to our friends back on the dock, I remembered how, as a child, I had always wanted to be a missionary on furlough—visiting churches, wearing exotic costumes, displaying unique collectibles, and telling thrilling stories about the advancement of the gospel. Now I was a missionary, and I was beginning my official furlough.

Contrary to my childish imaginings, being a missionary had been neither prestigious nor glamorous. There were no "heathen" in Lebanon; they were educated people who believed in God the Creator. But they had not greeted our message with open minds, nor had we baptized souls by the hundreds. It had been six and a half years of hard work fraught with dangers, disappointments and disease. We had been delivered from death only because God willed it so. (See the book, *Midge in Lebanon*).

The anticipation of "a big trip on a big ship to see big America" had overly stimulated our children, David and Ronnalee, ages five and seven. They were like Mexican jumping beans.

Wayne and I were exhausted. We had spent two hectic months buying gifts for relatives and shipping them, along with costumes and memorabilia, ahead of us. Now, after selling some of our goods and storing the rest of it with other missionaries, we were finally on the ship homeward bound. I had talked so much about America that David decided he'd rather go to America than to heaven. I felt ambivalent. I looked forward to seeing our relatives, but leaving our Lebanese friends and the other missionaries, who had become family, divided my allegiance.

When the pine-covered mountains of Lebanon slipped from our view, we went down to explore our cabins. They weren't "Hilton" class, but they would do until we reached Naples. Or so I thought. Suddenly David burst into the cabin.

"I've got to go to the toilet!" he exclaimed breathlessly—in Arabic, of course.

"Well, go," I answered. "It's right down the hall."

"But I want an ARABIC toilet with a hole in the floor, like the one we had in our house in Kafarhazier."

"David, you've seen stools in many of the houses in Lebanon. "

"But I didn't use them. I went outside."

I sucked in my breath. Where had I been when the urges had overtaken him? Why had this toilet situation taken me by surprise?

"David," I said, "you'll just have to use a stool. That's all they have on this ship."

"No, I'll wait until we get to Italy."

"Five days is a long time," I sighed as I pulled the reluctant customer down the hall to the facility.

That wasn't David's only complaint. He wanted Arabic or American food. He didn't like pastas, which is a tough condition when you're stuck on a small Italian liner. Fortunately, that situation resolved itself when David discovered the fun of eating spaghetti.

"Look, I'm pulling up the anchor," he laughed as he sucked up a long strand of spaghetti into this mouth.

"Poor manners; happy kid. When we get settled, I'll work on that lad," I thought.

The waiter patted David on the head and called our blond, blue-eyed boy a "little prince." David hardly deserved the compliment; he now complained about the Italian language. "They can't talk either English or Arabic."

"David," I scolded, "there are hundreds of languages in this world, and you'll hear more of them as we travel through Europe."

"Well, they talk Arabic in heaven, so that's the language I'll speak."

It suddenly dawned on us that Arabic WAS the only language David spoke fluently. He understood English reasonably well and sometimes spoke a little, even though he ridiculed it as "chicken talk." Now we'd have to reprogram our son to communicate in English with our friends and relatives in America. This furlough wasn't starting out that great, but I comforted myself with the thought that it could only get better.

Five days later we landed in Naples, unloaded our suitcases, and stuffed them into a taxi. Piling in around them, we sped off to Pompeii and Mt. Vesuvius. The remains of Pompeii are marvelous but we were repulsed by the lewd references made to perverted sex and reckless pleasure. No wonder God destroyed the city.

Then on to Rome. At St. Peter's Square, a pickpocket relieved Wayne of his billfold containing $100 in cash. Was this furlough really getting better?

Wayne bought Eurail Passes for our tour of Europe. By the time we relayed six suitcases and four carry-on bags down the train platform, we were frazzled. Wayne slumped into his seat in the compartment.

"Midge, I've already learned the basic furlough rule—travel light. Hiking all this baggage around is tuckering me out."

"Me, too. And the children are too small to handle the heavy things, but they do help by sitting guard on the bags while we transfer them from point "A" to point "B".

Cheer up, Wayne. We'll only be doing this a dozen more times."

"Yeah," Wayne sighed. "There'll be at least a dozen more stops as we make our way through Italy, Switzerland, Germany, Holland, and England. Well, we're stuck with the luggage for now. Next furlough we'll be smarter."

One of the highlights of the next two weeks was spending time with Pat and Arvil Bunch in Germany. She washed our clothes and fed us well. We left Bunches ready for the rest of the trip. The baggage, however, continued to plague us.

The kids had loved all the modes of transportation—train, bus, taxi, dog-cart, gondola, ferry, and two-decker buses—but the best was yet to come. When we boarded the luxury liner, the S.S. United States, in Southampton, England, the children were ecstatic. They loved the elevators, making as many trips as possible on them—with or without an excuse. The play rooms, the children's programs, and game time filled their days with joy.

Down in the dining room the waiters hung around David and Ronnalee; they enjoyed listening to the children chatter together in Arabic. They pampered the kids by giving them anything they wanted. David and Ronnie took advantage of their good fortune, requesting American ice cream at every meal. They called American white bread "silk bread" because it was so soft and squeezy. I didn't even attempt to lecture them on the nutritional value of whole-wheat versus white bread; I'd discuss that later at home—if we ever got there!

After a marvelous six-day passage, we were almost reluctant to leave the comforts of the S.S. United States and start our tussle with those plagued suitcases again. Fortunately, brotherin-law Clarence Christian met us at the docks. We piled into his car and found our way to a motel outside of New York. I couldn't sleep that night. There were no bars on the windows of the motel. After living six and a half years in Lebanon, I had grown accustomed to having bars on the windows of my abode.

Without that security, I was sure I had lived long enough only to be killed on American soil. But, like David and his complaints, I learned to adjust.

In Maryland we purchased a 1953 Chevy and felt like royalty as we drove across America. Since there were many miles to cover, we ate on the go. Wayne claimed that David and Ronnie could spot a Dairy Queen "a mile down the road and around the corner." Our furlough was definitely improving. We gave gifts to our relatives and whittled our suitcases down to three, plus, of course, the hand luggage that the kids thought was essential.

Furlough time was sharing time. We gave many programs in churches of different denominations. We dressed in costumes and showed our memorabilia just like other missionaries had done at my church when I was a child. But there was a difference. The missionaries of my childhood days had seemed so saintly, so "setapart." Why didn't I feel that way? I was just plain Midge—no different, no better, no saintlier than anyone else.

We were happy to tell what God had done for us and through us in soul winning, and display the interesting artifacts that related to Biblical customs or history. But the more I spoke about Lebanon, the more anxious I was to finish our furlough and return "home."

We settled for the winter in Takoma Park where Wayne completed his Master's program at the seminary. I studied education at Washington Missionary College. Ronnalee went to J.N. Andrews Elementary School completing both first and second grades that year.

By this time, David spoke English well. We sent him to public kindergarten along with two other boys who lived in our apartment building. David Clark and Laverne Schlehuber's parents had been missionaries in Africa. When those boys saw the huge, golden earrings worn by their teacher, they assumed she was a heathen. It wasn't difficult for them to persuade David that she was. Among the three "missionary-keteers," they passed the word along. At the first parent-teacher conference, the teacher informed me that she was not a "heathen" as our boys had labeled her. I apologized profusely. When I got David home, I explained the basics of Dale Carnegie's "How to Win Friends and Influence People." David wasn't impressed. Since David didn't care for the confinement of school, and his popularity with the teacher had obviously waned, we decided to keep him home second semester. Taking care of him was no problem; Wayne was at the apartment when I wasn't. Everyone was happier with this arrangement.

Both sets of parents came to visit us in Takoma Park for a month. We had a wonderful time showing them around Washington, D.C., and Virginia. Wayne took them up to New York to see the "Big Apple." Coming from the plains of South

Dakota and Kansas, the skyscrapers of New York overwhelmed them.

My mother wanted to see Ellis Island. It had been almost 50 years since she passed through this point of immigration as a 23-year-old German fraulein. It brought tears to her eyes as she viewed the place of her first contact in America. Passing through Ellis Island was a demeaning and fearful experience for most immigrants; but if they passed the physical, psychological, and work-eligibility tests it was a passport to their dreams.

"I came to America to fulfill my dream," she mused. "Wayne and Midge left it to fulfill their dream. I gave birth to her in America, and she had David in Lebanon. Life is an enigma, but wonderful if we let God lead."

Wayne took the foursome to Philadelphia so that my dad could see the point of his immigration. He had been a 13-year-old lad from Denmark then. Eleven years later he married the neighbor's hired girl, who had just immigrated from Germany. The serious German and the fun-loving Dane had made a good match. This was the year of my parents 50th anniversary.

Though all four of our parents were in their late sixties, they survived our packed agenda very well. We six adults and two children even drove down to Miami, Florida, to spend Thanksgiving with my sister Gladys and husband

Bill Ring. The month spent with our parents became the most memorable part of our furlough.

After Christmas Ronnie's tonsils gave her trouble again, so the doctor suggested that both children have their tonsils out. We informed the children of the decision, and they thought it sounded quite exciting: sleep overnight in a hospital, drink grape juice, and eat ice cream. Innocent darlings! We trundled them off to Washington Adventist Hospital and Wayne stayed with them. I was a basket case—the idea of someone cutting in my children's throats made me nauseous and scared. The children recovered and so did I, but they decided tonsillectomies were NO FUN. They wouldn't recommend it to anyone. Ronnie gave such a graphic account of her hospital experience to the neighbor boy that he vomited.

Our weekends were very busy. Almost every Friday night or Sabbath, we had appointments in various churches.

Sometimes we had quite a distance to travel. The children became weary of being away from home every weekend, of wearing costumes and singing Arabic songs. They didn't think being missionaries on furlough was all that great. During one evening program, David found release from his boredom. He had worn his costume, sung his songs, and was, I supposed, back sitting on his chair. But while Wayne was off the platform changing costumes and I was speaking, I noticed that the audience's attention was diverted to the right side of the stage. Snickers rippled through the crowd. I stopped talking and looked to their point of interest. There was David, sitting astride the banister, slapping the wooden rail behind him. He was completely oblivious to anyone or anything around him. He was a cowboy riding the plains. What was worse, he had pulled the plug out of his reed flute and pretended to be smoking it. I was humiliated. We were giving a program for a large Lutheran congregation, and we certainly didn't want them to think that Wayne smoked. I plucked David off his "horse" and handed him over to a teenage girl who liked caring for him. Never again did we let the children stay on the platform for any length of time. We had them do their part and then sent them to a back room where they could play quietly.

The winter passed quickly, and soon it was time to pack again. We didn't need to buy many things to take back with us. By 1954, almost anything from any place in the world could be purchased in Lebanon. We shipped our boxes and barrels to New York so they could go with us on the ship scheduled to sail in three months. In May, we headed West again.

General Conference was held at the Cow Palace in San Francisco that summer, and we were invited to attend. What a THRILL! Winona Olson, our sister-in-law, took care of the children so we could devote our fun time to the convention. That certainly was a blessing for me since I had written an hourlong play for our Middle East program. The play proved to be difficult to produce, however. There were no microphones to fasten to the actors, so we had to use a double cast the stage actors who mimed everything and the people backstage who read the script. The actors memorized their lines and said them to their cohorts on stage as the people on the microphones synchronized their lines with the actor's performance. Then to complicate things stiff further, we had to use labor union workers to do the lighting. Since there were no curtains to pull, the actors changed props in semi-darkness. I was thankful when it was over; the cast had carried it off successfully.

Then it was time to say our goodbyes. We visited the Olsons on their fruit farm on Appleton Road near MiltonFreewater. David and Ronnie liked to "truck" around behind Grandpa Ole as he irrigated his apple trees. They also found a few good trees to climb. When they were "starved" from their activities, they could always depend upon Grandma Ada to have a scrumptious meat waiting for them. Grandma increased her popularity by making delectable fruit pies smothered with sweet whipped cream. Grandma even made a fancy cake for Ronnie's eighth birthday.

Five days before heading back East, Ronnalee showed us her surprise. "Look at the mosquito bites on my tummy," she said as she pulled up her shirt.

"CHICKEN POX!" Wayne moaned. "What do we do?"

"Wait and see how long it takes her to get over them," I suggested.

A few more pox broke out on her face and arms, but Ronnie felt fine. We tried to keep David away from her, but they'd always been inseparable so he was thoroughly exposed. In five days Ronnie's pox had all but disappeared so we headed for South Dakota before David came down with them. We figured we had at least five days. However, the first day on the road David became lethargic. By evening pox were popping out all over him. We spent the night at my sister Jean Combes's house in Boise. Ile next morning David was worse. We were in a quandry. If we stayed until he recovered, we would miss the family reunion and my parents 50th wedding anniversary. We concluded that David would be no worse off lying on the back seat of the car as we drove to South Dakota, so we left. That night we stayed in a motel with the owner's knowledge that our son had chicken pox. We spent most of that night comforting David. He did not have just a CASE of chicken pox, he was literally plastered from head to toe. He had them in his ears, nose, mouth, and eyelids. It was simply incredible. Ronnie had gotten by so easy—never missed a meal nor a full day of play. Poor David suffered the agony of Job.

David recovered at my parents home in South Dakota. The children loved roaming about the 160-acre farm, watching the cows, sheep, horses, chickens, ducks, and geese, and playing with Fido, the collie dog. Running through the rows of tall corn and riding on the hay wagon or big John Deere tractor with Uncle Julius came pretty close to their idea of utopia.

A few days before the anniversary was the Thompson family reunion. It was fun being together—seven of us eight children, the in-laws, and most of the grandchildren. We chatted and played games together as we had when we were young. We prepared a special anniversary program for our parents which we gave for the 200 guests who came to celebrate with us. And then it was all over. It was the perfect ending for a busy furlough.

Wayne left for the Medical Cadet Corps Training Camp in Michigan. After a week, my parents put the children and me on the train bound for New York where we would rendezvous with Wayne. Ronnalee behaved like a little lady on the train, playing with her dolls and reading, while David practiced medicine with his little doctor's kit. He examined my heart. "Mommie, you don't have to worry. Your heart's not beating at all!" he exclaimed in a voice loud enough to entertain half the people in the car.

But my heart was beating. In fact, it was hurting. Though I would be happy to stop living out of a suitcase and set up housekeeping in Lebanon again, I would miss my family. To be separated for six years from one's kin is a very long time; so much can happen. I had a disturbing premonition. Every clack of the wheels on the track seemed to say, "Before you return to America someone dear to you will be missing."

I tried to push the thought from my mind. I tried to convince myself that nothing was likely to happen. It was ridiculous to borrow sorrow for tomorrow. Everyone was well. Our parents had given us their blessing to return to Lebanon.

It was a fine day in August when we boarded the Norwegian freighter S.S.[1] at Hoboken, New Jersey, and sailed for the Middle East. I was uncomfortable with this ship, however, because of a well-publicized incident connected with it. One of its crew members had murdered a passenger two days before the ship arrived in Boston. He'd thrown her body into the ocean and assumed that the fish would devour the evidence. Five days later, however, her body washed ashore. Investigators solved the crime quickly, and the perpetrator was incarcerated. But

---

[1] I chose not to the name the ship to protect its anonymity.

I worried that he might have a colleague left on the ship. Wayne's assurance that we were perfectly safe, didn't convince me of anything. What did a minister know about crime and criminals other than it was a sin to kill?

We enjoyed traveling on freighters because they carried only 12 passengers. We got well acquainted with the crew, ate at the Captain's table, and had the run of the whole ship. Wayne and the children especially enjoyed going down to the engine room to watch the motors work.

Freighters also made many stops. Ile first stop excited me—a scheduled, two-day layover in Casablanca. Quickly getting permission, we left the ship and toured the city. Then dock workers called a strike and our stay was extended three more days. This gave us time to tour the countryside, swim in the Atlantic Ocean, and visit other ships anchored in the harbor. We even attended the Adventist Church where Wayne delivered the Sabbath morning sermon.

Our next stop was in Tunis to unload freight. We enjoyed watching the young boys dive into the ocean for shells. They came up with some perfect specimens, and we purchased them. Of course, our cabins took on the smell of rotting fish as the creatures inside the shells deteriorated. When I could tolerate the smell no longer, the captain made a special place for them.

At Malta our ship delivered two coast-guard cutters. We had time to disembark and explore the island. When shipwrecked, the Apostle Paul had spent the winter here.

The next port of call was Beirut. When we saw the umbrella pine-covered mountains of Lebanon come into view, we knew we were almost home. Our furlough was over.

CHAPTER 2
GETTING BACK TO BUSINESS

When we left the states, we hadn't been told what our work assignments would be for our second term, but we were anxious to get back to business.

Ile harbor was full of ocean liners the day we arrived in Beirut, so our little freighter had to anchor outside the bay. There would be room for our ship to dock the next day, but we wanted to disembark immediately. We couldn't wait to put our feet back on Lebanese soil and see our friends. We gathered our luggage on deck and waited for a dingy to transfer us to land. The Mediterranean was calm as usual, so going down the wobbly gangway latched to the side of the ship should pose no problem. Except for me—I had an aversion to those steps that hung out over the sea. Furthermore, I hated the big, scary leap from the last step down into the boat. As I looked over the railing, I heard someone calling our names.

"Hi, Midge and Wayne! Down here." The Funds signaled to us from a little boat bobbing in the waves by the side of our ship.

Alice, how good to see you again!" I shouted excitedly, forgetting all about my fears. "Whose baby are you holding?"

"It's ours—Nancy Lee. Six months old now."

"She's surely a little doll."

Fund's six-year-old son stood in the middle of the boat, waving and grinning broadly. "Hi, Larry," David yelled. "Got any new Dinky cars?"

Larry held up three fingers.

"Come on down," Arthur said. "You're staying with us until you find a house. The crew will lower your luggage in a rope sling."

A ROPE! I wished they'd let me down in a net like they did the luggage, but I knew they wouldn't. So, in a spirit of generosity, I let David and Ronnie climb down the steps first just to try it out. They made it look so easy.

"Wayne, would you, ah, please go down ahead of me, and, ah, catch me in case I fall?" I begged.

"No, Midge. Get control of your fears and just do it."

Wayne cheered me on as I eased my way down the gangway. Arthur guided my feet as I dropped into the rocking dingy. I breathed a sigh of relief.

"Piece of cake," I bragged. But my nerves were still blowing fuses in my electrical system. I was happy to be in the boat and not in the water.

Wayne zipped down the steps and joined us. Then we motored to the wharf. At Funds' home, we enjoyed a great meal. Three weeks of Norwegian freighter food made us crave a change of menu.

As Wayne enjoyed second helpings of Alice's cooking, he regaled them with stories of our ship's cuisine. "The bread and cheese on the ship were good, and we managed the other food fine, until—" Wayne grinned and looked knowingly at me. "Until they served Midge's favorite dessert. All week long the captain talked about the Sunday dinner treat. He gave the Norwegian name for it which meant nothing to us. Finally, the first mate described it as a special pudding. Now that sounded good to all of us. Sunday noon came, and the pudding was served. We looked at it a bit suspiciously; it had a grayish color and strange odor. Finally, Midge followed the captain's lead and ate a few spoonfuls. I could tell by her facial expression that she had no intention of asking for seconds, so the children and I just sat there with our spoons in limbo, waiting for more information from her.

"'How do you like it?' the captain smiled, obviously relishing the dessert.

"'I, ah, well, it's different. VERY DIFFERENT.' Midge admitted.

"'Now I 'member the English vord' he said. 'It's bloot bloot putting.'

"With a look of disbelief and repulsion, Midge asked, 'BLOOD! Blood like from veins?'"

"Yah, fom da cows," he replied snarfing down his pudding.

"Midge dropped her spoon, rushed from the dining room, leaned over the railing, and you know the rest."

Everyone laughed—except me. It was not a pleasant memory.

The day after landing in Beirut, we met with Elder Hartwell, the union president. He told us the committee voted for Wayne to follow up Bible Correspondence School leads and work with the Beirut Arabic Church. This meant we would live in Mouseitbe, a suburb of Beirut. That situation was both good and problematic. It was good because we would live near Wayne's work and the Lebanese church members, but our children would have to live in an asphalt jungle. There was no yard connected with the rented apartment nor a nearby park where our lnds could run off their wiggles. The neighborhood children played on the streets and sidewalks, but that seemed dangerous to us.

Then we were presented with a partial solution to our problem. I was asked to teach the elementary school for missionaries' children up on the mountain slope where Middle East College was located. This would get the children and me out of the city for a good part of the day; but it also meant that the children and I would have to commute up to the college every day. I couldn't use our car since Wayne needed it to deliver correspondence school certificates and follow up leads.

Getting up to my school was a real problem since there was no public transportation. Finally, that dilemma was resolved. Two of our church members from Mouseitbe worked at Middle East Press which was also on the college hill. These men hired a regular taxi to take them to work every day. If I shared expenses, the children and I could ride with them. I didn't like having to get the children up so early every morning to catch our ride, but we had to make some concessions.

Another complication developed. Our unit on the second floor of a new apartment complex would not be ready for at least a month. The Funds had generously shared their quarters with us for two weeks, and we felt that to stay longer was imposing on them. So, when the Appels invited us to spend that month with them on the division compound, we accepted their offer. It was an ideal setup: Appel's house was adequately large; Elder Appel, who was the division president, would be gone most of the time; we could be of help to Mrs. Appel; and our children would be in the country where they could play with the other children living on the compound.

The Middle East Division compound was located near the bottom of Jabil Septia (Adventist Mountain). The mountain slope was named for the Adventists even though we did not own all the land. The college property extended over 70 acres near the top of the mountain. There was over a mile of privately owned property between the college and the five acres near the bottom of the hill where the division compound was located.

The compound was completely enclosed with an eight-foot high, chain-link fence. The gate opened onto the public road that led to the top of the mountain and Middle East College. Near the gate was the president's house with the office building across from it. The builders had filled in a ravine across from the parking lot and walled up the lower side of that short strip where the roadside dropped steeply into the valley, but they hadn't put a railing on top of the wall. Going up and around the loop was a triplex for single workers, a guest apartment, and four other houses. The only flat land on the compound was the parking lot. But the children considered the hill a plus; neat inclines allowed wagons to roll down to the parking lot. Of course, there was the less desirable task of pulling the wagons back up the hill, but the kids were able to balance the advantages with the disadvantages.

While in the states, David had been fitted with glasses. He loved his glasses. With them, he could SEE. But when David looked down under the rim of his glasses he couldn't judge distances very well. He had broken his arm when he fell off a wall in Takoma Park while playing follow-the-leader with the kids. Now he was on the compound where walls and trees challenged the climbing instincts of our adventurous, almost-six-year-old boy. We made David promise to take reasonable precautions. Eight-year-old Ronnalee volunteered to be security guard for her brother—she much enjoyed being big sister boss.

Wayne put David's new bicycle together, and the children on the compound took turns riding it. Ile compound was not an ideal place to ride a bike since it was hilly and there was that one steep retaining wall near the office building that had no protective railings. We warned the children to stay away from that area. But one day David came zipping down the hill on his bike, looked down through his glasses, and misjudged his distance from the wall. He soared off into space and crashed onto the stones and shrubs below.

The other children screamed, "David's killed himself." With that hysterical cry the division offices emptied as workers poured out of the doors and rushed to the scene. They recovered David, scratched and bruised, but fine other than another broken arm. The bicycle also survived the olympic leap.

While we waited for our apartment to be ready, the mission asked Wayne to be pastor for the Youth Camp up in the mountains. September 12 he went outside his tent to exercise, slipped on some slick pine needles, and fell forward on his head. This scrunched up his back and sprained his wrist. He didn't think the injury was serious just very painful. He continued to work four more days. Then the pain got so severe that he went down to AUB (American University of Beirut) Hospital. The x-ray showed that he had cracked a vertebrae. This curtailed his activity for the next six weeks.

The apartment was finally ready October 3. We went to garage Wes of embassy personnel and picked up some respectable, second-hand furniture. We gathered the things we had left with other missionaries and in the school attic—11 places in all. Then we bought a secondhand, four-door Opel car and were ready for business.

One day Mary Wehbe, a 17-year-old girl with hip dysplasia from a village in North Lebanon, came to our door. She wanted to go to our Mouseitbe Mission School. She hadn't gone to the school much in her village because it was too far for her to walk. She'd studied at home but now needed higher academics. She could easily walk the block from our home to the Mission School, but she didn't have the money for private education. We gladly took her in to live with us and paid her tuition. We both had paying jobs now, and it was an opportunity for us to share our blessings. (We were always happy that we had helped Mary. She was a bright girl and became an excellent teacher in our mission schools).

Before we were really settled, Alice Muellim came to us with her problem. She was a seamstress and had gotten work in a tailor shop in Beirut. She wasn't making enough money yet to rent an apartment so she needed a place to sleep and eat for a few months. It was our privilege to have her join our family, too. We put our two children in the same bedroom and gave the girls the extra room.

Hazel Geraty, wife of Dr. Thomas Geraty, president of Middle East College, started the school year while I got settled. In November, I took over the cherubs—and I do mean cherubs. It would be quite impossible to find a nicer group of children to teach. They were eager learners, cooperative, polite, fun, talented, and creative. I could exhaust my vocabulary of complimentary adjectives on them and not be exaggerating. I thought they were especially saintly, given the unique situation in which the school was housed. School was held in two, small, connecting offices at the end of the Industrial Arts Building of the college. Sometimes the whine of the saws made communication almost impossible. At such times, I'd have to write instructions on the chalkboard or give them a recess.

Since we arrived at the school early in the morning, I asked Graham Keough to come in then so I could teach him privately. He was 14 years old and in the seventh grade. He had lost some schooling due to a head injury. However, he had fully recovered from the accident, was a brilliant student, and eager to learn. I got permission from his parents to push him through both seventh and eighth grades that year. His savvy in math and sciences amazed me; it was sheer pleasure to tutor Graham. At 8 A.M. the rest of the students arrived.

Susan McCulloch and Charles Jones, both sixth graders, shared the smaller room with Graham. In the larger room were the younger children. David was still a free spirit, but had a private corner in the classroom. Alger Keough and Teresa Jones were in the first grade. Michael McCulloch, Ron Geraty, Norma Keough, and Ronnalee made up the third grade class. Those children learned their lessons very rapidly and then completed the enrichment program I had devised. I couldn't keep them occupied. We didn't have a library per se, but the children brought books from home and shared.

When the lower-grade children had put in their allotted school time, I let them out to play. David roamed the hills with them or with his sidekick, Tommy Gott. The children always came back with interesting trophies they found on the hillsides. One of their finds, which repulsed me a little, was the bleached, fleshless skull of a horse. They played with that head for days. They discovered that a small yank would remove the teeth, one at a time. Then the challenge for them was to put the teeth back in the right places. They mastered that puzzle in a few days.

Ron and Mike had the future of their classmates all mapped out. Ronnalee would marry Ron. He would become a doctor and she a nurse. Mike would marry Norma. She would become a teacher and he a businessman.[1]

---

[1] Norma became a teacher and a minister, Mike a businessman, Ron a doctor, and Ronnalee a nurse. Their childhood ambitions were realized, except they each married someone else. (See appendix at the end of this book.)

While we were occupied on the college hill, Wayne was having exciting experiences with the correspondence school leads. Delivering graduation certificates took him all over Lebanon. The correspondence courses were a popular past time for the villagers, and they answered the questions precisely. However, the end results were disappointing. People were convinced but not convicted. It was impossible to study further with each student individually because they were so widely scattered and Wayne was only one person. Some of the young people from the college went with him at times, but it was usually only a one-time visit. One new convert, Salim Husbani, went with Wayne to Baalbek to visit some leads. Salim was thrilled to tell what Jesus meant to him, and the people were impressed. But that was the end of it. It took a whole day to go to Baalbek and back. Salim was still in college and didn't have the time or the money to do more.

Elder George Keough, the head of the correspondence school, often wrote personal messages in the lessons he returned to the students. He had lived in the Middle East for many years, was fluent in the Arabic language, and knew the culture. The students enjoyed reading his encouraging missives but even that did not result in conversions. The students needed the personal touch and many more hours of study. Although they believed the doctrines to be right it was not convenient for them to change. One student's comment at the end of a lesson on baptism revealed his pitiful lack of comprehension: "I believe in baptism. Send it to me by mail?" Ile remark was humorous, yet pathetic. He really hadn't understood the significance of baptism.

Lebanon was a peaceful and prosperous country in those days. After World War 11, the Lebanese economy soared and international banking flourished. Merchant ships could once more ply the Mediterranean safely, and the Lebanese imported goods from all over the world. Since there were no trade barriers, choice products from foreign countries filled Lebanese shops. Lebanese had all the modern conveniences available to people anywhere. In a material way, Lebanese were better off than most people in the world. How different this stint was from our first term when common commodities had been at a premium, if they could be found at all. It was simply incredible how rapidly times had changed.

Television stations sprung up in Beirut, and people were glued to their sets. This new form of entertainment adversely affected the attendance at cinemas and nightclubs, and it had a devastating effect on religion. Arabs, who are known to be shrewd financiers, were either too busy earning money or enjoying entertainment. Therefore, although some students accepted the gospel message, the correspondence school lessons were not as effective as we would have liked them to be.

A 16-year-old lad from the village of Zaraphen (Zarapheth of Elijah's day) took the Bible correspondence lessons and was converted. His family, though moderately wealthy and educated, belonged to a fanatical religious group. They became very angry with Nasser because of his conviction. Routinely, his father beat him severely, but he always stopped before Nasser went unconscious. The father didn't want Nasser to die before he had forced him to change his mind. Finally, in a fit of anger, the father threw Nasser out of the home without even so much as a change of clothing. Nasser came down to our Arabic School in Mouseitbe and told his story. The principal gave the youth his books and tuition, and permission to sleep on the floor of a classroom. But this did not care for his physical needs. Occasionally his mother secretly sent some cooked food to her son with a friend, but Nasser had to eat it cold.

God let us minister to Nasser during this period. A mattress on our living room floor in a heated room was a luxury to him. His gratitude for warm food and showers were touching. This opportunity for sharing with Nasser cost us so little, but gave us much satisfaction. The first night I looked up to heaven and prayed, "Jesus, I never imagined I would have a young man from Zarapheth sleeping on my living room floor! Would you please tell Prophet Elijah about it since he lives up there with you now?"

The Dorcas ladies gave Nasser blankets, several changes of clothing, and a haircut. Nasser looked like a new man—his bruises had healed, his hair and eyes shone, and he was dressed in modem, clean clothes. Arabs am naturally hospitable and willing to help one another, so Nasser's stay in our home was short. Since we already had the two girls and couldn't give Nasser the benefit of a private room, another family took Nasser into their home. He finished the school year, got a job, and took care of himself after that. He was one trophy resulting from the Bible lessons.

One day Wayne was on a service taxi going down to old Tyre in southern Lebanon. (A service taxi has a specific route, somewhat like a city bus, but is more flexible.) Wayne wanted to take advantage of the hour-long ride to Tyre. He explained his work to his traveling companions. He was amazed to learn that, among the five men, two of them had taken the Bible lessons. They were happy to meet a representative of the correspondence school, but they didn't plan to change their religious philosophy.

When he reached Tyre, Wayne discovered that most of the Bible students lived near the sea. He walked into a business near the wharf and asked where he might find the individuals named on the certificates. Immediately he was surrounded by a citizens' guard. Since Tyre is close to Israel, people were very suspicious of him and his work. Was this foreigner some kind of spy? An agent for the CIA? Was he secretly compiling information on the town's people?

Repeatedly Wayne explained who he was and his mission. He told them why he wanted to see certain individuals. Even though the certificates validated his statements, yet some men followed him. They escorted him to the homes of the correspondence school graduates and listened to the conversation. Wayne tried to get his self-appointed guards interested in taking the Bible lessons, but with no success. At last, they were satisfied he was who he claimed to be and left.

When he was free to go on his own, Wayne walked down to the docks where the fishermen were gathering their nets, preparing for another night's fishing on the open sea. He told these Moslem men about God and the message of Jesus in the New Testament. "We'd like to sign up for these lessons about Allah," one man said, "but, sir, we can't read or write. Could someone just come and teach us?"

Like the Syro-Phoenician woman of Christ's day, they wanted some of the crumbs that fell from the master's table. Wayne turned away sorrowful because he knew the church did not have the resources to send a preacher with some "crumbs" to feed them. A few years later the mission voted a budget to send a worker to Tyre. Then the political trouble in Lebanon intensified and curtailed work in that area, but God knows the hearts and desires of the people of Tyre. Surely some of them are bound for heaven.

In spite of the fact that Wayne was sometimes frustrated with the impossible task of studying the Bible with all the correspondence school students, he was reaching some. I was thoroughly enjoying my job, too. It was good to be back in the business of winning souls in Lebanon.

CHAPTER 3
TRAGEDY STRIKES

It was the Easter season and time to buy summer shoes for the children. David hated going to town for anything except Dinky cars, so Wayne dropped Ronnie and me off at the shoe market, and he and David went home.

Since I had nearly died so many times during our pioneer days in North Lebanon, I was afraid I would not live to see my children grow into adulthood. Therefore, I started having them make their own decisions at a very young age. Ronnie took her time windowshopping for shoes, knowing the decision was hers to make. Finally, she saw just what she wanted—white slippers with daisy cut-outs across the toe.

The shop owner was taken with our vivacious, little eightyear old. He offered her all kinds of bonuses—candy, gum, and trinkets. But the toy that topped her list was the atomic bomb. It was a simple toy, like a cherry bomb, that made an explosive sound when dropped on the terracotta floor, hence its name.

"I'm going to share this with David," she informed the shop owner as she waved goodbye.

"And you come again, little princess," he said.

As usual, we went to the comer where the Sudanese vendor sold her fresh, hot-roasted peanuts. With Ronnie in town, the lady could be certain of a sale. "Atini miatain gram fistu, ifudleck," she said in Arabic. Then the two exchanged smiles while 200 grams of peanuts and 50 piasters exchanged hands.

That's what was special about Ronnie. Her ready smile and zest for life spread an aura of caring like a blanket of sunshine to those around her. And people melted under the love expressed in her soft, brown eyes. She did it innocently, unaffectedly. It was her God-given gift.

We walked to the busy street corner where we caught the service taxis for Mouseitbe. But when a service taxi stopped at the curb, other people crowded in ahead of us. In seconds the five passenger seats were taken, and the taxi was off. I tapped my foot impatiently while I waited. I was anxious to get home to prepare dinner for the family and grade papers. Ronnie, on the other hand, was relaxed and pleasant, smiling to all the passers-by.

"You know what, Mom?" she said, matter-of-factly, "I wouldn't care if I should die tonight."

I jerked to attention, startled by Ronnie's reference to death. "Whatever would make you say a thing like that, Child?" I gasped, trying to suppress my shock.

"Oh, it's Easter. Jesus died at Easter time and was resurrected and went to heaven. If I should die tonight, I'd see you in heaven. Jesus will resurrect me, you know," she stated confidently.

I was shaken by her statement. Why would the subject of death even enter the mind of a healthy, bubbly eight-year-old girl? Did she have a premonition of impending doom? A chill swept over me, and I shivered in spite of the warmth of the March evening. Ronnie's ominous words encircled me like a black cloud. No longer was I concerned about getting home, making dinner, or grading papers.

Then Ronnie startled me again. "Mom, I just prayed that Jesus would help us get a taxi right away 'cause you look pale and tired. "

Blessed innocent! Precious, observant child! How could she know that it was my fear for her life that creased my brow.

The next thing I knew, Ronnie and I were gently pushed into a taxi by a kind man. Then, two other passengers crawled into the empty seats, and we were off for Mouseitbe. As the driver careened through the crooked, narrow streets of old Beirut, I was glad I had sandwiched Ronnie between me and the pleasant fat man. That was the safest place for her, I thought.

"Jesus answered my prayer in a hurry, didn't he, Mom?" Ronnie was saying. "I'd hardly finished praying before the nice man helped us into the taxi."

"Yes, Darling," I murmured, marveling at her pure faith.

The taxi driver let us out at our street corner, and we climbed the steps to our second floor apartment. As we prepared dinner, Wayne and I discussed the day's events. I couldn't bring myself to tell him about Ronnie's bizarre conversation.

The dinner hour was pleasant, and the normalcy of our daily routine helped to push the strange foreboding into the far recesses of my mind.

After dinner Ronnie brought out the atomic bomb toy. David was delighted with the explosive sound. Then Ronnie, always anxious to improve upon a situation, thought the bomb would make an even louder sound if it was dropped from a greater height. So, she got the wooden ladder and placed it against the lintel of the bathroom door. Above the door was the opening to a storage area. From the top of the ladder, Ronnie dropped the bomb. David danced excitedly, retrieved the bomb, and tossed it back to his sister. When we observed what the children were doing, we sensed danger. But before we could stop them, David returned the bomb with a mighty sling. It landed in the storage room. Quick as a cat, Ronnie scaled the ladder, climbed onto the ledge of the storage door, stood up, and cracked her head on the low ceiling. The impact caused her to lose her balance. Filled with horror, we raced to catch her as she toppled from the storage door, head first toward the floor. But we couldn't reach her in time to save her. She fell with a thud to the floor. Her head hit the sharp, marble threshold (or sill), leaving a depression in her skull from the left temple to two inches behind her ear.

Her crumpled little body lay inert. Carefully Wayne rolled her onto her back. Was she dead? Her neck broken? Her back? Wayne finally found a weak pulse and tried counting her irregular heart beat. I hyperventilated, David cried, and Alice, our house guest, prayed.

Wayne covered Ronnie with a blanket and raced for the door. "I'm calling Dr. Nachman. I'll wait for him in front of the building. Don't move her!"

Wayne was back in twenty minutes with Dr. Nachman in tow. "Bad skull fracture," was the Doctor's temporary assessment. "Move her carefully to your car and rush her to the American University Hospital. I'll meet you at the emergency entrance with the best neurosurgeon in Lebanon."

"Is Ronnie going to die?" David sobbed as Wayne carried her to the car.

"We hope not," Wayne tried to assure him, though his confidence was clearly shaken. "We'll be back later, Davy. Pray like a big boy and be brave." Then we kissed our son and left him with Alice to share their tears and fears.

In ten minutes we were at the emergency entrance to the American University of Beirut Hospital (AUB Hospital). Dr. Nachman and two attendants met us outside. Gently they placed Ronnie on a gurney and wheeled her into x-ray. Dr. Fuad Haddad walked into the room and took charge. This brilliant young doctor had just returned from extensive neurosurgical residencies in Canada, England, and the United States.

After examining many x-rays, he faced us. "Honestly, I can't render a complete diagnosis since x-rays can't tell us exactly what is going on inside her skull. But her deep unconsciousness and other symptoms indicate that she has a serious skull fracture. The blow to her temple might have killed her immediately, but—ah—the accident still may be fatal."

I steadied myself on the gurney. Would she die tonight?

We were numb with fear as we followed Dr. Haddad and the gurney carrying Ronnie to the children's ward. They settled her into a bed. We waited.

At nine that night we called Elders Appel and Hartwell who came to the hospital, anointed Ronnie, and had special prayer. Then Wayne stayed with our darling while the men drove me home to get David. Elder Appel insisted that David and I go to the mission compound to spend the night.

Mrs. Appel, the mission's grandmother figure, helped David and me get settled in her spare bedroom. David's face was awash with tears, and sobs shook his little body. We prayed and cried together. I cuddled my son, finding comfort in holding his warm body in my arms.

David dropped off to sleep, but I could not rest. Ronnie's words haunted me, "If I should die tonight—Jesus will resurrect me—I'll see you in heaven."

Early in the morning David awoke. "Is Ronnie okay?"

I swallowed the lump in my throat and blinked back team. "I don't know, Davy. But Jesus will heal her if it is His will."

My classes were canceled for the duration of Ronnie's illness or—. I spent Friday in the hospital with Ronnie and Wayne; David stayed with Gordon and Evelyn Zytkoskee and played with Cherry and other children on the compound.

Late that afternoon Ronnie sat up in bed briefly, but she was not lucid. She didn't remember what had happened to her, nor much else. Still, I took this as a good omen. The doctor, however, cautioned us that our hopes were not justified. Soon I could see that he was right. Toward evening Ronnie became lethargic, then lapsed into unconsciousness.

Friday night Ronnie slipped into a deep coma. I went back to the division compound to an anxious little boy; Wayne stayed at the hospital with Ronnie. Saturday morning I was back in the children's ward. As I entered the room there was a flurry of activity around Ronnie's bed which frightened me.

"Mr. Olson," the doctor spoke hurriedly, "go down to the office and sign papers for immediate surgery. Either the brain is swelling or there is bleeding to the extent that it is affecting her involuntary muscles. We have to go in and relieve the pressure right away. Time is of essence."

Wayne was out the door in an instant. I stood helplessly by, listening, watching. The doctor gave orders in Arabic. "Make sure the operating theater is ready and call my assistants. Ask the cardiologist to come. This child's heartbeat is so erratic she may not even make it to surgery."

Was this it? I grasped the door casing for support. The room spun dizzily, but I didn't want to faint. I wanted to be there for Ronnie, even though I couldn't get close to her. The medical staff was so busy they didn't seem to notice I was there. Furthermore, no one guessed that I knew Arabic and understood perfectly what they were saying.

The cardiologist swept into the room. He gave Ronnie a cursory examination, straightened himself, and looked Dr. Haddad in the eye. "I'm not going into surgery with this patient," he said in Arabic. "She's as good as dead now. You can't get into her skull fast enough to relieve the pressure on the nerve centers controlling her involuntary muscles. Listen to her shallow, irregular breathing. Her heart is crazy. In the same minute it races, then almost quits. You know, Dr. Haddad,—"

"I know her parents believe in God. Thursday night a group of them had special prayer for her. I never heard such prayers. I have to try to save her. If I don't, I'll let her parents and God down. I'm going in, with or without you."

Then he signaled to the orderlies. "Get her up to surgery immediately."

Two orderlies whisked in with a gurney. They slid Ronnie's limp little body onto it and took off running. I supposed it was the last time I would see her alive. A few minutes later the orderlies wheeled Rome back into the room. She lay so still I was certain she had already died.

Dr. Haddad poked his head around the door. "Why isn't my patient in the operating room?"

Dr. K. said to take her back here to die,—they explained. "I'm going to operate on her! Get her upstairs PRONTO! Shave her head while I scrub," Dr. Haddad ordered.

I looked at my watch. It was a few minutes before 9 A.M. We called the Arabic Church, Middle East College Church, and the Armenian Church to update them on Ronnie's perilous condition. Elder Appel phoned churches in other parts of the Middle East. At I I A.M. Adventist Christians all over the division were praying for Ronnie's recovery. A few Lebanese and fellow missionaries came to the hospital to support us through the most difficult day of our lives.

At noon a young Polish doctor came into the waiting room. My heart stood still. "Dr. Haddad sent me down here to report that he is into the brain area." Then she detailed the surgery. "First he laid back the skin, then drilled three holes so that from the initial break he could saw out a rectangular piece of bone two by four inches. He found that a sliver of bone had punctured a large blood vessel. Now he is suctioning off the blood clot pressing on her brain. I'll be back to report to you again as soon as I have more information."

Wayne thanked her. My stomach turned—her graphic description of sawing Ronnie's skull open and suctioning out blood made me shiver and gag.

Though we didn't know how to process all the young doctor's information, we knew Ronnie was still alive. From the whispered conversation of the medical staff, we knew that as many of the doctors who could free themselves from their work were sitting in the operating theater watching Dr. Haddad perform a most delicate surgery.

By I P.M., more friends came to offer their love and concern. They almost filled the hospital waiting room. From time to time we gathered in groups for prayer. Then we waited for the next medical bulletin.

Every hour the Polish doctor appeared and assessed us of Ronnie's situation. Down deep in our heart we all knew everything was not right. It was what she wasn't saying.

Shortly after 4 P.M. Dr. Haddad himself appeared and called Wayne and me into his office. He looked exhausted, and well he should; he had spent the past two nights in the doctor's lounge to be near Ronnie. Now he had just completed a sixhour plus head surgery. We could tell by the distressed look on his face that he did not have good news for us.

"I left my assistants to close up. Ronnalee is still alive, but ... Well, things don't look good. Her comatose condition is so deep that I operated on her without anesthetic."

I gasped at the thought, but Dr. Haddad assured me that she felt nothing. He continued. "We found multiple cracks in her skull—some going up and over the top of her head and some through the base of the skull. Sort of like a cracked walnut. But our major concern is the obvious damage to the brain itself. First of all, it is a wonder the initial impact to the temple area didn't kill her. It was, however, those shattered pieces of bone in the temple area that were the real culprits. They ripped up brain tissue and punctured a major blood vessel. The oozing blood flooded the skull and depressed the brain, affecting the involuntary muscles. All the while her brain was deprived of the nourishment the ruptured vessel should have been supplying to her brain. This caused further damage to the brain. Do you know what this means?"

We held our breath. We dared not venture a guess.

Dr. Haddad sighed deeply. "This means—A—that she can never be normal. For instance, she will not be able to talk since the speech center is located on the left side of her brain. The left hemisphere of her brain is irreparably damaged; which means—A—she will never be able to function mentally." Dr.

Haddad paused a long time. He was tired, and he was sad. His devotion to Ronnie was touching. He had wanted it to turn out differently. "I'm sorry," he said with a slight tremor in his voice. "It would be better if she doesn't live. She will be only a vegetable. " He shook his head and rested his chin in his hands.

Although it was hard for us to talk, we thanked Dr. Haddad for his valiant effort and left to tell our friends the bad news. At that moment, as if to augment the report, two orderlies, followed by several nurses, came down the hallway wheeling Ronnie back to her room. She was a pitiful sight. Her head was swathed in bandages; her eyes and cheeks were swollen even with her nose. Tubes were attached to every limb. I groaned within me. "My baby! My precious child! How can I give you up? 'If you should die tonight . I'll see you in heaven.'" Then I wept uncontrollably.

Friends escorted me to Laura Appel's home. I could not face David. The Zytkoskees took care of his needs. George Gott stayed in the hospital with Wayne. Ronnie needed to be guarded constantly to keep her from hitting her head on the bed rails. Sometimes she tossed so violently that there was danger she might dislodge the bone piece that had been laid back onto the skull and held in place only by the skin. Further, the shattered pieces of bone had to be thrown away, leaving a hole over her temple the size of a silver dollar. In case she might live, Dr. Haddad would have to operate again to cover the hole with a silver plate; but at this juncture, it seemed like an unnecessary procedure.

That night we told our friends to pray Ronnie would not live UNLESS she could live a normal life. We knew this would take a miracle.

The next few days became routine. Ronnie remained comatose. Laura Appel and I stayed in the hospital with Ronnie during the day while Wayne went home to sleep. Some of the mission men took turns spending the night with Wayne at the hospital. It was a very stressful vigil.

Sunday, Monday, and Tuesday passed. No change. Wednesday morning Wayne claimed Ronnie responded to his questions which led him to believe that she heard and understood him. Wayne had put his finger in her hand and said, "Ronnie, if you hear me, squeeze my finger." He believed she squeezed his finger and informed the nurses of this. After Wayne left for home, the nurses said to me, "Mr. Olson has been here too long. He is hallucinating. He should stay away from the hospital for a few days lest he snap."

"Yes," I responded, "I suppose so, but I know he won't leave Ronnie."

Several times during the day I placed my finger in Ronnie's hand, but didn't get even a flicker of response. Night came and the men and we ladies exchanged guard duty again.

Everyone living on Jebil Septia and the college property knew of Ronnie's accident. A doctor who lived on the mountain discussed Ronnie's condition with Laura Appel. "I, along with several of my colleagues and a dozen medical students, watched the six-hour surgery. Dr. Haddad is a brilliant neurosurgeon, but even his skill could not change the Olson girl's outcome. The left lobe of her brain is chewed up."

We had accepted the fact and were praying that God would take Ronnie quickly or recreate her brain miraculously.

Early Thursday morning the phone rang. I-aura tensed as she handed the receiver to me. "It's from the hospital." I took the phone in my trembling hands and held my breath.

"Midge, MIDGE!" It was Wayne's voice. Words tumbled from his lips. "Come to the hospital immediately. Ronnie's talking! She's becoming alert and making sense. I asked her a question, and she answered it. I told the nurse. At first she wouldn't even come to the room because she didn't believe me. Now she's excited, too, and has called the doctor. He's coming over." Wayne paused for breath.

"I'll be right down to the hospital!" I said, hanging up the phone. I shook as I dialed the Zytkoskees to tell them the news.

"Great news!" Gordon exclaimed. "Let's go to the hospital. I'll stop by Appel's house in five minutes to pick you up."

I hopped into the car with Gordon, still trembling with excitement. Gordon covered the ten miles to the AUB Hospital in about as many minutes. Then he left me at the hospital entrance while he parked the car. My heart beat wildly as I sprinted through the lobby and down the hall to the children's ward. I burst into the room on the heels of Dr. Haddad. I watched intently as he examined Ronnie.

"I'm your doctor, Honey. Will you talk to me?"

"I don' wanna talk. I'm tired," a faint little voice mumbled.

"Praise Allah!" Dr. Haddad exclaimed. "This is absolutely amazing! I've got to tell my colleagues. They won't believe this. The child can talk! And clearly, too." Then, turning to me he added, "Kiss the ground."

I knew what he meant. When an Arab knows he has seen the hand of God at work, he kisses the basic substance of God's handiwork, the earth, acknowledging Him as the creator of all. Though he may not literally kiss the ground, his reference to the act is his testimony of faith. Dr. Haddad was telling us that he had seen a miracle.

The news of the miracle spread throughout the hospital like sand whipped by a strong west wind. All day long a procession of nurses, doctors, hospital personnel, staff, and friends paraded through the children's ward. The object of their attention was busy gorging herself on juices sucked through a straw, or sleeping. Conversing with people was not high on her priority of "do's. "

Dr. Haddad came into her room every hour and plied Ronnie with questions. She answered him as briefly as possible, if at all. However, by afternoon Ronnie had some questions of her own. "Am I in a hospital?"

"Yes, Sweetheart," Dr. Haddad answered, rubbing her cheek gently with his finger.

"Why do I have a cap on?" she queried feeling of her bandaged head.

"Because you fell and hurt your head. I operated on it and God fixed it up for you."

"Oh." And Ronnie lapsed back into sleep.

By late afternoon she awakened and told Dr. Haddad, "I want to go home."

"Why? What's special there?" Dr. Haddad asked, testing her memory.

"A brother and a new puppy."

"What are their names?"

"My brother is David, and my dog is Teddy."

Dr. Haddad winked at me and whispered, "Is it true?" I nodded. "Then she is remembering, too. Terrific!" he smiled.

"When can I go home?"

"Tomorrow, if you can walk a straight line."

"I can do that, but I can't see unless I turn my head."

"I know," Dr. Haddad sympathized. "You bumped your head so hard that your eyes are stuck in the left side of their sockets. But, in a month or so, they will gradually move back into place."

Then he turned to me. "Since God took over her case, her recovery is incredible. God must have re-created her brain—a miracle is what I wrote on her chart. I can't do anything more for her. She may as well go home tomorrow."

Thursday afternoon I telephoned the news of Ronnie's remarkable recovery to the college and division offices.

Friday held still more surprises for us. I watched as Dr. Haddad took off the bandages. When the incision was exposed, Dr. Haddad drew back and let out a low whistle. "Wow! Would you look at that? Not a bloody spot. Stitches dissolved. It's clean and white—looks like a three-month-old scar. This is another miracle."

Then he picked Ronnie up and balanced her for a few minutes. When she was steady on her feet he told her to walk down the line.

Ronnie cocked her head so she could see the floor from the left corner of her eyes. Carefully she placed one bare foot in front of the other and walked a perfect line. Everyone in the room cheered.

Dr. Haddad turned to Wayne. "Go to the office, pay your bill, and take her home. "

Dr. Haddad and I chatted while I dressed Ronnie. Shortly Wayne returned. "Dr. Haddad," Wayne said, "I'm sure there is a mistake in the billing. They charged me 100 Lebanese Lira for the surgery instead of 10,000. This bill is only $33 American dollars."

"There is no mistake, Mr. Olson. I took only a token fee, and I feel guilty about that," the good man said as tears welled up in his eyes. "How can I take money for what God did? The damage done to her brain tissue by the splintered bone was irreparable. Then there was the matter of the severed blood vessel. Auxiliary vessels can develop to do the work, but how did it happen so quickly? It doesn't take a specialist to tell you that the brain goes dead when it doesn't get fed properly. Until yesterday I was a nominal Christian. Now I am really a believer. I've seen a miracle. I guess, after almost 2,000 years, it was time we saw another resurrection, wasn't it? Happy Easter!"

CHAPTER 4
THE BEST OF TIMES AND THE WORST OF TIMES

We had seen the worst of times with Ronnalee's skull fracture. Now we were ready for better times. Two weeks after Ronnie's accident we returned to school. It felt good to be back to a normal routine, but fife for most of us would never be NORMAL again. We had all been sobered by the tragedy and amazed by the miracle. We realized more acutely that life was a precious gift from God, something to be cherished and enjoyed. Ronnie's naked head was a daily reminder of that.

The school children seemed more thankful, more thoughtful, more loving, more Christlike. Each child tried his or her best to help Ronnie adapt to her circumstances. Ronnie wanted to play softball with the children. Ron brought a helmet for her to wear so the ball would not hit the damaged area on her head. Graham pitched the ball so gently and patiently that even though Ronnie could scarcely see, she was able to connect with the ball. Norma and Mike read to her when her eyes could no longer focus. Each day her eyes appeared to be drifting more to the right, but improvement was slow. When Ronnie's nerves wore thin and weariness overtook her, Susan fixed a bed for Ronnie by her desk. She rubbed her back gently, and Ronnie relaxed. Charles, Teresa, or Alger held Ronnie's hand when she walked down the hill so she would not stumble and fall. What amazing, loving children!

Besides my schoolwork, I did what I could to be of service in the Arabic Church and at the college. I gave readings, helped with banquets, picnics, Dorcas, and wrote plays for special occasions. I sometimes spoke for vespers, chapels, or class presentations.

Wayne's program was even more involved. In March he was asked to be acting president of the Lebanon-Syrian mission.

This meant he would spend many Sabbaths speaking at the churches in the field and attending to the needs of the schools. He continued to arrange speakers for the Mouseitbe Arabic Church when he wasn't able to be there. He spent time consulting with Ibrahim and Najeeb Ghazal, the Adventist contractors, who were building the church in Mouseitbe. He was busy setting up mission offices in Mouseitbe for himself and treasurer George Yared. And last of all, he had to plat a graveyard on the useless hillside below Middle East College campus.

Sometimes our work involved unusual but interesting diversions. Matchmaking was one of them. By special request, we had been initiated into this business when we were in North Lebanon. Arranged marriages were not new to the Middle East. The Biblical story of Abraham's concern to find a proper wife for Isaac is proof of this custom. Today it works something like this: After a young man and young lady are attracted to each other, the young man divulges his choice to his father. If his parents believe the choice is a good one, his father will ask her father for the daughter's hand in marriage. Ile arrangement must be agreeable to all parties—the young people and their parents. If not, the process begins again. Often Christian young people select their own life partner and make the arrangements themselves just as we do in the states.

But what about the young people who were new Adventists? Since their Adventist acquaintances were limited, they needed a pseudoparent to direct them to suitable marriage partners. That was where we came in as matchmakers.

Ramon Bitar, a new Adventist from Syria, was engaged to a young lady whose faith differed greatly from his. We visited with the young couple and soon discovered that she was not suited for him socially or spiritually. We finally persuaded him to break the engagement.

She concurred with the idea. We promised to help him find someone more suited to his faith and talents.

One very dear girl came to our minds—Mary Nessimian. She had stayed with us during our first two summers in Lebanon and cared for Ronnie while I helped Wayne with evangelistic meetings. We thought Mary and Ramon were ideally suited for one another, but their paths hadn't crossed. Ramon was in business and Mary taught in our Armenian Church School. one Sunday in April we invited both Ramon and Mary to our home for dinner. After we introduced them to each other, they were suspicious of our motives. At first things were a bit strained, but soon the two outgoing young people didn't need us around. We celebrated their engagement in June and their wedding in September.

Helping with engagements and weddings became one of my favorite pastimes. They are the best of times. Ronnie reveled in participating in the weddings, but they bored David. Held rather be out in the country collecting frogs and chameleons with Tommy Gott. David, the Bible boy, and Cherry Zytkoskee, the flower girl, became regular choices for local weddings. When I informed David that he and Cherry were asked to help with Mary's wedding, he groaned, "Do I have to marry Cherry again?"

Summers in Lebanon are the best of times. I drove my children and their friends to the beach at least three times a week. The water along the Mediterranean shore is almost bathtub warm in the summer, and the waves are gentle. Some days we went inland to the sand dunes.

The summer sun and fresh air helped Ronnie's healing process. Her eyes moved back into place, and once again she was our carefree, vivacious little girl.

In July we took Ronnie to her appointment with Dr. Haddad. He placed her on the examining table and tested her mentally and physically to determine what permanent damage might have resulted from her skull fracture.

"Well, Mr. and Mrs. Olson," he said, obviously elated, "she is absolutely normal in every way—good muscle control, eye movement, and speech. Now let's see about that hole in her skull that needs the silver plate."

"Dr. Haddad," I interrupted, "when I wash her hair I've noticed that the hole has filled in."

"Well, it may have just a little, but skull bone doesn't HOLY MOTHER MARY! What is this? The hole HAS filled in! I can't believe it! When God does a miracle He doesn't stop halfway, does He? I'll add another 'miracle' to her chart."

Then, with tears in his eyes, he kissed Ronnie, and shook our hands. "It's been a thrill for me to have Ronnie as a patient. Through her miracle I got better acquainted with God."

We thanked Dr. Haddad and God. It was a big relief to know that Ronnie did not need surgery. Now we could lay specific plans for the rest of the summer.

That summer we had developed a fascination for Mount Hermon. Moses, Joshua, David and other Bible writers referred to it. Hermon marked the northernmost edge of Israel and the inheritance of Dan. Other writers spoke of the eternal snow that capped the mount. We saw and admired this majestic mountain every time we drove over the Anti-Lebanon mountain range to Damascus, Syria. The mountain became an obsession with us. We determined to climb it and view Israel, Lebanon, and Syria from its summit. Trying to get information about Mount Hermon was virtually impossible. No one we knew or met had ever climbed it. Someone told us that there were guides in a settlement at the base of the mountain that could help us find the right trails. Other than that, we had only the facts: Mount Hermon, located at the southern portion of the Anti-Lebanon Mountain range, is 15 miles long and rises over 9,000 feet above sea level.

The first part of August seemed like the best time to attempt the climb—the snow was mostly melted by then and the weather was as warm as it would get. Thirteen of us left hot Beirut packing heavy jackets, food, and water. Ile distance to the foot of the mountain was much greater than we had been told, and the last twenty miles of the road were almost impossible. By the time we arranged for guides and donkeys to carry our baggage, it was well after sundown. The night was ideal for the climb: a full moon rose over the snow-capped ridge, the breeze was comfortably cool, and two loaded donkeys and a jolly guide were willing and ready to go. We began the ascent in good spirits, fired with ambition. We expected to scale Hermon in a few hours. It didn't look very far.

We chatted and laughed as we started up the trail. After a few hours, our energy ebbed, and there was less chatting and laughing. Three hours later we became mutes. The climb challenged every fiber in our bodies, and the elevation caused us to suck air into our aching lungs. It took seven hours of huffing and puffing to reach the summit. Completely exhausted, we flopped on the ground and slept. Even the donkeys dropped their heads in weariness. We were reasonably certain that few other idiots had ever scaled this mountain. How surprised we were to find the remains of an old Roman temple on the crest of Mount Hermon!

The Bible tells us that pagans built altars on the "high places." Mt. Hermon must have been the highest of them all. Perhaps high-place worship was a throw-back to the Tower of Babel. But never could Babel, built on the plains of Iraq, vie with the heights of Hermon.

"This is incredible!" I exclaimed. "To think people actually put themselves through the agony of climbing this mountain to worship Baal!"

No one answered me. They were either too tired or too busy studying the graffiti on the stones—probably made by Americans. "Bob made it" was spray-painted on one rock. I wished I'd have a magic marker. I'd have inscribed, "Midge made it, too, and lost 10 pounds doing it."

We could see far south into Israel. To the east was Syria, and to the west was Sidon and the Mediterranean Sea. The view was breathtaking. It was a "best of times" experience. I was glad I had made the climb once, but I knew there would never be a repeat performance.

It took us only five hours to descend Hermon the Great, but we pampered sore muscles and squeaky knees for a week.

We were still in the limping stage of our "climb-recovery period" when one of the biggest thrills of our ministry occurred—the dedication of the new church in North Lebanon on August 20, 1955. Almost six years of our lives had been spent in pioneering the work in that area. There had been no Adventists when we went there in 1947; now there were enough to build a church. We had suffered all kinds of persecution to bring the gospel to the people of North Lebanon. The opposition had tried to stop us with stones, bombs, gunfire, dynamite, and ambush, but God had preserved our lives to raise up a people for His kingdom. When men failed in their attempts to stop us, a heart attack and colitis almost took my life.

We had wanted to build the first church in North Lebanon before we left on furlough. In March of 1953, George Yared, Arthur Fund, and Elders Hartwell and Appel had gone with Wayne to look over the available pieces of land. They selected a lot and proceeded to work on building permits. But it was the privilege of Dan and Gladys Kubrock, who took our place, to oversee the building of the church. A year later a junior academy was begun for the children of our new members in North Lebanon.

Both Wayne and I had grown up on farms, and we missed living in a rural environment. Living in the city of Beirut had been a trial for us. The division president agreed that it would be better for our family to move closer to my work on the college hill. So, in September we moved to Chafic Srour's duplex which was situated between the division compound and the college. Now the children and I could walk to school, and Wayne had full use of the car.

Wayne finished platting the Adventist Cemetery in October, which was none too soon. A beloved Armenian member died on an October Friday, and because there is no embalming in the Middle East, the government requires that interment be made within 24 hours. The funeral had to take place on Sabbath afternoon. This posed a big problem. Since summers in the Middle East are completely dry, the ground is too hard to dig a grave. But they HAD to dig a grave, even though it was like chiseling out cement. The family of the bereaved had asked other churches to allow them to bury their loved one in their cemeteries, but had been refused permission.

The Armenian pastor hired two porters from the city to dig the grave for his relative in our cemetery. They started Sabbath morning but by noon they had hewn out a grave less that a foot deep. College students came to the aid of the weary gravediggers. Some carried buckets of water down from the college and dumped it into the grave, trying to soften the dirt. The boys dug as fast and hard as they could with picks and shovels. When one tired, he crawled out and another youth took his place. By 1:30 P.M. the college students had excavated another four inches of dirt. But the grave had to be deep enough to hold the casket with an added foot of dirt to cover it.

Wayne looked at what appeared to be a hopeless situation. "How long do you think it will be before you're down three feet on the high side of the slope?" he asked.

"Tomorrow," one weary student volunteered.

"That's what I'm afraid of, " Wayne said as he kicked a rock from the path. "The funeral is scheduled to take place at the Armenian Church at 2:30 this afternoon. After the service we'll take the deceased up here for burial. We'll need the grave deep enough to hold the casket."

"Well, why don't you just tell the people about the problem we're having up here at the cemetery?" one student asked.

"I'd like to, but I can't," Wayne said. "There are people who will attend the funeral from other religions. Both the Protestants and Armenian Orthodox refused to bury our Adventist brother in their cemeteries. If I explain this at the service, they'll feel offended that I mentioned their prejudices. So I can't explain our problem. We'll need to wait until this grave is ready."

"I've got a solution," one young man volunteered. "Go ahead with the service as planned and keep going until we send a courier to the back of the church to notify you that the grave is ready. You may have to prolong the service a bit."

"I'd guess quite a bit," Wayne sighed. "I've thought about it all morning and have come to the same conclusion. I'll prolong the service, but let me know the instant you are within 20 minutes of finishing the gravesite. "

Down in the city, friends and relatives were already crowding the Armenian Church. It was very hot that October day, so everyone, except Wayne and the gravediggers, was prepared for a short service.

Wayne and Aram took the platform, noticeably late. "We'll begin the service this afternoon by singing some of our deceased brother's favorite hymns," Wayne announced in his best ministerial form.

Everyone who understood English gasped audibly and looked at one another in dismay. Congregational singing might be a novel idea, but not very acceptable.

Aram, noting the reception Wayne's announcement received, fidgeted nervously. Then he swallowed hard and translated into Armenian, "Ah, we, we'll begin the s-service by ssinging some of our b-brother's favorite hymns." Now the Armenian speaking part of the congregation gasped and looked at one another in dismay.

I was so embarrassed by Wayne's obvious deviation from the normal service that I wanted to evaporate into the stuffy air of the packed Armenian Church.

Six hymns later, Aram got desperate. "I'm not getting much cooperation from the congregation, " he whispered. "Can't you start with prayer or something?

"I started with prayer six hours ago," Wayne whispered back. "When the grave is deep enough for burial my prayer will have been answered. You go ahead and pray now and make it long."

Aram blinked, took a deep breath, and invited the congregation to pray with him. Aram prayed one of the longest prayers in the annals of funeral history. He reminded God of all the good deeds of the deceased, his family, his friends, his enemies, and everyone he could name in the congregation. I didn't understand Armenian, but I understood the restless mood of the crowd. Occasionally someone would peek to see if Aram was running out of verbiage. There were many amen "hints" from the congregation before Aram concluded his prayer.

Then Wayne launched into his longest funeral sermon, paraphrased, revised, and elaborated. He even included some illustrations and stories that were completely irrelevant. But it lengthened his sermon.

Next Mary Nessimian Bitar sang a solo which met with "amen" approval by the congregation.

When there was stiff no sign of a courier, Wayne launched into another sermon. It was extremely repetitious, but it used up more time. Aram did an amazing job of translating, but his energy was waning. "I'm, I'm about to faint. My throat is sore. I can't go on," he whispered hoarsely.

Wayne's brain shifted into high gear. He called upon the church elder to give an extemporaneous obituary. The amazed elder walked slowly to the platform.

"Elaborate, tell everything you can remember about him," Wayne spoke quietly into the ear of the good man.

"Why?" the elder, still in a state of shock, asked.

"Because the grave's not deep enough," Wayne whispered.

"You're joking!" the elder exclaimed in a voice loud enough for everyone to hear. Then he leaned back and, in disbelief, peered into Wayne's face.

"Sh," Wayne cautioned. "Just talk. Don't ask questions."

Joking! Now that's an inappropriate word to use at a funeral service. A buzz of whispered disapprovals rippled through the congregation as they chewed on that one. They wondered what was going on with the usually reserved Elder Olson. Death is not a joking matter.

"Please talk NOW," Wayne begged as he stumped into a chair on the platform and wiped beads of sweat from his face. Aram wilted into another chair. Both men had perspired through the armpits of their jackets. Ministers must wear black suits at funerals even when the temperature exceeds 90 degrees and the humidity hovers in the same range.

Crowded as we were in the pews, our bodies generated a lot of heat and perspiration. Fresh air became a premium. Even massive amounts of deodorant could not have purified the foul air. So, we waited and hoped to survive. Funerals are always the worst of times, but this was the absolute WORST.

After eleven minutes the Elder turned the meeting back to Wayne, who had kept his eyes peeled on the back door for the appearance of the courier. Wayne got to his feet, but Aram was done in. He couldn't translate or sing anymore. Wayne fumbled mentally for more ideas to prolong the service. He came up with another unpopular solution. "Let's have a few testimonials from the congregation about our brother," Wayne announced.

The audience groaned audibly. No one volunteered so Wayne called upon certain individuals to speak.

By this time, more than two hours had passed. Still no courier. People, who were still awake, yawned and raised their watch arm high. It would be disrespectful to the family of the deceased for them to leave the funeral service, but they obviously couldn't stand much more delay. Since Aram still hadn't recovered, Wayne called upon Mary Bitar to lead out in a few more hymns. The people were tired of sitting so Wayne had them stand. This awakened some of the sleepers, and they droned through the songs.

One lady behind me said to her companion, "That preacher has sung, prayed, preached, and eulogized the deceased for over two hours. I declare I think he's waiting for the resurrection so he won't have to bury Brother

It was 4:45 P.M. when the courier finally poked his head in at the back door. Wayne was jubilant. The congregation had barely sung the last words of the hymn when Wayne dismissed them with an unusually short prayer,

"Dear Father, please comfort the family of Brother . I thank you for the friends who help, ah, helped us. We long for heaven when no graves will ever have to be dug. In Jesus name, Amen."

Friends and family drove the five miles behind the hearse to the cemetery. By 5:15 we were at the gravesite and lowered the casket into its place. Because the grave was on a mountain side, the diggers were able to pile stones and dirt on the lower side making the hole appear deeper than it really was. After the crowd left, college students set the casket aside and worked through the night to make the grave deeper. Finally they were able to cover the casket with about 18 inches of soil.

Few people ever knew about the problem at the cemetery nor why Wayne had prolonged the funeral service that day. When the winter rains came and digging was easier, Wayne had several graves dug, then filled them in with brush. That way a grave was always ready for a casket.

The following Monday school began. The college decided they needed the two office rooms in the Industrial Arts Building, so our Beirut English Church School was moved to an end of the first floor of the girls dormitory. I had two rooms with a hallway between them. David, Tommy Gott, and Cherry Zytkoskee were in first grade. Alger Keough, Teresa Jones, and Roger Nolte, son of an American embassy family living on the hill, were in second grade. The Geratys had gone on furlough so the fourth grade had only Norma Keough, Mike McCulloch, and Ronnalee. David Rice and Charles Jones were in the upper grades. The children had no play equipment and only a small gravel spot for a playground. They were happy playing group games and never knew they were "deprived."

While we were practicing for our Christmas program, the worst of times struck Tripoli, North Lebanon. Three days of excessive rainfall in the mountains sent torrents of water rushing down the canyon. It overflowed the river's banks and flooded the estuary at Tripoli. Many homes were washed out to sea, drowning 119 people in mud or water. Hundreds of survivors were desperate for clothing, bedding, housing, and food. We spent the last days of the year in Tripoli giving out clothing, blankets, and food, but we could never replace what they had lost.

It had been a year filled with blessings, disasters, miracles, and progress. The events of that year had reinforced our trust in God; He had seen us through the best of times and the worst of times.

CHAPTER 5
BEWARE THE IDES OF MARCH

The 1955–56 school year began with the dedication of the new Administration Building on the Middle East College campus. Up until that time, the college dining room had been used for everything, and dormitory rooms were crowded in order that offices and classrooms might have space. Even with the new Administration Building it was a sacrifice for the college to give the English Church School the use of the two end rooms on the first floor of the girls dormitory. It wasn't convenient for us either. My students had to run through the dormitory hallway to use the unisex toilet. Some of them got conveniently lost on the way. Even this was certainly better than what they had in the Industrial Arts Building the year before; there they had to run outside in the rain, around the corner, into the building, and to the far end of the shop.

I was happy when Elders Appel and Keough asked me to draw up plans for an elementary school that would be built on the division compound. "It's a pity to shift those poor little kids from one building to another—never knowing for sure where they'll study the next school year," Elder Appel said.

"Amen!" I agreed. "It's also difficult for a teacher to split her attention between two rooms. It only works because the children are naturally good."

Drawing plans for a new school building was one of the happiest assignments ever given to me. Our enrollment of 10 pupils was small, but we needed to plan for the future. Besides the little ones waiting until they were old enough to go to school, there were other children on the college hill that wanted to attend our one-room school.

I drew a large class room and a smaller room that could be used for classes, teacher's office, or library. Then I added the luxury of separate toilets for boys and girls.

The blueprints were drawn up and given to a contractor. He promised to have the school building ready in time for the 1956-57 school year. With that pledge, the children happily endured the inconveniences of cold, unheated schoolrooms, long journeys to the toilet, no playground equipment, and makeshift desks. Next year they would have a permanent school, new desks, a real playground, and a warm room. How they anticipated these luxuries!

Wayne's appointment book was very full. The men at the mission and college worked full time during the week, preached on Sabbaths, provided entertainment for students and friends on Saturday nights, and had committee meetings on Sundays.

Sometimes, Wayne and Arthur Keough would squeeze a few hours out of their day to take my students on a field trip. The children enjoyed touring the tile factory and the diamond factory, a prosperous industry in Lebanon. Another favorite spot was the ocean reef north of Nahar el-Kalb (Dog River). There they observed colorful sea anemones, ink-squirting squid, and exotic fish.

All too soon it was that time of the year—MARCH. I dreaded for March to come because that was the month our family always seemed to have some serious problem. This year was no different—I came down with a bad case of viral pneumonia. Wayne took me to the AUB Hospital with a temperature of 104. In spite of penicillin injections, my temperature hovered around 104 for days. Lethargically, I slept the days away, forgetting to drink water. The nurses let me sleep. When Wayne came to visit he forced me to drink several glasses of water. His persistence saved me from having urinary problems.

School was canceled temporarily again this March.

During my second week in the hospital I learned of another Olson incident. While playing "kick-the-can" with the kids on the compound, Ronnalee had slipped and broken her elbow. Fortunately, it was just an arm instead of the job she had done on her head the March before.

Two weeks later I was home again, and we were rejoicing that March was almost over. Then the third disaster struck. Friday night while we were getting ready for bed, we heard a deep, fearful rumble that seemed to come up from the bowels of the earth. Then the house began to rock.

"Quick! To the hallway everyone," Wayne shouted. "It's an earthquake!"

It lasted only a few seconds, but it did its damage. Our area did not suffer much, but a few miles south it wreaked havoc with the old houses in the mountain villages. Whole families were buried in the rubble. Animals rotted where they had been struck with flying objects. In one place the earth cracked open, taking people, houses, and animals with it. Before they could climb out of their earthen tomb, another quake shook the crack closed.

The survivors needed help, and we had within our grasp what was needed to relieve their misery—three tons of used clothing in the wharf warehouse. But the government would not release the freight without our paying heavy customs. The mission couldn't afford the cost of the customs they demanded. This was both ironic and frustrating. The clothing was to be given to Lebanese people, yet the Lebanese government wouldn't allow us to bring it into the country; they believed they were protecting the interests of the three textile factories. Ile officials didn't seem to realize that people who had nothing could buy nothing.

The mission had exhausted the Community Service supplies for disaster relief during the December flood in Tripoli. Wayne had sent an SOS to the states for used clothing and blankets. Providentially, the General Conference responded immediately and shipped the goods. The bales were in the customs shed; now if we could only get them out.

Since Mr. Noujaim, Elder Appel, and Wayne could make no progress with the customs officials, they finally got an appointment with the president of the Lebanese Republic. The men were greeted cordially by President Camil Chamoun. After listening to their request, he proposed that they work through the Red Cross which was exempt from customs. The mission finally did this.

The Red Cross was happy with the windfall from us. They didn't have anything on hand to give the earthquake victims. They processed our relief supplies duty free and then proceeded to take the credit for supplying the needs of the victims. They dropped off only a few bales of clothing at the mission for us to distribute. We were disappointed that we could not have more contact with the victims, but were satisfied that most of the supplies were given to the needy.

"This March has served as a triple whammy, " Wayne said. "Next year let's just skip from February to April, or lock ourselves in the house during March."

I disagreed. "No, then we'd probably get poisoned on water or choke on a raisin. Julius Caesar was warned to 'Beware the Ides of March.' I guess we need to do the same. "

CHAPTER 6

SUMMERS, SEA, SAND, AND SURFING

Summers were always the best of times. The children sprouted proverbial fins as they spent time in the water. Wayne built a cement storage tank in our backyard that never filled more than two feet deep. It was a marvelous place for the children to splash and cool off. Their friends from up the hill or down on the compound often joined them at their private little swimmin' hole.

For real swimming, San Simone was our favorite beach. There I taught the children to swim. How I did that is a wonder considering the fact that I personally swam about as well as a kangaroo. I knew the rudiments of swimming, but didn't practice them very well. I hated getting salt water in my eyes and ears, so I kept my head above water. (The Mediterranean Sea is saltier than either the Pacific or Atlantic Ocean)

Every few weeks church folks would get together for a beach party. It wasn't necessarily an organized affair—just a come-if-you-wish sort of thing. Wayne would join us as often as he could. Ronnie and David liked it when Dad was there because they could go out further into the ocean and not stick with Mom in waist-deep water. While everyone else swam, I stayed near shore. The usual excuse for my cowardice was that I was "guarding everyone's stuff."

Another favorite sport of the children was to play on the sand dunes. About once a week I'd fill my car with as many kids as it would hold and head for the dunes. For two hours the children played—sliding down the steep dunes and then racing back up. When it was time to go home, I counted them—Eileen and Martha Lesher, Alger and Norma Keough, Mike McCulloch, Roger and Mae Nolte, Ronnalee and David. I'd brush as much sand as possible out of their clothes and hair, then stuff them into the car. I always ended up with a generous supply of sand on the seats and floor of the car, but the kids were happy and tired.

One day when the children were otherwise occupied, Dorothy Oster suggested that we go to the beach and go surfing. Of course, I had heard of surfing but had no desire to do it. Somehow that indomitable lady persuaded me to try it. "It's lots of fun, Midge," she promised.

Now Dorothy is one of the best swimmers I have ever known. I should have considered that carefully, and perhaps prayerfully, before I accepted the surfboard from her outstretched hands. As a child and youth I had always been willing to try anything that sounded like fun. Age and experience should have taught me to be more cautious, but it hadn't.

After Dorothy's pep talk, I had only one question: "How do you use it?"

"Just paddle out on it, catch a wave, and ride it in," she explained.

"Now what could be easier than that?" I thought. Just to be sure I understood her explanation correctly, I stayed on the beach to observe Dorothy's demonstration. She went WAY out, caught a wave, and rode it in. Wow! It looked like great fun!

"Lie on your tummy the first time you ride the board. That will help you get the feel of it," she suggested, her eyes dancing with pleasure.

I grasped the surfboard, battled the waves, and got out—oh, a little more than waist deep. I finally mustered up the courage to catch a wave. Lying on my tummy, I gripped the edges of the surfboard, which seemed to have no sense of direction, and made it safely to shore. It had been a bit scary but fun.

"Come on," Dorothy called over her shoulder as she headed for the surf. "Try kneeling on the board this time."

"Sure," I told myself. "I was barely able to hang onto the bucking bronco when I lay on my tummy. This neophyte better just stick to basics for now." And I headed out into the ocean again with that vacillating plank bobbing in every direction.

This time I went out a little further and waited to catch the perfect wave. But while I waited, two separate waves converged on one another causing an undertow. The waves tossed me and my surfboard straight down into the sand. I scraped bottom, leaving skin from my face, arms, and chest on the ocean floor. Just when I thought I would never breathe again, the water spun me to the surface. As I fought my way toward shore, the surfboard came after me. Ile waves lifted the board on high and then threw it down on my head. It nearly knocked me senseless, but my innate desire to live kept me going. I finally pulled myself onto term firma—if a sandy beach can be called term or firma.

As I was spewing water from my nose and mouth, and wiping salt from my eyes, the surfboard shot out of the water and hit me on the shins. I could not believe the vengeance of that hunk of wood. I wasn't even safe on shore! That board had an insatiable desire to "get me." When I came to my senses, I was bleeding, had bumps on my head and shins, and, to my embarrassment, found that my bathing suit had settled at my waist. I hurriedly pulled the suit up into place, ignoring the rips and snags.

Dorothy appeared. "You had a rough ride that time, didn't you?" (an understatement) "Better try again," she encouraged.

"No, thanks," I replied. "I'm getting dressed. No more surfing for me."

Dorothy went blissfully on with her sport, completely oblivious of my moments of terror in the deep. It was just as well. She had the knack and I didn't. Ever since that day, I have viewed surfboard riders with a reverent awe.

I continued to fill my summer days with sun, sand, and sea, but no more surfing EVER for me.

CHAPTER 7
PAUL NEVER HAD IT THIS GOOD

I was quite content to leave the sea behind to tour Greece and Turkey. We had saved vacation time for two years so that we could visit the cities Paul named in Acts and the seven churches John mentioned in Revelation.

July 30 we loaded our Chevy with the usual travel gear food box, plastic cereal bowls, glasses, flatware, water jug, medicines, pillows, blankets, and clothing. The next mo i g we left the college hill and headed north along the seacoast. At the border, the Lebanese checked our passports and car papers, then cheerfully waved us on to Syria. The Syrian gendarmes took their job seriously. They investigated the contents of our suitcases and food box, kicked the tires, lifted the hood and looked under the car. After an hour and a half they completed their inspection. We drove on to Aleppo where we spent the night.

The next morning, after a banana, cereal, and powdered milk breakfast, we drove on to the Turkish border. We managed to get through that hurdle fine. The modem road lies parallel to, or sometimes crosses, the old Roman road of Paul's day. The road was still in excellent condition. Large stones, many 24 inches in diameter, formed both the base and surface of the road. The Romans built for eternity; modem men build asphalt roads which deteriorate in a few years, but are better for vulcanized tires.

Wayne stopped and took pictures of the once-heavily trafficked road that led from Rome to Asia. It had been built for the convenience of armies, merchants, government officers, and caravans. Christian missionaries used it, too. The dusty footsteps of Paul, Barnabas, John Mark, and Peter were obscured, but in my mind I saw those worthy men trudging along on the old Roman road, discussing evangelistic plans.

Our next stop was Tarsus, Paul's home town. Tarsus, founded by the Phoenicians about 2000 B.C., was the chief city of Cilicia. After being ruled by several world empires, it was annexed by Rome in 64 B.C. Thus, Paul was born a Roman citizen.

When the Greeks settled in the city they founded the philosophical school of Tarsus, which in Paul's day was rivaled only by those of Alexandria and Athens.

Young Saul (Paul) probably studied philosophy, science, education, and culture at the famous Tarsus University. He learned Greek, Latin, Hebrew and Aramaic. It's assumed that he also studied religion at the local Synagogue. We found no trace of either of those sites. In fact, there is very little left above ground of Paul's Tarsus except the old gate to the city.

In Paul's day seagoing ships came down the narrow but deep Cydnus River 12 miles to the docks of Tarsus. Today, the river is reduced to a mere trickle. During the centuries, rain has washed silt into the river and earthquakes have broken up the terrain to the extent that old springs no longer feed the river. There is still a water hole where young boys swim, and water buffalo wallow in deeper pools and soft mud.

It was hot and sticky in Tarsus, and we were hungry. In a little mompop restaurant we dined on beans, rice, bread, fruit, and lemonade. Then we drove to the cool hills and rented a room in a country hotel. The next morning the hotel manager's wife served us eggs, bread, jam, hot milk, cherries, peaches, and summer apples. That day we drove through the beautiful Taurus Mountains which reminded us of the Colorado Rockies. Along the way there were numerous pipes driven into the red rock where mountain springs provided cool and refreshing water. We filled our water jug and washed our dishes and fruit with Tide soap at these springs.

Not far from Tarsus we passed through the Cicilian Gates in the Taurus Mountains. The "Gates" are a narrow passage in a canyon between two high mountain ridges, just barely wide enough for two vehicles to pass. Some believe the gorge was caused by water erosion; others theorize that engineers about 1000 B.C. cut the opening in order to avoid going up and over the rugged peaks.

Turkey is an enchanting land of mountains, plateaus, valleys, and small villages. We saw shepherds herding sheep and angora goats, watched farmers load hay onto ox carts, and laughed at the clumsy storks tottering beside their nests on top of ancient columns. From the province of Cilicia we passed into Galatia, which had been settled by Gauls from France three thousand years earlier. Perhaps this is the reason some Galatians are fair.

We got to Ankara early in the afternoon and explored the modem capital of Turkey. First we went to the Mausoleum of Ataturk who is called "the father of Turkey." He was born Mustafa Kamel and is to Turkey what Lenin was to the USSR. Following World War I, Ataturk and his Nationalist Forces snatched the power from the Ottoman Sultans, and in 1923 established the Turkish republic. (See the book DIAMONDOLA AND ARAM).

Soldiers stood guard at the Mausoleum, which is a marvel of artistic beauty. The roof and ceiling is inlaid with red and turquoise colored stones and decorated with gold. From its vantage point, we looked down on this splendid, well-planned city of wide streets and boulevards, statues and monuments, city parks and squares, swank hotels and stadium, opera house and zoo. Quaint, arched bridges span streams of slow-moving water which circulate through the city. Trees strung with lights line the avenues, giving the whole city a gala affect.

The children enjoyed riding the ferris wheel, twirling airplanes, and bumper cars at the amusement park.

The next day we passed through more scenic mountain country which reminded us of the Swiss Alps and German plateaus. We reached Istanbul on the Asian side and crossed the Bosporus Straits via ferry boat to European Istanbul. We stayed at the mission with Connard and Beulah Rasmussen. Our children were happy to play with Connard, Jr., Maynard, and little Ron. It thrilled us to see the new chapel/church being built by mission president Rasmussen. The space for the building was very limited, but the members rejoiced that they had received permission to build the first Christian house of worship in Turkey since 1914.

During our three days in Istanbul, we visited the famous St. Sophia Mosque. It had been a Christian church with beautiful paintings on the walls; but when the Moslems confiscated it in 1453, they plastered over the pictures. (Moslems believe they should not make an image or likeness of anything that might be worshipped in place of God). They built four minarets from which to call the faithful to prayer. Then, in 1920, Ataturk turned St. Sophia into a museum and had the plaster removed from the ancient paintings. Some paintings are still in fair condition.

The Blue Mosque is the only one in the world with six minarets and is covered with blue ceramic tile. Handwoven, intricately designed Turkish carpets cover the floors. It was Friday noon, and rows of Islamic adherents were kneeling in prayer with their foreheads touching the ground. In the antichamber the women were worshipping Allah, too. I admired the reverence they had for God.

We visited the Sultan's treasury, museum, and the old Roman aqueduct. Finally we went to the Grand Bazaar, a labyrinth of over 4,000 shops. Tourists find many things they can do without, but, like me, they can't resist the temptation to buy something. The only bazaar to equal or surpass the one in Istanbul is Cairo's El Khalili Bazaar.

Wayne preached to the small congregation on Sabbath. The next day we took a boat ride up the Bosporus to the opening of the Black Sea. Elaborately decorated palaces and villas almost touch the shoreline.

Monday night was spent in Alexandropolis. The next morning we drove down to Kavalla (Neapolis of Paul's day) where Paul landed when his ship pulled in from Troas. Kavalla is a typical Greek city with whitewashed buildings and little outdoor cafes facing the waterfront. Red-checkered cloths cover the small round tables where the Greeks congregate to chat and feast on gourmet cuisine. The harbor, lined with pleasure and fishing craft, is a buzz of activity. Beyond it all is the blue expanse of the Aegean Sea, calm and sparkling in the morning sun. The old Roman aqueduct is almost perfectly preserved, and the wall surrounding the city on the three land sides is mostly intact.

We forced ourselves to leave idyllic Kavalla\Neapolis to drive on through Macedonia. The children had Wayne stop so they could get out of the car and walk on the Roman Imperial Post Road that runs parallel to the modem highway.

"How did the Romans move such large stones that fit together so perfectly?" Ronnie wanted to know.

"Slave labor, probably," Wayne answered.

Then, to the children's delight, they spotted two box turtles ambling along the Roman road near them. They each picked up a turtle and claimed it as a pet.

"I'm calling mine Macey because I found him in Macedonia," Ronnie explained.

"And I'm calling mine Donia," David said.

"Wait a minute," I objected. "Who said you kids could have those turtles? They're as big as a cereal bowl. How can we get them back home?"

The children didn't attempt an answer; they contorted their faces into pitiful looks of longing desire and stroked the shells of their turtles. Two pairs of eyes looked pleadingly at their father. Did those kids know how to work him? They knew he liked critters as well as they did. It didn't surprise them nor me when Wayne relented.

"Oh, well, all right," Wayne agreed - too quickly, I thought.

"Just a minute," I argued. "What will we feed them and where will we carry them? I don't want them loose around my feet in the car."

"I'll find a box, and we'll feed them vegetables," Wayne answered.

"Thanks, Dad!" The children were jubilant over their victory.

Two turtles, two happy kids, Wayne, and a muttering mother went on their way through Macedonia, intending to visit all the sites mentioned in Acts 15 through 18.

The road leading into Philippi was lined with tall, deciduous trees that kissed at their tops. We drove almost a mile under this canopy of green. What a welcome relief this was from the August sun.

First we sought out the Gangites River where the women met on the Sabbath day for prayer (Acts 15). As we stood in the shade of a grove of trees, Wayne remarked, "Since there was no Jewish synagogue in Philippi, how appropriate for the women to meet in God's outdoor cathedral."

"Yes," I agreed. "It's so quiet and peaceful here. I wish I could have heard the messages Paul gave to the women."

"Well, why didn't you, Mom? Weren't you listening?" David asked accusingly.

I could hear myself speaking to David in that question. "Of course, I was listening," I stated defensively. "I mean, I didn't hear Paul because that was long ago. I wasn't even born, and I didn't live here."

"We are referring to the Bible story about the Apostle Paul, David," Wayne patiently explained. "It was here that Lydia and her household were converted and baptized.

"Oh. Where? Right there?" David asked pointing to a spot where the river seemed unusually tranquil.

"David, we can't be absolutely certain about some of the places of antiquity, but it was in this area," Wayne said a bit less patiently. "Now just follow along and imagine what it was like here 2,000 years ago."

Seven-year-old David lacked enthusiasm for the archaeological sites which fascinated us. He and his turtle Donia would just have to bear with us.

We drove up into the city which is relatively small compared to what it was in Paul's day. Philippi was situated on a steep mountain overlooking the Gangites River valley. Numerous mountain springs fed water into the city. The Athenians founded "Crenides" in the 7th century B.C. Philip II of Macedonia captured it in 357 B.C., named it after himself, and built his residence here. Gold and silver were mined in the surrounding mountains, which gave the city more prominence. In 168 B.C. Philippi fell to the Romans.

Since both Wayne and I were avid ancient history buffs, we knew that one of the most famous events in Roman history took place in this vicinity in 42 B.C. We tried to imagine just where the battle between Octavian and Anthony, Caesar's avengers, and Brutus and Cassias, his murderers, took place. Since each faction had a large army, the battle had to be fought outside of Philippi - probably in the valley and on the lower mountain slopes. The victors, Octavian and Anthony, then enlarged the city and Philippi flourished more than before.

During Paul's day about half the population was Roman since many soldiers retired there. The rest were Macedonians along with a few Jews. In New Testament times, Philippi was a great trading center. It was favorably situated near the Via Egnatia, the Roman highway which crossed all of Macedonia from the east (Aegean Sea) to the west (Adriatic Sea) coast. Lydia, who was a seller of purple cloth, moved from Thyatira in Asia Minor to ply her trade in Philippi.

We entered the old city and were amazed at the mass and beauty of the white marble and green stone ruins of old Philippi. Perhaps Lydia's home lay amid those remains; she was a wealthy, prominent woman of Philippi. According to Acts, Paul's entire evangelistic team stayed in her villa and preached to guests in the atrium of her home.

Parts of the walls of the old city were still intact. We made our way around fallen pillars, stones, and walls. It seemed there were more ruins of the old city than buildings in new. Modern Philippi has lost the grandeur and importance that it had in New Testament times.

The ancient marketplace was made of less elaborate materials than the wealthy residential area, yet the massive granite stones were impressive. It was in this market square where Paul and Silas met with an incident that halted their work in Philippi. A slave girl, supposedly possessing supernatural abilities that were used for the financial advantage of her masters, followed them crying, "These are the servants of the most high God, which shew unto us the way of salvation."

The girl's presence was disconcerting, so Paul, in the name of Jesus, commanded the evil spirit to leave her. Since her oracular powers were now destroyed, her masters were incensed with Paul whom they blamed for their loss of income. They dragged Paul and Silas to the Forum and accused them before the civil magistrates of being Jews who taught things contrary to the Roman law. The authorities had Paul and Silas flogged and placed in the local prison. Luke tells the story of the apostles singing hymns of praises, of the earthquake that destroyed the jail, and of the conversion of the jailer and his family. The next day the officials were discomfited when they learned that they had beaten and imprisoned a Roman citizen without a hearing. We found that old jail. My flesh rippled with goose bumps as I viewed the ruins of the place that had been rocked by mighty angels.

Although the early Christians suffered persecution in Philippi, yet the converts multiplied. Within the first century, a Christian church was established. The remains of a large basilica built about 400 A.D. stands prominently among the ruins near the old jail, a witness to the world that Christianity had enveloped the city by that time. Today, Philippi, as well as most of Greece, claims Christianity as its religion.

We drove on to Salonica. (old Thessalonike) and rented a room for the night. Wayne found a box for the turtles; they spent the night scratching the sides of the box, and I determined they and their noise would spend future nights in the car.

The next morning we explored old Thessalonike, but there was so much to see it was almost overwhelming. Even David and Ronnalee were impressed with the humongous walls, the towers, and the citadel. Statues, sculptures, and works of art were everywhere. The children showed the turtles the sites who gave us no clue as to their impressions.

Some of the streets leading into the modem metropolis are still on the same level as they were in ancient times. The Arch of Galerius opens onto one of these streets. This 2000-year-old Arch is covered with hundreds of beautiful figures carved in bas relief into the stone. I would guess that Kodak profits have soared since the archaeologists reconstructed the Arch.

Cassander, one of the successors of Alexander the Great, made Thermae his capital in 315 B.C. He renamed it Thessalonike, in honor of, his wife, Alexander's sister. When it fell into Roman hands in 168 B.C., Thessalonike experienced its greatest expansion. After the Battle of Philippi in 42 B.C., Thessalonike was made a free city administered by magistrates called "rulers of the city." (Note Acts 17:6 and 8.)

We did not locate the synagogue in which Paul preached. In spite of persecution, Christian gentiles, a few Jews, and some of the leading women established a church. Converts were regularly added to the membership. Two of them, Aristarchus and Secundus, became Paul's traveling companions -

We visited the Thessalonike Adventist Church. It is a turn-of-thecentury architectural structure with a ground and first floor. In the 1920's the Adventist mission moved the orphans from Istanbul to this building. When stability was restored in Istanbul, they all moved back there.

Thessalonike was an important military and commercial city in Paul's day. Not only was it on the east-west overland route, the Via Egnatia, leading through central Greece, but it had a fine seaport.

The modem seaport, which was filled with countless kinds of seacraft, intrigued our children. We placated their interests by spending several hours at the waterfront. They watched the fishermen unload their catch, viewed the luxury yachts, and saw a cruise ship dock and the passengers disembark. I was willing to offer the tourists two turtles, but I knew I'd have opposition.

About 50 miles from Thessalonike is Berea. Paul spoke of the Jews in this town as being more noble than the Thessalonians in that they received the gospel with joy. His ministry there was successful; he established a church of Jews and noble Greek women and men. Then some Jews came from Thessalonike and stirred up trouble, forcing him to leave Berea. Not much is left to see in this town except some steps leading to a platform at the agora. The Greeks told us that Paul preached from this platform, which is possible. During the first century A.D. Berea was a large city but was never very important.

Corinth is one of the most exciting places in Greece to visit because it is extensively excavated. Archaeologists have scraped away the debris so that one walks on the same stone pavement of Paul's day. The restorations make it possible to get an amazingly accurate picture of life in ancient Corinth.

The history of this city is too long to relate. It existed before the days of Abraham. In later times, Julius Caesar rebuilt the city in 44 B.C. and brought it to prominence. We enjoyed our walk around the agora (market square). The northwest side of the agora is 500 feet long. The 33 shops, each of which had a storeroom and a supply of cold water, are relatively well preserved or restored. The roof (now destroyed) of the covered sidewalk in front of these shops was supported by 71 Doric columns. Back of it was the Temple of Apollo.

In another area of the agora were many taverns with 40-foot-deep wells which were connected at the bottom. Containers of milk, meat, and wine were lowered into the wells where running spring water kept them cool. Wine jars, mixing bowls, drinking cups, gambling devices, dice, and flutes have been recovered from the wells of the taverns. Every vice known to man could be found within the agora at the taverns, casinos, or brothels.

Across the agora were other shops whose owners might have sold cloth, perfumery and cosmetics, soap, bread, vegetables, tailor shops, or other services.

A prominent place along one side of the agora was the raised platform of the bema or judgement seat of the proconsul. (An inscription positively identifies this place). Wayne ascended the steps to the bema and acted the part of Gallio while I stood below representing Paul who had been brought before him.

"If it were a case of wrongdoing or crime, I would bear you, O, Jews; but since it is a question of words ... I refuse to be a judge of these things."

I cheered my victory (or Paul's), and the children were amused at our acting. "Now, kids, the next thing that happened was that the people took Sosthenes, the ruler of the synagogue and the instigator of this riot, and beat him up."

"That was good! He got what he deserved," Ronnalee decided. "I'll bet Justus and Crispus were glad they were on Paul's side that day."

"You can be sure of that," Wayne agreed.

"Dad, you haven't showed us where Paul made his tents," Ronnalee said.

"He made the black goat's hair tents in the home of his friends, Aquila and Priscilla. They might have lived over there in the residential area, but they probably sold some of their tents right here in the agora. On market days, local craftsmen often set up their booths on the streets."

Beyond the agora, was the theater (which seated 18,000 spectators), the Odeum, and the Temple of Asclepias. One place we did not choose to visit was the Temple of Aphrodite standing on top of the 1,800 foot high acropolis south of Corinth.

"It is said that two thirds of the population of Corinth were slaves, and 1,000 of them were temple prostitutes who lived right up there on that mountain," Wayne explained.

"What's a temple prostitute?" David asked.

I held my breath, waiting for Wayne to explain that one.

"It's a Corinthian girl," Wayne stated simply. "And before you ask another question, let me say there were Corinthian girls living here in the city too - some good, some bad." David was satisfied with that answer.

We left the agora and walked down Lechaeum. Road. Sailors, citizens, or visitors entering the city through the Lechaeum Gate could refresh themselves at the wine and food shops. They could also use the public toilet which had at least 10 seats available. It was interesting how the Corinthian engineers had channeled water to run continuously in a trough about 6 feet below the toilet seats to keep the facility flushed at all times.

I suppose the next stop for the people might have been the public bath. Below a ledge of rocks were fashioned covered cubicles where springs of water gushed out into stone troughs. People could draw water out of these troughs or put their jars directly under one of the springs. The excess water overflowed into a large pool built of stone and mortar. It appeared to me that this was the public bath. The water was constantly changing because the pools overflowed into channels that probably led to the toilet flushing system. From there the sewage was piped out to the sea.

After a good bath, a Jew might choose to worship at the Synagogue. A stone lintel with a fragmentary inscription "[Syna]gogue of the Hebr[ews]" was found written in a script that dates back to the 4th century A.D. The synagogue of Paul's day was possibly in the same location.

The immorality that existed in Corinth rivaled that of Pompeii. The location of Corinth, built on the only land connection between northern Greece and the Peloponnesus may have contributed to their sordid moral behavior. Corinth had two harbors - Cenchreae, seven miles east of the city on the Sardonic Gulf, and Lechaeum, one and a half miles west on the Corinthian Gulf. These busy harbors were filled with transient men willing to support the red-light district of Corinth.

We learned that Corinthian engineers ingeniously figured out a method of transporting ships overland. Parallel tracks were built on which they pulled small ships overland from Lechaeum to Cenchreae, and vice versa. This was a life-saving service since the seas around the south end of the Peloponnesus was usually very choppy, and the danger of getting shipwrecked on the rocks or in the waves was real. This problem was solved in modern times (1881–1893) by building the Corinth Canal through the five-mile isthmus. Even in modern times this is quite an engineering feat since the canal had to be dug through 70 feet or more of solid rock and needed to be wide enough for a ship to pass from the Corinthian Gulf to the Sardonic Gulf.

Our day of thrills was over and Sabbath was upon us. We rented a room in the Bel Vue Hotel and slept comfortably as cool ocean breezes wafted over us. The next morning we drove the 45 miles to Athens where Wayne preached in the Adventist church. We spent the day with new friends; that evening we shopped for souvenirs.

Sunday we visited the usual tourist spots in Athens. First we climbed 60 feet to the Areopagus or Mars Hill. (It was named after the Greek god of war, Ares, and the Roman god, Mars). From there we got a good overall view of the agora with the reconstructed Stoa Basileios in the center. In Paul's day, the administrative offices and the seat of the high court of justice was in the Stoa. Trials were conducted in the Basileios but the sentences were pronounced from Mars Hill. (Acts 17:19, Luke says Paul was taken before the council of Areopagus). It is believed that the authorities recognized Paul as a learned man and a Christian philosopher, therefore he was privileged to lecture from Mars Hill. From the hill he could be heard by more people than in the crowded agora. Today the Basileios is a museum.

Athens, founded in the 16th century B.C., is the capital and most illustrious city in all of Greece. The Persians, Greeks, and Romans have all left their mark on the city. Sculptures and statues are everywhere. In Paul's day there were at least 3,000 shrines dedicated to various deities. I don't know how many there are today, but we would have used a lot of film had we attempted to photograph a fraction of them.

The climb to the top of the Acropolis was strenuous. I thought that I had completely recovered from the heart attack I had six years earlier, but my heart let me know that I should think again.

Wayne stopped. "Would you really like to get to the top of the Acropolis and see the Parthenon?"

"Yes," I answered between puffs.

"Alright. Relax and let me pull you."

At the top of the Acropolis, I saw the Parthenon spectacular, immense, imposing. No other building in the world outside of the Taj Mahal in India excites me more. On the trek back down the hill we stopped often to get glimpses of the 15 other temples within that area.

We drove past the residence of the president of Greece. The children enjoyed that most because the uniformed guards were dressed in the national Greek garb. This was living Greece - not just ruins of the past.

After a full day of sightseeing in Athens, we were tired. In twelve days we had traveled through country that must have taken months for Paul to cover on foot. As I slid into our Chevy, I patted the comfortable seats and sighed, "Paul never had it so good. Yes, indeed, Paul NEVER had it this good."

"Macey and Donia never had it so good, either," Ronnie said. "If it hadn't been for David and me, they'd never have seen Athens."

I groaned, "Had it been up to me, they'd NEVER have seen Athens or anything else in Greece."

CHAPTER 8

CHECKING OUT THE SEVEN CHURCHES AND PATMOS

(John never had it so good)

Sunday night, August 12, we met Elder R. Allan Anderson of the General Conference Ministerial Association at the Athens airport. This rendezvous had been pre-planned. Anderson was anxious to join us in touring southwest Turkey since he was in the process of writing a book, UNFOLDING REVELATION. He wanted to visit the Seven Churches of Revelation before publishing his work. He was coming to the Middle East for a ministerial convention from August 23 through September 2 anyway, so when he learned of our plans, he asked to join us. It was our pleasure to have this knowledgeable friend with us.

From the airport we drove directly to the seaport at Pireus and loaded our car onto the deck of a cruise ship. The children kissed their turtles good night and followed us to our cabins. The Aegean Sea was calm, and the gentle waves rocked us to sleep. The next morning the children had to check on Macey and Dome. Of course, the turtles were doing fine, but when you're the guardians of such lovable pets you can't take any chances. (When I was their age, I had the good sense to own cats and dogs who were cuddly and responsive).

Monday afternoon we stood on the deck as our ship left the Aegean Sea, entered Izmir Bay, and then slipped into the 30-mile-long inlet that ends at Izmir (ancient Smyrna). The tongue of still, blue water is contained by the hillocks on either side. The shoreline is breathtakingly beautiful—trees, grass, and flower-covered hills reflect their shimmering images on the glassy sea. Soon Izmir came into view, and we docked at one of the best harbors in the world.

We disembarked, hired a taxi, found a hotel, and ate supper. The men returned to the dock for the car, while the children and I explored our environs. We decided that Turkey's third largest city would be a marvelous place to live—ideal climate, good food, modern buildings, and intriguing bazaars.

"John never had it this good," I commented aloud.

"Huh? John who?" David asked.

"Oh, John the Apostle. I'm just thinking to myself. Paul and John never had hot running water in their rooms, electricity, handy canned food, and a car."

"I guess that's true," Ronnalee agreed. "I'm glad I don't have to live in the ruins they did. And I don't have to WALK from one ruined town to another."

It took a bit of my explaining and a lot of their imagining to convince the kids that the "ruins" were once beautiful cities with temples, markets, palaces, and houses for real people and that our purpose for visiting these places was to identify with places and people of New Testament times.

The men returned with the car about 11:30 P.M. Elder Anderson sputtered, "What a bungling mess! Those customs officials don't know what they are doing. I don't see how you could be so patient with them, Wayne."

"He can't help it," I laughed. "It's his nature."

"Well," Wayne drawled, "getting upset wouldn't have hurried things along. I've learned that patience pays off. Did you notice? They processed our papers first."

"Uh," Elder Anderson grunted, still not completely appeased.

EPHESUS

The next morning we drove south to Ephesus, taking the seven churches in the order John gives them in Revelation. Ephesus was a settlement as early as 2000 B.C. In later centuries it experienced rule by Persians, Greeks, and Romans. It was the most important city of the Roman province of Asia because it was situated at the junction of natural trade routes, both land and sea. Besides international trade, Ephesus had the great temple of Artemis (Diana), the famous magical books (the Ephesia grammata), and the economic power of its banking association. By the third century B.C. the census was 250,000 inhabitants. During Roman times the population may have increased to a million.

Toward the end of Paul's second missionary journey (52 A.D.), he, Aquila, and Priscilla (fellow workers in the tentmaking business) sailed from Cenchrea, Greece, to Ephesus. At that time, Ephesus was accessible from the west by sea and by overland trade routes from the east and north. Merchant ships from all over the then-known world docked at the Ephesian harbor to unload their cargo. Seamen and travelers stepping off their ships must have been dazzled by the glistening, white marble pavement of the Arcadian Way. Ibis street was onethird of a mile long (1,735 feet) and 36 feet wide. Colonnaded, covered sidewalks fronted the shops, public bath and toilets. The Arcadian Way sloped up to the city, and its lampstands were lighted at night. Signs carved in the pavement directed sexually active men to the brothels within the city.

At the end of the Arcadian Way was the spectacular Great Theater built on the slope of Mount Pion. The theater had 66 rows of seats which accommodated 24,500 people. The semicircular auditorium was immense—495 feet in diameter. I mounted the 110 by 22 foot stage and gave a reading. The acoustics were amazing—even my whisper could be heard in the uppermost tier of seats. In ancient times the sculptured, stone backdrop for the stage was three stories high. Either this theater or the sports arena was the scene of the riot instigated by Demitrius, the silversmith, against Paul (Acts 19:23-41).

We were hot, tired, and hungry so we sat down on the theater seats and discussed that long-ago event as we ate our lunch—sandwiches, canned beans, and watermelon. We wished we could have had access to the food and juice shops, the bath house, and toilet facilities that once operated on the Arcadian Way, but we didn't. In this respect, Paul and John had it better than we did.

The water and sewage system used throughout Ephesus amazed us. Ephesian engineers laid four-inch diameter clay pipes with enough slope so gravity would carry fresh water into the city and the sewage down to the sea. Convenience and sanitation was enjoyed by the Ephesians 2,000 years ago. Only in the past few centuries have European and American cities developed sewage systems equal to that of some ancient cultures.

Paul's brief visit to Ephesus in 52 A.D. aroused an interest in Christianity. Aquila and Priscilla stayed on to continue the ministry. Later Paul spent about three years in Ephesus (approximately 54 to 57 A.D.). He taught in the Jewish synagogue for three months until he was ousted from there. For the next two years he taught in the school of Tyrannus until the episode with the silversmiths mentioned above. Many visitors, politicians, and business people who came to Ephesus during this time, heard Paul preach, believed his message, and carried the gospel to their cities. After Timothy's stint as Bishop of Ephesus, the Apostle John came to take over that position. It is believed that John and Jesus mother lived in Ephesus from 65 A.D. until their deaths.

During the first century A.D., Christian communities sprung up in many cities of Asia Minor, and churches were built. We went in search of the old church in Ephesus. Perpendicular to the Arcadian Way is Marble Street which fronts the Great Theater. Going north we found a huge gymnasium, a stadium, and baths. Our most thrilling discovery, however, was the remains of the large church of the Virgin Mary, which was built over the first, much smaller Christian Church. Nearby was the Church of St. John.

The immense Basilica of St. John stands on a high hill some distance away. A marble container under the altar of the church was supposed to contain the apostle's bones, but they have been stolen. At the Counsel of Ephesus held in the Basilica in 431 A.D. Mary was declared the "Mother of God."

Though located some distance apart, these large churches testify to the strength of Christianity in Ephesus during the early centuries. All the churches had sizable baptisteries for immersion. Elder Anderson and I walked down into one of them, and he pretended to perform the rite for me. Then he stood by a stone pulpit and read the message John wrote to the church of Ephesus (Revelation 2:1-7) during his exile in Patmos.

We retraced our steps and walked south along Marble Street into the heart of old Ephesus. We wandered through the humongous agora—a shopping mall so large it could satisfy the most avid female American shopper. This agora must have had everything! Even a walk-in medical clinic with apothecaries nearby. There were stalls for fortunetellers; bookstores which included books of magic (an Ephesian specialty); craft, shoe, and cloth shops; and countless other nooks and crannies. Several gymnasia were available for the young men in Olympic training or for the wealthy who just wanted to work off the calories ingested in the fast-food shops. From this agora Onesimus escaped from his master Philemon and stowed away on a ship bound for Rome. Considering the size of the agora, it must have been easy for Onesimus to elude his master.

The Celsus Library at the end of Marble Street appears to be a twostory building, but on the inside it was three stories. There the reader could study special manuscripts kept in the alcoves, browse the shelves behind the main room, or attend a program in the lecture hall. The card catalog was not visible and neither were the manuscripts, but this building represented a culture of educated, intelligent people. The Celsus Library rivaled that of Alexandria, Egypt, and Pergamum.

A door inside the library lobby had enclosed steps that led down to an underground tunnel that ended at the brothel. Unfaithful husbands could sneak through the tunnel to the brothel across the street without being seen.

How handy! They could honestly tell their wives, "I've just been to the library, Honey." A slight deviation from truth, but who could argue the point?

At the library we made a left turn up Curetes Street which leads steeply upward to the elite section of town. Here the rich, the rulers, and the politicians held meetings, music concerts, and plays in the odium. The agora was not really a marketplace but a "Capitol Hill" for the politicians of Ephesus. Fountains, baths, gymnasia, multi-story office complexes, temples, eateries, hotels, and other luxuries indicated that the "senators" of the Asian Roman Empire spent tax money on themselves. So what's new?

The ruins of Ephesus seemed endless, but we wanted to see the site of the great temple dedicated to the worship of Artemis (Diana). We drove down to what had once been the bay area (today a fertile valley) to see the remains. This building was four times the size of the Parthenon at Athens. It was considered one of the seven wonders of the world. The structure had 117 columns, each 66 feet high. Thirty-six of them had sculptured, life-size figures around the lower part. The temple was elaborately decorated with red, white, yellow, black, and green marble.

"Supposedly, gold was used for mortar," Wayne informed me.

"Seeing is believing, and I see no gold here." I said skeptically.

"Well, gifts for building the temple were enormous, " Wayne contended. "One man contributed $850,000. "

"Humph! That man needed psychiatric help or brain surgery, " I stated. "That figure would baffle the bookkeepers. "

"Over 100,000 pilgrims from other Asian cities attended March-April festivals in the temple to worship the many-breasted goddess of fertility," Wayne continued, undaunted by my skepticism. "There were many temples throughout Asia Minor dedicated to Diana, but Ephesus was the MOTHER TEMPLE. Supposedly Diana's statue fell from heaven on Ephesus."

"Now, who would believe that?" I muttered.

"Obviously not you! But this legend made Ephesus the Rome or Jerusalem or Mecca of all Asia." Wayne was now relieved of his burden of information.

Nothing of the temple of Artemis/Diana is visible today. Rapid acceptance of Christianity was basically the cause of its demise. The fears of Demitrius and the silversmiths were realized. The people lost interest in the worship of Diana and no longer supported the temple. It was destroyed by the Goths in 250 A.D., and was never completely rebuilt. It is interesting that some of the columns and stones were used in Christian churches or carried away by local residents to use in other buildings. Archaeologists had to dig down 24 feet to recover some of the statues. Today there is nothing left of the temple except a marshy hole that, during the dry season, reveals some foundation stones.

Through the centuries Ephesus lost it importance. The Caystar River washed silt down until, in spite of the valiant efforts of ancient engineers, it filled the harbor. By that time, Smyrna had developed a sheltered, safe harbor that was much better than that of Ephesus. Merchants, therefore, routed their business through Smyrna. Gradually the world-famous Ephesus was deserted. Today, near the ruins of old Ephesus, is the town of Seljuk.

That evening we drove to Kusadasi, 12 miles south of Ephesus, and inquired about transportation to the Island of Patmos. Since Patmos is a Greek Island, and the Turks and Greeks were/are at odds, no Turkish boat plied the Greek waters to Patmos. We were disappointed that our chances of getting to Patmos were nil. We rented rooms for the night and prayed about the matter.

The next morning Wayne walked down to the wharf, hoping to get a glimpse of the distant isle. His attention was diverted by a Greek fisherman and his son trying to bargain off their catch of fish to the local Turks.

When the business transaction was done, Wayne asked the Greek captain if he would take us to Patmos. The man jerked to attention.

"No ting dere. Why 'Mericani go dere?" the perplexed Greek asked.

"To see Patmos. Saint John was, ah, he wrote there," Wayne stammered as he tried to communicate with the captain.

"He gone. He morte," the Greek frowned, trying to understand this enigma.

"I KNOW he's dead. We just want to see Patmos," Wayne tried to explain. "You take us?"

The Greek turned and consulted with his son. Then he nodded to Wayne. "We take five peoples dere and back for $65 dolla."

In 1956 the price seemed exorbitant, but Wayne couldn't forfeit the opportunity—it was either this 30-foot vessel with the Greek or NO Patmos.

Wayne hurried back to the hotel and checked us out. We expected to be gone no more than one night, so we threw a few things into a small case and locked the rest in the trunk of the car. We sought exit permits from the Turkish officials, and, after much bickering, Wayne got their permission to leave the country temporarily. The next ordeal was passing through customs. The two men even examined our water jug and Wayne's electric shaver. We finally left at 1:30 P.M. and arrived at Samos three hours later. Since we now had entered Greek territory, we had to get Greek visas. This little errand took us clear across the island to the largest town. By 7 P.M. Greek visas were stamped in our passports, but it was too late to leave for Patmos. We bedded down in a hotel and promised the captain we would be ready to leave at 5 A.M.

PATMOS

The sky was clear and the sea was calm as we left Samos the next morning and skimmed across the water. Five hours later we pulled into the harbor of Patmos. The porpoises who played around the boat excited -us but angered the captain. By pantomime he indicated that the porpoises were big and his craft was small. He shouted some pretty hefty swear words at them. Since the children didn't know Greek, they weren't polluted by his language, and the dolphins didn't care.

Patmos is a barren, volcanic island in the Aegean Sea. It is only 10 miles long and 7 miles across at its widest spot. In Roman times, Patmos was a penal colony. In the times of Domitian, John was banished there—about 95 A.D. Today, about 2,600 people live in five hamlets on the 13-square-mile land area, only a fraction of which is tillable. Its coastline is extremely indented, irregular, and rocky; the only safe place for a ship to enter is the harbor on the protected east side of the island. The land mass is steep and treacherous.

When we stepped off the boat, we were lucky to find one of only two motor vehicles on the island ready to make a trip to the top. We climbed aboard the rickety machine and held our breath as it inched around hairpin curves worthy of the name. The switchbacks were so severe the bus had to back up to make the turns. There was only a hair's width of road between us and the edge.

"Man! It's a long drop over these sharp, steep cliffs!" Wayne commented.

"Hush!" I scolded. "I'm trying not to faint."

When it was impossible for the omnibus to go higher, we were very relieved to get out and plant our feet on terra firma and scale the heights to the monastery on our own steam. The monastery was built in 1088 A.D. by the monk Christodulus. The chapel is decorated with old icons and objects of worship. Devout pilgrims light candles, and smoke saturates the air. In the living quarters of the monastery, the children found what they thought was a two by six foot wooden bathtub. But with the scarcity of fresh water on Patmos, common sense told us that folks would be lucky to get a weekly "spit bath." It actually was a bread trough carved out of the trunk of a tree.

Down the hill, we came to the cave that supposedly sheltered John when he lived on the island and wrote the book of Revelation. We stepped to a rise where we could look west to the sea. In his vision, John saw the righteous standing beside a "sea of glass mingled with fire." (Rev.

15:2-4) His words described the scene he probably saw daily—the sun's rays reflecting off the water, making it look like a fiery sea of glass.

After eating a delicious dinner of Greek cuisine in a harbor cafe, we told our boat captain we were ready to leave. It was already 1 P.M. We wanted to reach Samos early so we could get back to Turkey that night.

The experienced captain put his hand over his eyes and surveyed the seas. "No good."

"What's he saying?" Elder Anderson asked anxiously. "Is he suggesting that we can't leave?"

"I think so," Wayne answered, "but let's go over to the pharmacy and see if someone can speak enough English to translate for us."

The pharmacist, who spoke fairly good English, confirmed that the captain did NOT want to leave Patmos at this time because his trained eye detected a storm brewing in the west.

"Is it dangerous to sail now?" Wayne inquired.

"Ah, he says that it would be very uncomfortable for you," the pharmacist interpreted.

"But we HAVE to leave now or I'll be late for my speaking appointments in Beirut," Elder Anderson insisted. "Are you AFRAID to sail to Samos?"

Although Elder Anderson did not mean it that way, the captain took this as insinuation of his cowardice.

"Greek not 'fraid," he scoffed angrily. "Get. in boat."

We got into the 30-foot craft and sailed away. We skirted the eastern coast of Patmos. The sailing was relatively smooth, but we couldn't have imagined how rough the sea would become once we left the shelter of Patmos. About an hour into the trip we understood what the captain had tried to tell us. The wind swept in from the west, tossing the craft mercilessly upon the foaming billows. The children were in danger of falling overboard since they didn't have the strength to hold on, so we put them down the hatch. They didn't complain about the fish scales and smell; they were thankful for the protection of the hold. As the boat bounced from side to side and up and down, David and Ronnalee were tossed around, banging themselves on the sides. But no one complained; no one spoke; everyone prayed.

Wayne and I sat on the edge of the hatch, dangling our feet in the hold and hanging on for dear life. When the waves reached 20 feet, we despaired of ever surviving the trip. Many thoughts raced through our minds as we believed we were living our last moments. I examined my heart and wondered if I was ready to meet my Maker. I regretted not heeding the captain's warning because our lives were now in jeopardy.

I looked back at the captain, his son, and Elder Anderson standing together in the minuscule cabin. Their faces were grim. The captain struggled to steer the craft into the curling waves. One moment we were in the trough of the wave, and the next second we were riding the crest. We teetered on the crest for an endless moment, then crashed down into the trough. The water poured over us, and the wind chilled us to the bone. My arms ached from the cold and from gripping the edge of the hatch, but I knew I was doomed if I relaxed my hold for a split second.

Then the sea and waves got worse. The boat was swamped, and the motor died. The son bailed out water with a bucket in one hand and hung onto the edge of the boat with the other. The captain somehow managed to put up a sail and tried to keep the boat steered into the waves. Then he lost control and the boat went sideways. We tipped at such an angle that we were shaded from the sun. This happened repeatedly. Each time we thought we would slip into the sea. It seemed that the devil was determined to destroy us by whipping up the worst of storms. We knew that if God did not deliver us, all hope was gone. At this point, the old seaman despaired of survival. He and his son cried out to God for deliverance.

The captain viewed us suspiciously. "God mad at you? God kill us 'cause we take you? I never see so bad storm."

"It's not God. It's Satan's storm. He hates us. We're preachers," Elder Anderson tried to explain to the captain.

I don't know if he understood. Besides the noise of the winds and the waves, there was the language barrier. The craft had no radio nor any other means of sending out a distress signal. Therefore, if our boat capsized, no one would ever know what really happened to us nor where we went down.

The boat began moving along with the sail, yet there was grave danger since the storm had not ceased. After four hours we passed along the east coast of some uninhabited islands; they broke the fury of the waves to some extent. The captain estimated the waves now to be less than 15 feet high. Even so, with water towering above our heads, it still was frightening. After an hour of free sailing, the captain was able to start the boat's motor again.

It had seemed like an eternity, but Samos finally came into view. We had spent six harrowing hours in the deep. When we docked, excited islanders gathered around us wanting to know who we were and how we had made it through the storm. The captain pointed to the sky and made the sign of the cross, indicating that God had delivered us. AMEN!

The crowd gasped when we pulled Ronnalee and David up from the hold. They were shocked that we had children with us. They patted and kissed the kids, making the sign of the cross and rejoicing for their deliverance. In spite of their bruises, being wet and cold, scared half to death, covered with scales, and smelling of fish, the children had survived the ordeal quite well.

We were a pitiful sight—dripping wet with salt water, covered with soot, and green at the gills. Elder Anderson's felt hat flopped like a mop, but that was the least of his worries.

We made our way to the hotel we had occupied the night before. The owner couldn't recognize us in our new, wet look, but she graciously led us down to the facilities and asked us to bath before we occupied a room. There was no hot water, but cold water and lots of soap cleansed us.

I developed a high temperature during the night which made us more anxious than ever to get back to the luggage and medicines we had left in the trunk of our car in Turkey. The next morning we got exit permits from the Greeks and headed back to Turkey.

The seas were reasonably calm. After three hours we landed at Kusadasi. The customs official escorted us into his little shed. He was suspicious because we had gone with a Greek fisherman in his small boat to who knows where. He interrogated us and examined everything. He even went through the men's billfolds. Since we seemed to be his only customers for the day, he must have felt obligated to make his time worth his pay. We'll never know what he was looking for, but he seemed to be having a good time doing it. Three hours later he released us. He had exhausted our patience and reduced our cash reserves by "accepting" a tip.

We got into our car, and the kids checked on their turtles. "Macy and Donia really missed us," David said as he stroked Donia's shell.

"How can you know that?" I asked. I thought this to be a logical question.

"Well, they've pulled in their heads and don't even want to talk with us," was David's perfectly illogical answer.

"I hope that makes sense to you," I replied. "I've never had a conversation with a turtle."

The children comforted their turtles while we drove to a hotel in Smyrna.

SMYRNA

Alexander the Great brought Smyrna into prominence. Two centuries before Christ it was one of the richest coastal cities of Asia. Smyrna was ideally located in the fertile Meles River Valley which still produces an abundance of all kinds of grains, fruits, and vegetables.

Symrna was easily accessible from the east by the Imperial Post Road. And from the west, ocean
going vessels sailed down the Hermaic Gulf bringing with them merchandizing powers. The warm mineral springs were a medicinal treat for arthritic patients, and the surrounding mountains contained valuable minerals.

Since Smyrna is near Ephesus, Paul probably preached the gospel there, too. By the end of the first century, a Christian church was built in Smyrna. The population then was over 250,000; today Izmir has about a million people. It is the only continuously inhabited city of the seven churches mentioned by John in Revelation.

Sabbath morning we climbed the heights to the citadel and explored it. We sat down on Mt. Pagus and viewed the city where Christians had endured the most severe persecutions. I imagined the crowd that gathered on this hillside to jeer Polycarp, a convert of John's, as he was burned at the stake (156 A.D.). I saw the Orthodox Church where clergy were impaled on the walls in the 1920's. Beyond the city lay the harbor where hundreds of Armenian youth met their death in watery graves. They had fled from their persecutors and had swum out to the English ships anchored in the harbor. They begged to be taken aboard, but the English crews had been ordered not to help any of them. As I gazed upon the peaceful, picturesque surroundings, it was difficult to imagine the atrocities Christians had endured in this city through the ages.

From the inception of Christianity, the believers in Smyrna suffered persecution. The Roman emperor Trajan (98-117 A.D.) gave the first official orders against Christianity. From 303 to 313 A.D. Diocletian tried to wipe Christianity from the face of the earth. A respite was enjoyed by Christians in the entire Roman Empire when Constantine gave them liberty to practice their religion (about 315 A.D.). That all changed with the Seljuks (11th century), the Ottomans, and other Turkish regimes.

Today, however, there are more Christians per capita in Smyrna than in any other Turkish city in Asia.

Smyrna was the second church John addressed in writing his message from the Isle of Patmos (Rev. 2:8-11). The promise "Be faithful unto death, and I (Jesus) will give you a crown of life," must have been precious to the thousands of Christians who have lost their lives in Symrna.

Modem buildings encroach upon the ruins of the old, but archaeologists finally discovered Smyrna's ancient agora under the heart of today's business district. Although not the largest, Symrna's three-story agora was the most unique marketplace of the ancient world. The subterranean halls and shops of the lowest level are so well preserved that merchants could almost use them today. The ground floor has few remains, and the second story is obliterated. Statues uncovered by Smyrna's builders can be seen at the ancient sites or in the museum.

We visited Smyrna's fabulous fairgrounds which are the nicest I have seen anywhere. Then we drove to Pergamum, or Bergama, as it is called today, and checked into a hotel for the night.

PERGAMUM

The next morning we went to Bergama's market to replenish our food supply. A gourmet cook could become completely unhinged there. The variety of foods on the stands was surpassed only by the size and flavor of the fresh fruits and vegetables. Elder Anderson chose grapes and softball-size peaches; Wayne selected plums and pears; I purchased bread, cheese, boiled eggs, jam, butter, tomatoes, cucumbers, and cookies; and the children begged some lettuce from the vendor for—guess who? Yes, those turtles were still enjoying Olson Welfare Assistance, free transportation, food, and lodging. And their scratching on the box stiff annoyed me.

The Turks claimed they grew 56 varieties of grapes in Bergama's Caicus Valley. Or was it five or six? How would I know, and what did I care? The sight of perfect, oversized fruit and their delightful aromas overloaded my senses. I hadn't expected to see fruit like this until I reached heaven. One sliced peach filled a dinner plate. What an incredible breakfast we had!

Ephesus and Corinth had been my favorite ancient cities until I saw Pergamum. During its prominence in the third and second century B.C., Pergamum was acclaimed the richest city of Asia Minor. Kings deposited their wealth in Pergamum's fortress because the city stood at an elevation of 1,000 feet which they considered a natural defense and, therefore, impregnable. When Lysimachus, one of Alexander's generals, ruled the city, he deposited his state treasure of 9,000 golden talents ($10,000,000) in the fortress. I doubt that ten million dollars would impress a Rockefeller, but it was awesome to me.

From Mysia, Lydia, Caria, Pamphylia, Phrygia and Galatia the kings of Pergamum exacted tribute. They used this income to beautify the palace, temples, gymnasia, theaters, and other public buildings. The Pergamum hospital\medical center was the best in the world and their aqueduct was an engineering feat unequalled anywhere for several more centuries. Pergamum remained a center of culture and wealth until John's day when it began losing some of it's position and importance to Ephesus.

All of the important buildings in Pergamum. stood on top of Acropolis Hill or on its slopes. The residential area was at the foot of the hill or in the plain as it is today. The population in John's time was well over 100,000; today, the valley city of Bergama has only 35,000.

"Come," Wayne said, "let's go take a look at the library which boasted of having over 200,000 manuscripts."

"Didn't they have any books?" David inquired.

"Manuscripts were their books, Davy!" Wayne sighed a bit impatiently. "Good grief! I'm just trying to make this interesting and educational for you. Now listen! The library stood where those stones are scattered. Pergamum's large collection of manuscripts aroused the jealousy of Ptolemy V of Egypt. Fearing that Pergamum's collection

Checking Out The Seven Churches And Patmos • 85

would soon exceed his Alexandrian library, Ptolemy imposed an embargo on papyrus. Since Egypt was the sole producer of papyrus, Pergamum was forced to develop an alternative material on which to write. This necessity led bookmakers to invent parchment, which was superior to papyrus and leather. Before you ask, let me explain that parchment is made from the hides of young animals—lambs, kids, or calves. After a special tanning process, it's ready for use. However, after this effort to foil Ptolemy's embargo, it is disgusting that Mark Anthony gave Pergamum's library collection to Cleopatra of Egypt."

"WHAT?" I exploded. "What would make a man do a stupid thing like that?'

"Love, Midge, LOVE," Wayne laughed. "What's worse, the guide book says that those books, along with thousands of others, were destroyed by the Arabs during their conquest of Egypt. "

Now my ire was full blown. "How could they?" I sputtered. "Valuable information of antiquity obliterated forever! As a librarian and collector of old books, I'd give the gold crown off my molar for just one page of such a manuscript. "

Since it was thousands of years too late for me to do anything about it, I walked off my "mad" on the pathway that led to the remains of the incredible Temple of Zeus. Since a poisonous, living serpent was always kept in this temple as an object of worship, I warned everyone to be on the lookout for their offspring.

The steps to the Great Altar of Zeus are still there, but the German government transported the actual altar to Berlin where it was reconstructed. In John's day the Altar was a two-story masterpiece of architecture and art. Shaped like a horse shoe, this altar was 127 by 120 feet and 40 feet high. The lower story had slabs of relief sculptures all around its sides which depicted the war between the gods and the giants. The upper portion had beautifully designed colonnades. Although the Great Altar to Zeus is better protected within the confines of the Pergamum Museum in Berlin, I would liked to have seen it as it was in John's day—standing on Pergamum's acropolis, glistening in the Sun.

The amphitheater in Pergamum is the steepest in the world. From the top it made me dizzy to look down on the stage. On the descent, I had to concentrate on my movement to keep from falling.

The palace, temples, theaters, gymnasia, stadiums, public buildings, agora, and the amphitheater rival those of Ephesus for size. The white marble slabs with names inscribed on them captured Wayne's interest. In Revelation John said that God would give the overcomers a "white stone" engraved with a "new name." The people of Pergamum could easily understand that analogy—every important person, it seems, had their names and titles inscribed on white marble.

Nowhere does John mention the medical school nor the hospital. We drove a mile across the valley to see this medical center which was dedicated to the god of healing, Asclepias. It was an amazing complex—much larger than I had anticipated. Beside the medical school was the hospital with treatment rooms, an underground dream room where patients spent a night to get divine messages about the treatment they should receive, a theater or odeum for entertaining the patients or teaching classes, and a chapel dedicated to Asclepias. Galen, the great physician of antiquity, got his education in Pergamum's medical school. He wrote 500 medical articles and developed methods of treatment that were used for more than 1,000 years. Some of his medical statements were still practiced in George Washington's day.

The doctors of Pergamum used natural remedies. The apothecary had all kinds of jars for herbs, and mortars and pestles to crush and mix the compounds. Water from the hot mineral springs were routed into baths. Cold spring water was conveniently available. In the courtyard we photographed the monument of caduceus. The medical profession still uses the serpent entwined around the pole as their symbol.

THYATIRA

We had driven beside the Roman Imperial Post Road that led from Ephesus all the way north through Symrna and Pergamum. But outside Pergamum the nice asphalt road deteriorated into a dusty gravel trail. As we entered Akhisar, the site of ancient Thyatira, Elder Anderson yelled "Stop, STOP! "

Wayne slammed on the brakes and skidded to an abrupt stop. Clouds of dust billowed around us. Since Elder Anderson joined us, I had been relegated to the back seat with the kids and the turtles. We slid off the seat onto the floor and knocked over the turtles' box. I sat on Macey, but it didn't hurt him.

"What's wrong?" Wayne asked, still badly shaken.

"There! Don't you see that?" Elder Anderson pointed in the direction of a pottery factory.

"Yes. That's one of the pottery factories for which Akhisar is known. Old Thyatira was also known for its pottery as well as its blast furnaces, purple dye, and .

"No, no!" Elder Anderson interrupted. "See that heap of broken pottery beside the building? John wrote, 'I will give him power over the nations, and he shall rule them with a rod of iron, as when earthen pots are broken in pieces.' That broken pottery is symbolic. It represents the sinners who reject salvation. Their lives are broken shards—worth nothing."

"Wow!" Ronnie exclaimed. "John says all that about those shards?"

While the theologians took pictures of the broken pottery, they explained to the children that weak pots break in the kiln and cannot be fixed. Weak Christians break under the fire of trials and can't be fixed, either.

The children just said, "Oh," as if they understood. Maybe they did. But the Turks who came out of the factory and saw Wayne and Elder Anderson taking pictures of broken pottery did not understand at all. They threw up their hands and shook their heads in disbelief, talking rapidly to each other about the crazy Americans. I shrugged my shoulders and smiled as if I agreed with the Turks. They concluded that I was the intelligent one in the crowd and invited the children and me into the factory to watch them make pottery. Reluctantly they allowed the men to follow.

One kind man, who spoke a little English, showed us around the town. Almost the only thing of antiquity was the sarcophagus with the Greek name of "Thyatira" inscribed on its side and some fenced-in ruins that might be the remains of a Christian Church or the Temple of Sambathe.

"Where's the OLD city?" I asked.

He pointed down to the ground. "Under dirt. Sometime we dig hole for house and find old tings." It was evident that folks in Akhisar weren't very interested in old Thyatira. Making a living for the here and now absorbed their time and thoughts.

Thyatira never had the fame or size of the other six churches, but it was an important center of trade and industry on the road between Pergamum and Sardis. The city was distinguished by their guilds of weavers and dyers of wool and linen textiles. Lydia, one of Paul's first converts in Philippi, was from Thyatira and a "seller of purple" cloth. The people of Thyatira had developed a bright red dye from the madder root.

Why it was called "purple" is a point for speculation.

Copper and brass objects and leather goods were also a source of income for the Thyatirans. Some ore is still mined from the hills around Akhisar. The population of Thyatira in John's day must have been about the same as that of Akhisar today—62,000.

What really interested the children and the turtles was the melons being loaded onto freight cars headed for Istanbul. The workers baited us by cutting up a melon for us to sample. UMM! We were caught! The melons were so sweet and juicy and cheap that we couldn't resist buying far too many. Now, besides the two turtles and their box, two children and their toys, I had melons rolling around my feet. But I was having a marvelous time.

John commends the Thyatirans for their love, faith, service, and patient endurance. Most early Christians suffered persecution, but it was the patient endurance of their trials that made converts of the pagans. Asia Minor was considered a stronghold of Christianity for many centuries even though sporadic persecution thinned their ranks. The downfall of some of Thyatira's Christians was their "toleration of the woman Jezebel, who calls herself a prophetess . . . " Some Bible scholars believe that John is referring to the oracle-giving prophetess of Thyatira's Temple of Sambathe. As Jezebel brought Baal worship into Israel, the amalgamation of pagan practices with Christianity brought a weakness into the church of Thyatira, causing its demise. To my knowledge, there are no Christians in Akhisar today.

We waved goodbye to our self-appointed guide and left. Down the road we checked into a nice hotel.

SARDIS

On the road to Sardis we inhaled the real estate and then sneezed it out. "Are we going through this dust to see some more ruins?" Ronnie asked.

"We hope there are some ruins excavated in Sardis," Wayne answered.

"Ruins! Ruins!" David exclaimed. "They're ruining me."

"I'm sorry, David," I sympathized. "I know it isn't as interesting to you as it is to us, but we'll be home in just a few more days. So bear with us."

That day we were all plagued with the Turkey Trots. Maybe it was too much melon or some bug, but we all had our moments. Since there were no public toilets available, the one with the urge simply called for "time out," and Wayne stopped by the side of the seldom-traveled road. The four of us would then stand on the left side of the car to give the trotter privacy. We didn't let this malady slow us down; a few doses of medicine plus white bread and boiled rice ended the problem.

The ruins of Sardis were in the process of being excavated and restored. We investigated the remains of the magnificent temple, half of which was dedicated to Cybele (the mother goddess of Asia Minor who equated Artemis or Diana), and the other half was devoted to Zeus. The temple was about the same size as that in Ephesus—330 by 165 feet. Two of the original 66 foot columns with their capitols in place tower into the sky. Thirty feet of many of the other columns stand on their ninefoot-diameter bases which are exquisitely sculptured with leaf designs. Excavating this edifice was a challenge since all but a few feet of the temple was buried beneath 50 feet of debris.

Beside the temples is a small, sixth century Christian Church which stands as a memorial to what had been. It may have been built over the church of the first Christians. In his letter, John told the church of Sardis that though they were alive they were spiritually dead. I suspect the Christians in Sardis were the weakest of those in the seven churches because John does not commend them. Since the Christian church is so small in comparison to the humongous size of the pagan temples and Jewish Synagogue, I assume the Christian membership was small, as, well.

Sardisians distinguished themselves by inventing and minting the first coins (7th century B.C.). Money is frequently found in the vicinity. David, who had an affinity for money, was happy when we bought some old coins from a shepherd herding his goats on the ruins. The shepherd was equally happy with the exchange.

David and Ronnalee discovered that swinging on a chain hanging from an old excavating machine was fine sport. While they were thus occupied, I was fascinated by the beautiful red rock in the vicinity. The rocks varied in shade from pink to deep maroon. I picked up more than Wayne was willing to put in the trunk, so I slipped a few pieces in by my feet. There they shared space with the melons, the turtles, and the kid's toys.

Wayne and Elder Anderson studied the guidebook. "Old Sardis was built on the slopes of Mt. Tmolus with a wall surrounding it. The Pactolus River formed a natural moat on two sides. Before and after the days of the fabulously rich King Croesus, Sardis was a very wealthy city; however, it never equaled Ephesus or Symrna in importance. The Mongolians, under Tamerlane, finally destroyed Sardis in 1402 A.D. Sart, the modem village, lies near the ruins. Poor Turkish farmers plow over the ancient remains of the residential part of Sardis. The Roman theater at the base of the hill . . ."

"Cannot be compared to what we've seen in other places," I interrupted. "I think we should move on."

Due to my haste, we missed the Hall of Justice, the huge gymnasium, swimming pool, baths, shops, and the largest ancient synagogue ever found. It is 190 feet by 68 feet, and it was found with a mosaic floor still intact.

PHILADELPHIA

The sixth church on our agenda was Philadelphia. It stands at the other end of the base of Mt. Tmolus, about 25 miles southeast of Sardis on the way to Colossae. The founder of the city, Attalus II Philadelphus of Pergamum, named it Philadelphia, city of "brotherly love," in honor of his brother Eumenes 11. We drove through a cloud of dust and reached Philadelphia, about noon. People poured from their houses to see the strangers who drove a car with Lebanese license plates. We were covered with so much dust they couldn't be certain of our nationality. One lady patronized me by patting the dust off my shoulders and hair. I smiled at her, and she returned a toothless grin.

Alashehir, modem Philadelphia, is still the city of "brotherly love." Those dear people were so anxious to assist us that they almost trampled one another to get near us. We were "pressed about," and there were times when a deep breath would have felt good. At this point, I envied the turtles their hard, impregnable shells. We couldn't communicate with the friendly crowd—they spoke no English and we spoke no Turkish. We tried Arabic words, even a little German. They finally understood that we wanted to see relics of antiquity.

While Wayne and Elder Anderson photographed the remains of an early Christian church, I left with a young man who promised to take me to the government office. I hoped someone there could translate for us. We wound through a maize of streets and alleys. I knew I could never find my way back; even the FBI would be stymied in their search for me.

We did reach the government office which was secreted in such an out-of-the-way place that I felt deep respect for a guide who could actually locate it. After all that effort, the official looked quizzically at me, shook his head, and accompanied us back to the village square.

Meanwhile, "brotherly love" in the square had escalated. David objected to being hugged and kissed by the old ladies, and Ronnalee didn't want her blondish hair brushed by any more rough hands. Then the women began on me, a fresh candidate for their affections. They invited me into their homes to drink tea, taste their bread, and sample their dolma—a delightful Turkish specialty made with rice and seasonings wrapped in grape leaves and boiled. Since I love dolma, and it was lunch time, I allowed myself to sample quite a bit.

Since we couldn't find the old city wall, Wayne decided we should drive on to Laodicea. Moreover, he was hungry and wanted to get out of the city before opening the trunk and exposing its contents to curious eyes.

As we drove south out of town, there stood the old city wall for which we had been hunting. We could have saved time and effort if we'd just left Alashehir immediately. But then we would have missed an experience, and I'd have missed my dolma luncheon.

John had nothing but good to say about the church of Philadelphia, and we could say nothing but good about the friendly Moslem Turks in Alashehir today.

LAODICEA

It was hot. We opened the car windows and enjoyed the wind (but not the dust) as we drove forty miles south to Laodicea. The city was founded by King Antiochus Il (261 246 B.C.) and named in honor of his wife/sister, Laodice. Like all the cities in which the seven churches were located, Laodicea was also a prosperous commercial center on the Post Imperial Road, a trade route that went from Rome to Mesopotamia. Laodicea, like many of the cities in western Asia, had been destroyed in the big earthquake in 17 A.D. All were rebuilt by the Romans on a grander scale with temples, stadiums, circuses, amphitheaters, gymnasia, agoras, schools with advanced education, and cultural centers. Christianity had been established in this area by Paul or his fellow ministers (beginning about 50 A.D.), and the membership grew rapidly. Though some Laodiceans were punished or martyred, most of them escaped the atrocities inflicted upon many Christians in the other churches. Perhaps that is why they were "lukewarm."

John's message to Laodicea refers to a number of specifics to which those people could certainly relate. The citizens were wealthy and proud. They felt they had "need of nothing." Laodiceans had plenty of the valuable metal, but John counsels them to "buy gold tried in the fire." The gold they banked could not save them. They needed the priceless gift of salvation.

In part, Laodiceans were wealthy because of their specialty cloth made from the glossy, long wool of black sheep. They cashed in on their fine product by exporting it to other lands. Only the wealthy Laodiceans wore the black cloaks. John counseled them to buy "white robes that they may be clothed." They wore their beautiful black garments proudly as an outward display of their wealth and prestige. Figuratively, they needed to acknowledge their spiritual poverty and humbly accept the white robe of Christ's righteousness. The white robe, worn by the poor and the slaves, signified their admission of poverty.

John urged the Laodiceans to "buy eye salve that they may see." This advice which referred to their spiritual blindness, might also have offended their pride. After all, the whole world sought the famous Phrygian eye powder produced in Laodicea.

It worked to cure the eye diseases and trachoma problems that plagued the people of those days.

A modem naturopathic doctor in Lebanon gave us his "Phrygian powder" to heal the eye infections that were so prevalent during the fig season. It healed the infection better and faster than any medication we got from the pharmacy.

Laodicea was devastated by the earthquake of 60 A.D. The emperor Nero offered financial assistance to help rebuild their illustrious city, but the haughty and wealthy citizens sent word that they did not need resources from outside. They could do it themselves, and they did.

Old Laodicea's ruins are not excavated. The only remains visible is the crumbled amphitheater. However, the ruins of the nearby sister city of Hierapolis is extensively uncovered. Excavations reveal the same magnificent Grecian-Roman buildings as described in the other locations. Unique to Hierapolis, however, is the huge necropolis (cemetery). There are hundreds of family tombs, sarcophagi, as well as other types of graves where thousands of people have been laid to rest.

Laodicea, Hierapolis, and Colossae are within close proximity of each other. They lie about 100 miles east of Ephesus. Paul never visited these towns, but he wrote letters to Colossae (Col. 2:1), Laodecia and Hierapolis (Col 4:13) in A.D. 62 when imprisoned in Rome (Col. 4:16). The letters have been lost.

Laodicea was situated in the fertile Lycus River valley at an elevation of 800 feet. It rested between mountain peaks towering 8,000 to 9,000 feet. After it was destroyed by the Seijuks (11th century), the Crusaders (12th century), and the Turks (13th century), it was never rebuilt. Since that time it has lain in ruins and has served as a quarry for Denizli, the modem thriving city of 136,000, standing in the vicinity of Laodicea.

The wool from their black sheep and white angora goats no longer earns them fame or wealth. Also gone is the medical school built near the temple of Men Karou. Phrygian eye powder has been replaced by sulfa and other medications.

We still had a few hours before sunset, so we drove back to Hierapolis to swim in the hot mineral springs. After traveling the dusty roads we certainly needed a cleansing. The water was hot when it left Hierapolis, but as it flowed through the Lycus Valley it cooled to lukewarm by the time it reached Laodecia. Lukewarm water was thus a familiar phenomenon to the Laodecians.

When we reached the warm water pool, we donned our swimming suits and dove in. Elder Anderson didn't have a swim suit so he wore the salty slacks that had basically been ruined from our trip to Patmos. The mineral water finished them off. He now bad holey pants, that he could not wear them in holy places.

A man standing on the edge of the pool yelled, "Open your eyes and submerge them in the water." Of course, I did it. It was amazing. At first it burned, but soon it felt very soothing. Then I did a stupid thing that caused me instant regret. I tasted that lukewarm water. I not only "spewed it out of my mouth," I almost vomited.

There was no fresh water to rinse off the minerals, so we had to pull our clothes on over sticky bodies. But we were refreshed. As we drove from the site, we stopped to take pictures of the spectacular cascade-like formations of Pamukkale. Hierapolis's hot mineral water trickles down the hillside into turquoise colored pools. The pool water then spills over the stepped terraces leaving white calcium deposits of pure travertine marble that resembles frozen waterfalls. Wayne took too many pictures of the awesome, natural formations, but then, who could blame him.

Laodicea and Hierapolis ended our educational and inspirational tour. For us, our visit to the seven churches illuminated the messages given by John in his letters to them. We left the area of western Asia Minor with an added appreciation for the Bible. We were more convinced than ever that its writers were truly inspired by God.

*In the spring of 1995 1 took a tour group to visit west Anatolia. Time has wrought changes in western Turkey, but, in some ways, I preferred it the way it was in 1956. Buildings in Philadelphia have been torn down to make wide roads through the city. I missed the village square with its hubbub of humanity pressing around us. The Great Theater in Ephesus is closed to the public. We had to view it through a fence. We weren't allowed to wander through the agora, either. We never saw the sarcophagus at Thyatira nor the pottery factory with its heap of shards. Some of Heirapolis's hot mineral water has been channeled into a great indoor swimming pool in a modem hotel. I missed seeing the apothecary shop in Pergamum. In Sardis, the machine left by the archaeologists on which David and Ronnie played is still there—a bit more rusty. Kasadasi is no longer a sleepy little hamlet with a dock. It has become a bustling, modern city with a large seaport that caters to cruise ships. Progress has taken away the quaintness of these Turkish towns, but not the friendliness of the people. Modernization has made travel more pleasant and Turkey more prosperous. Riding in comfortable motor coaches over asphalt highways, sleeping and dining in deluxe hotels, traveling with a knowledgeable, Englishspeaking guide is a luxury we all enjoyed. Just ask Jack and Beth Betz, Pat Bunch, Lela and Ray Cronk, Ken and Joyce Emerick, Betty Farley, Agnus and Loren Montgomery, David Olson, Loraine Richmond, Peggy Riethmiller, Mary Stewart, Steven and Esther Tarangle, Mary Lou Wooley, and me. We all agree that Turkey is terrific.

CHAPTER 9
HOME AGAIN

Monday evening we left Laodicea and drove the 11 miles to Colossae. A few remains of antiquity are visible near the village of Honaz. Since the ministerial meetings in Beirut were to begin on Thursday evening, and we had many miles to go, we hurried through Colossae, the home of Epaphras, Philemon, and his slave Onesimus. Paul never preached in Colossae but he wrote them a letter during his first imprisonment in Rome. If Paul's letter of love didn't encourage them, visits from the Apostle John must have bolstered their faith.

The next few miles from Colossae to Afyon were the absolutely most abominable roads I had ever seen. Alternately, we drove through creek beds filled with large stones, water, mud, or four inches of fine silt. We prayed we would make it without breaking an axle or puncturing the oil pan. We were very relieved to arrive safely at Afyon, a large modem city. The name Afyon means opium. Fields of poppies are everywhere, and it is no secret that they produce the best opium.

We found a hotel that had just enough beds for our family. All five of us had often slept in the same room, but this time there wasn't bed space for Elder Anderson. He found lodging in a small hotel a block away.

We were filthy beyond words. Taking a bath helped, but we had no, clean clothes to put on—silt had infiltrated everything in our suitcases. We consoled ourselves with the thought that we would be home in just two more days. Then we could dump our clothes into the washing machine, take a good bath, and be clean from skin to outer garment.

Meanwhile, Elder Anderson wasn't faring very well in his hotel. About 4:30 in the morning, he walked over to our hotel. When Wayne heard him talking to the clerk in the lobby, he went out to check on Elder Anderson.

"Why are you up so early?" Wayne asked.

"Bedbugs," he answered. "The mattress in my hotel room was infested with the little nibblers." He pointed to the bite spots on his arms and face to prove it.

We got up then, ate a hurried breakfast and went on our way to Antioch of Pisidia, Iconium, Lystra, and Derbe. There wasn't much to see in any of those places.

Tuesday noon Elder Anderson developed a fever. We were concerned that it might be the result of the bedbug bites. Throughout the afternoon he became more ill. In spite of the fact that we were short on time, we had to stop early that evening to give Elder Anderson rest and medication. Again we all slept in the same room.

Wayne became "Doctor Olson" as he took over Elder Anderson's case. He had the patient soak in a hot tub of water, then gave him hot and cold fomentations every three hours. Elder Anderson drank the juice and flu/cold medicine that Wayne handed him. We all prayed. During the night his fever broke, and Elder Anderson felt well enough the next morning to continue the journey.

Again we passed through the Cicilian Gates, stopped at Tarsus, and ate at the mom-pop restaurant. It was late Wednesday afternoon when we pulled into Antioch of Syria. Even so, Elder Anderson wanted to stop. The museum was closed, but we were fortunate to find a man with a key. We were even happier that the man was willing to use the key and give us a special tour of the museum. He spoke Arabic well, so we could translate the information to Elder Anderson.

Our guide showed us the old Roman bridge, then took us to the east side of the city where hills graduate into mountains.

"Look up. there," he said as he pointed to a solid rock hill. "See the earliest Christian church in the side of that rock?"

"No, where?" we asked.

"Aha! So, you don't see it! " Our guide sounded pleased that we had missed the site. "That church is well camouflaged. It is believed by some that it was established as early as 40 A.D. by Christians fleeing here from Jerusalem. Whenever it was built, it is certain the Christians were worried about persecution. They never disturbed the outer rock facing. That wall follows the natural contour of the rock cliff, so you can't see it. However, notice what seems like small holes in the rock? Those are actually little windows that ventilate the large room the Christians hollowed out inside the mountain. Would you like to see it?"

Would we? He had piqued our curiosity beyond measure.

The guide had us drive to the top of the mountain, which didn't make any sense until we got out. He led us down a path through thorny, dried shrubs to crudely hewn steps that went down into the mountain. It took careful footwork to descend the uneven steps, but soon we found ourselves in a large room—the early Christians' Church.

"You see," the guide said, his eyes dancing with delight, "Christians sneaked from the city up to this mountain, and then they went DOWN to their church."

We decided that the early Christians were very resourceful. No one could easily find the entrance to this church; neither would people even suspect there was a church inside the mountain. It must have taken the Christians many days and excessive effort to carve this church out of the living rock.

Signs of the cross were above the altar, and a baptistery for immersion was in front of it. Christians had also prepared for the worst scenario. In case they were betrayed or discovered, they built a secret tunnel for a hasty escape in the back of the church. We followed it only a short way. It was getting quite dark, our flashlight was going dead, and we needed to hurry along. The stop had taken more time than we had to spare, but it was well worth it.

When we got back in the car, Elder Anderson commented, "I don't know when the secret church was used, but Gibbons says that within the first century one fifth of the population, or 100,000 people, of Antioch were Christians. By the second century there were five million Christians throughout the Roman Empire. Fifty thousand of them in Rome. Christianity spread like wildfire. "

We left Antioch (Antakyah in Turkish) and got to the border by 8 P.M. The Turks sent us on our way in a few minutes, and so did the Syrians. Next we were at the SyrianLebanese border. They, too, were in a charitable mood and didn't delay us. We were happy to be driving along the Mediterranean Sea coast on the last leg of our journey home. We entered our front door about 4 A.M. and seared Ray Bitar, who was caring for our house and pets, almost out of his wits.

"I expected you to arrive in the daytime," he laughed nervously. "Only Americans are crazy enough to drive all night to get home to go to work the same day. By the way, Mary had our baby girl."

"Oh, Ray, I'm so happy for you both!" I exclaimed as I hugged him. "My 'sister' Mary who took care of Ronnie, now has a daughter of her own. Congratulations!"

That day we bathed, slept, and washed clothes. Elder Anderson had arrived in time for his ministerial meetings which began Thursday night. The ten days of meetings were a blessing to the ministers who had come from all over the Middle East Division.

We were sorry when we had to part with Elder Anderson on September 4. He had become a Grandpa to our children and a father to us.

Our dog, Teddy, was happy to see the children; the parakeets were, well, who could tell? Teddy was curious about the box turtles. He barked at them, rolled them over, and licked them, but he got no response. Macy and Donia simply pulled their appendages into their shells and let the dog act like an idiot. We finally had to keep the turtles out on our balcony to keep the dog from losing his mind. The turtles were more comfortable without the attention of Teddy, too. Though how could I be sure? Turtles, to my mind, are the most unresponsive creatures in the universe. Keeping turtles for pets, however, has its pluses. They aren't messy or smelly, and their food is cheap.

The children read about turtles and learned some things from keeping them, or so they claimed. They proudly displayed Macy and Donia to all their friends, who took turns holding them. I concluded that if the turtles made the kids happy I would tolerate the newest pets on the college hill. However, I thought it would have been interesting to know if the turtles ever wondered how they got from a Roman road in Macedonia to a balcony in Lebanon.

CHAPTER 10
MEDICAL CADET CORPS AT MIDDLE EAST COLLEGE

The ministerial meetings were scarcely over before Wayne had to implement a new and unusual assignment. Since war is always imminent in the Middle East, several countries had instituted compulsory military training. For young men not in school, the stint was for two years. For senior high school students and/or freshmen college students, this involved monthly bivouacs plus two weeks of compulsory and intensive training during the summers - similar to the ROTC in America.

The mission had not taken the government's edict too seriously until one day when a jeep arrived on the college campus loaded with rifles. They had come to teach our boys. Now it was certain that bearing arms and Sabbath observance would be a problem for our Adventist young men. That's when the division asked Wayne (who had been a lieutenant in the Medical Cadet Corps at Union College) to resolve this problem.

Wayne spent the next six months working with government officials to arrange an alternative training. He went to the Ministry of Military Affairs and talked with the officers. Also present was an English employee who was their technical advisor for civil defense. They listened intently as Wayne explained the stand of the Adventist church on bearing arms and how our MCC program was intended to train men to save lives. After showing the gentlemen brochures and pictures of our Medical Cadet Corps programs in the States, they were duly impressed. Wayne finally convinced them to give his plan a try - substitute Civil Defense and the Adventist Medical Cadet Corps program in lieu of their military training.

The government had two conditions however, that Wayne must meet. First, he had to accept students from other schools who preferred our program to bearing arms. Wayne agreed, providing the students wouldn't drink or smoke during the entire two-week training program. Second, the government insisted that two of their officers would be responsible for discipline and emergencies. Wayne gladly accepted that offer; it relieved him of the job.

Then Wayne discovered that the Lebanese government had no military drill manual for medical personal. Anees Haddad[1] hurdled that problem by translating the regular American manual into Arabic. By summer, everything was in place.

The Lebanese government got more involved as time passed. In the end, they furnished tents, fatigues, uniforms, boots, helmets, litters and all the Red Cross supplies, plus two lira a day per person to feed the cadets. Thus God and the government relieved the mission of the financial burden. Wayne paid only to make a Medical Cadet Corps flag and the emblems for their uniforms.

Sunday, September 9, several regular soldiers from the Lebanese Army came up to the college and helped Wayne and the 40 cadets set up camp. All the little boys on the compound and college hill were there to watch the excitement; their sisters and fathers discretely stood a short distance away. This was the first time anything of this nature had been done throughout the Middle East Division.

During the days that followed, the Lebanese Civil Defense unit sent their men to teach that aspect of army life; embassies provided civil defense films to show the cadets. Red Cross staff taught First Aid courses and presented certificates to the cadets at the final ceremony. Michael Nabti and Anees Haddad were Wayne's invaluable assistants throughout the entire program.

---

1 In the spring of 1957 the cadets marched in the Lebanese Independence Day Parade. A second MCC camp was held the following summer. Once again Anees Haddad, Youth Leader for Middle East Division, and Michael Nabti, teacher at Middle East College, were Wayne's chief assistants.

The head of the army also made himself available. He was amazed at the vitality and skill of our boys. Toward the end of the encampment the cadets put on a demonstration. They marched, put out fires, rescued people from steep hills, and showed other maneuvers needed to save lives.

Ile English Civil Defense expert remarked, "These boys are remarkable. I don't see how you ever taught them all of this is just two weeks."

"Christians put forth their best efforts for deserving causes," Wayne said.

Besides cameramen from the Civil Defense Corps, the Lebanese army, the American Embassy, the Red Cross, and the division, there was a host of onlookers from our churches and the college hill.

After such an impressive demonstration, our cadets were praised. They were invited to participate in the September 24 parade in Beirut. The cadets certainly enjoyed the cheers they received from the crowd as they passed in review. They were a sharp looking corps, and their performance was flawless.

Then the camp was over. It had been a whopping success. Our relations with the governments of Egypt, Syria, and Lebanon had definitely been improved. The cadets and Wayne were exhausted, but they were pleased with their success.

CHAPTER 11
NEW YEAR, NEW SCHOOL, NEW STUDENTS

One of the first things I did when we got back from our journey was to go to the division compound. The new school building was almost finished. I wanted to dance with excitement and jump for joy, but I maintained my dignity because the kids were there; otherwise, I would have exploded into jubilant footwork.

The builders had followed my plans explicitly. Bookcases covered with formica were below the bank of east windows. Chalkboards, with cork bulletin boards on either end, lined the front of the room. High windows on the west wall ventilated the room while the covered veranda protected them from rain. The children's desks were modeled after modem school desks in the states. Separate boys and girls bathrooms were stocked with paper. Balls, bats, and play equipment sat in a box.

A new school! What a luxury for the children and me! After the two little rooms in the Industrial Arts building one year, and the two end rooms in the girls dormitory the past year, this would be a blessed change. The children would have plenty of room to spread out in the large school room or do pet projects in the smaller room.

School began October 1 with ten students: Alger and Norma Keough, Mike McCulloch, Cherry Zytkoskee, Tommy Gott, David and Ronnalee Olson, David Rice, and Roger and Max Nolte (two American Embassy children). The children had fun settling into their new school and new desks. They brought books from home to start a library—probably 150 volumes in all. Colorful bulletin boards and a few plants completed the decor.

No one minded that Tommy, Roger, and David always brought chameleons, frogs, and lizards into the classroom, but the girls wanted some ordinary pets. I satisfied their wishes by purchasing two parakeets. They named the green bird Shadow and the yellow one Sunshine. When we closed all the windows and doors, the children took the parakeets out of their cages and carried them around on their hands or shoulders. The birds became very tame and flew from one child to another. They didn't seem to distract the children from their lessons.

We had never had a play field before, so recesses on the large field on the compound spelled pleasure. 'Me younger children were sometimes excused early to play outside. Tommy, Cherry, and David had immense imaginations which showed up in their "bear-cubcrawling-through-the-grass" routine. A scream from the grassy noll one day notified us that a lizard had taken refuge in Cherry's pant leg. Cherry loved all kinds of critters, but this critter had carried his luck too far.

One afternoon Mike, Norma, Alger, Ronnie, and David decided to play after the others left for home. I stepped out of the school's back door just in time to see Mike and Norma crash into each other. Both of them wore glasses, which were crushed into the other's face. Norma staggered backwards, blood streaming down her face. Alger lost his cool altogether and screamed, "Mother, Norma is dying! Come quick."

Mrs. Keough didn't hear him, but the men in the division office heard Alger's cry of desperation and came rushing up to the playground. Someone wiped the blood from Norma's face and brushed away glass slivers.

I turned to Mike who was bravely standing by watching us help Norma. I was more than alarmed when I saw slivers of glass protruding from his eye lids.

"Mike," I said as calmly as possible. "Stand real still and don't blink your eyes. I have to pull some glass out of your eye lids before it scratches your cornea. This is very important."

One of the men heard what I said and came over to help me. "This could mean trouble," he said. "He's got to get to a doctor right away. If we don't get all the glass out, he could lose his vision. Ronnalee, go down to the division office and ask someone to call Mike's father at the press," Ronnalee was off, the call was made, and moments later Mr. McCulloch drove up. He rushed Mike to the hospital where a doctor removed the last few minute pieces of glass. Mike's vision was saved. Other than a few bruises and broken glasses, Norma was all right, too. Thank God for the presence of angels.

We celebrated Wayne's and David's birthdays October 17 and 18. The parties had been fun. But the next day our joy turned to sorrow. The telegram from Oregon read: "Dad Olson killed October 18 on Milton-Freewater highway."

"What a terrible thing to happen on David's birthday!—I mused.

"I don't know what to do," Wayne wept. "I can't get to the funeral. I can't get my family by telephone. Here I sit, not knowing exactly what happened to my father. I'm mourning and frustrated at the same time. Midge, do you remember when we left America you had the distinct impression that we would never see all our family again? Well, it's happened. We'll never see my father again."

Two weeks later letters arrived from Wayne's family telling us more details: "Dad Olson was making a missionary visit after supper the night of October 18. The home was nearby so he decided to walk there. He was on the left shoulder of the road when he was struck by a speeding pickup. The college student driver lost control as he passed a car, swerved onto the shoulder and struck Dad. The mirror tore Dad's right arm, but the young man did not stop to help him. Dad was bleeding profusely and must have been dazed. There was a light in the house across the road and, we believe, he was going there for help. He walked out into the traffic and was hit by a big Buick that threw him 100 feet. His body was mangled badly, and his skull had multiple fractures."

In spite of our sagging spirits, we had to accept what we could not change. God never makes a mistake. He is with us through sunshine and shadow.

Two new students, Dick and Kenny Osborn, arrived the middle of November. Their father, Bob, was the new division treasurer, and their mother, Evelyn, was scheduled to work in the division office. They came to look over the school midmorning on the day they got to Beirut. I assigned them desks and assured them I'd have their school books by Monday.

Unfortunately, the Suez Canal dispute between France, England, and Egypt reached a crisis that day. Since Beirut was concerned about the possibility of an air raid, the sirens started blowing. It was just a practice drill, but the two recently arrived American boys must have thought we spent half of our school days under our desks with our hands over our head.

Trouble in the Suez Canal Zone escalated during November and December. Egypt wanted to nationalize the canal and take the revenue. After all, the canal was in Egypt's territory. England and France still wanted to keep control of the canal claiming they had paid the initial investment and upkeep. When political maneuvering became overly tense, foreign embassies urged their citizens to send their dependents out of Egypt. Thus it was that several more children were added to our roster: Ardis and Malcolm Russell and Ted Wilson.

Thanksgiving was always a happy holiday for the missionaries. It was the only time when all of us met without involving our national workers. There were over 60 of us in all—English, Australians, Swiss, and Americans. The men usually had an afternoon softball game, while we women spent the day cooking and visiting. This year the day was even more special with all the new arrivals.

In early December the Lesher family arrived from the states. They were on their way to Aden but lacked visas. They were told to wait in Beirut until the necessary papers could be secured. They had two daughters, Martha and Eileen. The original female threesome, Norma, Ronnalee, and Cherry were pleased to have their number doubled by adding Ardis, Eileen, and Martha. Now the six girls could have fun together, while the boys ran their

Dinky cars on "their clay bank" back of the school. The boys had developed an elaborate road system complete with bridges and tunnels, curves and parking lots. The ultimate in shopping for the boys in those days was to go to the Mickey Mouse Store in Beirut to buy the newest production in Dinky cars—an English manufactured toy.

Then the Christmas season was upon us. I wanted a Christmas tree at school, but I believed it was impossible to get one. In Lebanon at that time, it was forbidden to cut down an evergreen tree without permission. But Kenny and David had no problem with that law, nor the fact that there were only a few young evergreen trees growing on the compound. They took a saw, selected their favorite tree, and cut it down. Kenny sawed his hand in the process, but that didn't dampen his spirits. The two tree-napers dragged their trophy triumphantly into the school and dropped it at my feet.

I was flabbergasted. What could I say? Their little chests were swelled with pride; they had done their school and me a big favor. Their eyes sparkled with pleasure as they waited for my accolades. Their spirit of thoughtfulness deserved praise, yet I had to tell them that trees in Lebanon were too precious to be cut for decoration.

The boys handled my little speech far too well—I got the distinct impression that nothing I said diminished their feeling of accomplishment. They were the heroes of the day to the other students. They had brought home the tannenbaum for the school. Excited children enthusiastically gathered around the tree to decorate it with paper chains and popcorn strings, while I worried if I could get arrested for this infraction.

I had written a Christmas play for my ten students. When the seven new kids arrived, I had to re-write the play to include them. They all played in the rhythm band under the direction of David Rice (the only seventh-grader). I sewed caps and capes out of blue crepe paper trimmed with gold. They looked quite sharp and enjoyed being a "uniformed band."

Kenny was a rather shy child, so I was quite surprised when he came to me with an offer, "Mrs. Olson, if you have an extra poem, I'll say it for you."

I couldn't resist that sweet little boy. I made up a poem especially for Kenny. The program was set for Sunday night, December 23. All the children were ready, especially Kenny. Before the children went on stage, both Kenny's parents and I had advised him to speak loudly. And Kenny did just that. He shouted out his poem to the amusement of the audience. When he got back stage he asked me, "Why were people laughing? It wasn't a funny poem."

What could I say? Kenny needed positive strokes to overcome his shyness. "Kenny," I said, "I think they were smiling loudly because they were happy they could hear you.

You did such a good job!" Kenny was satisfied and made it through the rest of the program in style.

David, Tommy, and Kenny were the lowly shepherds in the play. They envied the fancy costumes of the wise men (Mike, Max, and David Rice) until Kenny reminded his pals that there was one worse part they could have been given—being Joseph (Roger), the husband of Mary (Cherry). Obviously the hormones hadn't kicked in yet because none of the second graders wanted a "wife" EVER!

The children performed well, making their teacher and parents proud.

New Year's day was also special. Many of us drove high up on the mountains to find snow. We slid down the hills on makeshift sleds dishpans, plastic, copper trays, anything! We drank hot chocolate, and ate sandwiches and fruit. We got wet, but we didn't care. We had fun!

Veda and Dick Lesher were living in the union building down in Ashrafiah (suburb of Beirut), but they basically had no furniture, no heat, no warm clothing, and no transportation. After they had patiently endured that situation for a month, we invited the Leshers to live with us until they received their Aden visas. On January 7 they took over Ronnie's room, and Ronnie moved in with David. Since Dick had ulcers, and we ate a lot of Arabic food, I was afraid to cook for them. So we agreed they could have the run of the house and use of our appliances, but do their own cooking. Veda kept her things in half of the refrigerator and made her meals before we ate. On weekends, we usually had our meals together. The Leshers were such amiable people. We enjoyed their company, and our children were happy to have live-in playmates.

In January the union committee voted for Wayne to become union evangelist. He was given permission to study Arabic for six months which would end when my school was out. Dick, Veda and Wayne all started Arabic lessons in our house, while the four children and I were busy down at the school.

I now had 17 students in six grades. I needed a little extra help, so Janet Russell, Indra Ashod, and Veda Lesher came to help me with some of the classes.

The first graders, Ardis, Martha, and Ted, were eager learners. In the first month they mastered all the Dick and Jane books and were ready for more advanced reading. They were the perfect class.

I could not say the same for the second graders. Oh, they cooperated very well, but their personalities were vastly different. They were both challenging and fun to teach. One day when I was teaching grades one and two a class on safety, I explained that the "cat's eyes" in the pavement on the road between Beirut and Sidon were there to delineate the lanes of traffic. Sensitive little Cherry got tears in her eyes.

"What's wrong with you?" David asked, trying to figure out why she was distressed. "Why are you crying?"

"Oh, I'm just thinking about those poor cats," she sniffed. "How many cats did they have to kill to get all of those eyes?"

"How can you be so stupid, Cherry!" Tommy exploded. "Those aren't real cat's eyes, they just call those reflectors cat's eyes because they shine in the dark like a cat's eye."

"Oh," Cherry said meekly, as she drew back embarrassed.

"You hurt her feelings, Tommy," Eileen said.

"Yeah, that wasn't very nice," Kenny agreed.

I was amused at the discussion, and so was Veda. The first graders just sat quietly with their hands folded and never got involved. The interesting thing about the five second graders was that they could settle any dispute amicably without adult interference. They were thinkers, but they didn't think the same way very much of the time.

The three third graders were bound for great things. Roger promised to be an anthropologist or naturalist. He drew whales and dinosaurs all over his papers and workbooks. He didn't always get his school work done, but I could always tell which papers were his.

Malcolm was headed for a professorship. He kept a BOOK OF KNOWLEDGE in his desk to which he reverted whenever his other lessons bored him. He knew so much trivia that he could have been a Jeopardy contestant.

I called Alger Keough my "Little Churchill." He was a diplomat, and he tended to business—not always his own. He was always the first in his class to get his work done. One day when he handed his math paper to me he said, "Here is my paper, Mrs. Olson. It's all done. Ah, not like some other people." He looked knowingly at his two classmates—one with eyes riveted on the BOOK OF KNOWLEDGE and the other leisurely sketching whales.

"Thanks, Alger," I said. "You have a good sense of responsibility. Maybe we should encourage your classmates to understand theirs." I walked down the aisle, took Malcolm's book temporarily and suggested that Roger and he do their math.

"Oh, sure," they agreed pleasantly and turned their attention to what they were supposed to be doing.

Dick was the only one in the fourth grade. He was very outgoing, very sure, very ambitious, and very mature. He was not only good in history and geography, he was excellent. Dick was headed for success, too.

Max, Norma, Mike, and Ronnie were a unique fifth-grade quartet. The comradeship they shared was beautiful. They played together, studied together, and stuck together. They always helped whichever one needed assistance.

David Rice, a seventh grader, was the oldest student in school. He was good natured and tried to arbitrate in little disputes. He assumed the "big brother" role by helping the younger children.

One day the clouds rolled in, and the sky turned a frightening color. Then we heard the pounding of hail on the school's roof. Marble-size stones of ice covered the ground. In the years we had been in Lebanon, it had never been cold enough in Beirut to hail or snow. The children were enthralled with the spectacle. They stood at the windows for 15 minutes watching the weather perform.

"Children, do you know what to do when life gives you a lemon?" I asked.

"Sure. Make lemonade," Dick answered immediately.

"And what should you do when it hails?"

They looked perplexed. That was a new one to them. It was new to me, too, but I had a nifty little plan. "I say we should make ice cream! Let's go up to my house, pick up hail stones, and use them to freeze homemade ice cream."

"Yeah," they all shouted enthusiastically. The children scrambled to get their coats on and raced up the hill. When we reached the house, Dick Lesher and Wayne got down our gallon ice cream freezer from the attic while Veda and I made the recipe. Recipe? What recipe? Veda and I substituted canned milk for cream, whole powdered milk (a little thicker than usual), sugar (the genuine thing), and vanilla. We sampled the mixture and it tasted very good.

Every child had a turn at the crank while Wayne regulated the amount of table salt added to the hail to make it freeze. Veda and I made fudge topping for the double batches of ice cream and chopped up walnuts. We fed the kids ice cream and topping until they were stuffed. None of the parents objected to our deviation from the normal school day, or the unhealthy food we fed their children. They knew that day and event would be etched in the memory bank of their children forever.

Interestingly enough, the hail only fell in a swath that crossed the division compound and college hill. In Beirut below us, they saw practically nothing of the phenomenon. Some of the children were convinced that God had sent them the hail just to make them happy. And none of us parents disputed that lovely thought.

All the children had pets or access to their friends' pets. Tommy's dog, Gink, was an interesting specimen, even for a mongrel. He showed his teeth and seemed to grin whenever the children talked to him. Gink was acceptable, but Gotts had one pet that was not popular with the adults on the college hill. Their donkey assumed the role of the proverbial rooster. Every morning his loud bray awakened everyone much earlier than they cared to get up. The mission children liked to ride him, but he bucked enough to keep them off more than on. The donkey's residency on the college hill was short-lived.

Macy and Donia finally came out of their winter's hibernation. After not eating anything from December to March, they began to nibble on almost any fruit or vegetable offered them. The children's interest in turtles was revived.

The weather warmed early that year. We opened the windows to enjoy the spring air. Sunshine and Shadow were out of their cage as usual, flying from one favorite student to the next. We forgot about the open windows. Suddenly the birds discovered their opportunity and flew to freedom.

"Oh, no! Sunshine and Shadow just flew away," Martha cried.

Like one unit, the children rose from their seats and ran out the door, chasing their birds in flight. Some were crying for the birds; some were calling to the birds; everyone was anxious to recapture the pets. Emotions ran from disbelief to hopeless sorrow as the birds flew from one tree to another and finally over the compound fence. We never saw them again.

April 17 the Leshers moved into a vacant house on the hill. After three and a half months of co-existence, it was lonely without them. They never did get their visas for Aden. That summer they moved to Egypt to work at Nile Union Academy.

We also moved. The division changed its mind about Wayne becoming union evangelist. They decided that moving a family frequently from one Middle East country to another would be very complicated. Visas, work permits, housing, and other details seemed too cumbersome and expensive. Furthermore, the time didn't seem right. They then voted for Wayne to be the chaplain at Dar Es Salaam hospital in Baghdad, Iraq, teach the nursing students Bible, and be pastor of the English Church. I was asked to teach the Baghdad English Elementary School.

At the same time, Charles Crider was invited to Lebanon from Iraq to take over the union's educational program. Criders and we agreed to exchange houses—they'd move into our apartment on the college hill, and we'd move into their house in Baghdad.

The college and division people had farewell parties for the Leshers and us. I cried as I packed. Lebanon had been our home since 1947, and I could hardly bear the thought of leaving it. Ronnalee, David, and I had spent only one year in the new school. I'd miss my dear little students, the college students and faculty, the mission and division workers, plus all our Lebanese friends. I was sure I could never be as happy in Iraq.

It was a blessing that none of us could see into the future, especially the people of Iraq. A time of trouble awaited us there.

CHAPTER 12

LIVING IN DANIEL'S LAND

I couldn't believe I was moving to Daniel's land, Iraq. As I packed, I rebelled inwardly, wishing it was only a bad dream. I never wanted to leave Lebanon.

"Midge, " Wayne chided, "we are missionaries, and we must be willing to go where we are needed."

"Or someone thinks we're needed," I grumbled still hoping for a reprieve.

One of our last acts was to give Macey and Donia their freedom. They had been with us for over a year, and the parting was sad especially for the children. Even I found some damp spots under my eyes as I watched the turtles amble up the mountain through the dry grass. They had grown accustomed to the welfare benefits we had doled out to them. Now I hoped their natural instincts would help them fend for themselves.

Our move seemed a reality when Wayne applied for our Iraqi visas. Then a truck came and loaded our goods. The next noon our family, along with our two parakeets in their cage, boarded the Nairn Bus and spent the night traveling over the dusty, rocky trail to Baghdad. The desert route was much shorter than going through Jordan on the asphalt highway. The bus was comfortable, and it was surprising how well the tightfitting doors and air conditioning kept out the dust and heat.

I sat in my seat, brooding about my situation. I had fought this move all the way. As I meditated, I remembered Paul's admonition—that Christians should be content in any situation in which they find themselves. I wanted to believe I was a Christian who was willing to take Paul's advice.

"But then Paul never had to move to Iraq," I argued the point with myself

"What did you say, Midge?" Wayne asked.

"Ah, Paul never moved to Iraq," I answered carefully, knowing he hadn't heard my disgruntled remark. "Wayne you're such a saint!"

"Wh-what? Whatever triggered that thought?" Wayne stuttered looking bewildered.

"Just, ah, just knowing how willing you are to go anywhere, do anything."

"I guess we're not on the same wavelength, Midge, Wayne said wrinkling his forehead. "But, but --- Hey, we're pulling into the bus station now. We're in Baghdad! Grab your things, kids! "

"Good!" the kids squealed, shouldering their travel bags.

There were no shouts of jubilation emerging from my lips lips that were firmly pursed into resignation. I hadn't been able to whip myself up into an enthusiastic mood yet. The bumpy, 22-hour ride across the desert hadn't stimulated optimistic feelings in me.

Dr. Bill Wagner met us at the depot and took us home for lunch. While our children got acquainted with Billy, Jeannie, and Ruthie, Kathleen put on a delicious meal. I wondered how she did it. I had heard they couldn't grow anything in Iraq except eggplant, oranges, and dates. I soon learned that Iraq grew many wonderful foods, plus producing three-fourths of the world's dates.

Three days after we arrived, the truck came with our goods. Porters moved our furniture into the house that Criders had lived in before they moved to our house in Beirut. Surrounding the house was a sixfoot-high cement wall with sharp glass pieces protruding from the top. The wall, along with the heavy iron gate, should keep out any thieves. There was, however, another presence that would discourage the boldest robbers. It was the. dog Criders had left behind. Shushka was a bad inheritance; she was a mean mongrel. We had to tranquilize her while the men moved the furniture into our house. Worse yet, the dog would never let the children and me into the house. Wayne had to go home with us and hold her off with sticks while we dashed through the front door. Wayne claimed that colporteur work had taught him how to make friends with ANY dog. He gave her food treats, but she'd rather have his hand than the food.

We never ventured into the garden nor yard. No one could come and visit us because they couldn't get into the house. This was ridiculous. The dog ruled our lives. We were not free to come and go; Wayne couldn't have cottage meetings in our home because he feared the dog would rip someone. After a month of working with the wild creature, Wayne gave up. "I could have tamed a lion by this time," he sighed, "but that dog is a hopeless demon."

Although Wayne hated to do it, he finally had a policeman come and shoot Shuska before she bit someone. At last we were free from the Canine Reign of Terror. We could walk in our garden filled with beautiful flowers—not to be compared to the Hanging Gardens of Babylon, but it satisfied my horticultural instincts. Now folks dropped around to visit. I learned that Iraqi people were just as friendly as the Lebanese, and I was happy I had moved to Iraq. In fact, I seemed to remember I had always wanted to live in Baghdad.

We missed the moderate climate of Lebanon, which is tempered by the Mediterranean Sea. It was hot in Iraq—like 120 degrees fahrenheit hot! When we got out of the club's swimming pool, we shivered because the water dried from our bodies so rapidly. When we were dry, the heat hit us again, and we sought shade and lemonade. When we walked across the street, my high heels sunk into the asphalt, and I walked out of my shoes onto the sizzling road. I soon learned the trick of walking on the balls of my feet.

Fortunately, the hospital and chapel were made comfortable with swamp coolers. In desert countries these installations put moisture into the air which in turn cools the atmosphere. This pushes the water bills up during the summer, but it makes living in hot; dry climates endurable. Our house had a swamp cooler in a huge downstairs bedroom; so, until the temperatures moderated, the children slept in our bedroom. Large ceiling fans in every room circulated the moist air which helped keep the house cooler.

The hospital workers were outstanding people. We enjoyed many social events together. We didn't always have a reason for a fling, but birthdays and special holidays certainly motivated us.

The Arabic church people were an educated, stimulating, and interesting group. Some of them owned lucrative businesses in Baghdad or factories in the suburbs, but they never flaunted their wealth. They were generous with their contributions and supported the mission and the Adventist Arabic School. As loyal Iraqi citizens, they were equally concerned that the people of their country have the advantages of modem technology. Building a hospital that would serve the people of Iraq was their dream. The actual project, however, was funded by the General Conference of Seventh-day Adventists.

The Adventist Dar Es Salaam Hospital had an excellent reputation. People came from everywhere for the services of our four reputable doctors. The nursing staff and students were from different countries and cultures—Armenian, Iraqi, Lebanese, Egyptian, Syrian, Jordanian, Palestinian, American, and Norwegian—but they nursed the sick in the spirit of Jesus. The physiotherapy department was run by Leif and Esther Jensen of Denmark. They did wonders with the patients. Ayoub Azar of Jordan was the pleasant pharmacist. Wayne, as hospital chaplain, enjoyed sharing the love of God with patients in the waiting room or in hospital beds.

Dar Es Salaam, a 60-bed hospital, was nearly always filled to capacity. The patient waiting room was usually crowded. Every day as many as 70 of Iraq's poor received loving attention at the free clinic. Dar Es Salaam's staff earned nation-wide recognition for their fine services. Embassy and professional people from many different countries, wealthy sheiks, oil-rich barons, Iraqi government officials, the average Iraqi, and Arab paupers walked through the doors of Dar Es Salaam Hospital sick and came away feeling better physically and refreshed spiritually.

The last of September I began teaching eleven students in the Baghdad English Church School located in the back corner of the hospital compound. Dick Karmy was a first grader; Paul Karmy, Buster Ubbink, and David were an interesting threesome in grade three; Ann Ubbink was the only fourth grader; Jim Karmy and Sylvia Aldrich enjoyed fifth grade classes; Ronnalee and Billy Wagner were in the sixth grade; Jeannie Wagner and Bob Karmy were the teenage eighth graders.

I tried challenging my students with every innovative program in my repertoire. But nothing I did interested the boys half as much as climbing the date trees during recess and picking the delectable fruit. Since that was their interest (or their desire to satisfy their appetite), I took the children to visit a date packaging factory. We were surprised at the sanitary way they packaged the dates. They rinsed off the dust, dried them, and then sanitized them in a special room for 24 hours. Then they packed them in boxes or tins.

The children were impressed, but they still ate the dates they picked right off the trees without washing them. I often wondered how to teach kids the concept that soap and water were meant to run interference with germs. But why should they worry? They stayed healthier than we adults who took precautions. I learned from the date packaging plant manager that the sweetness in dates kills any living organism on them. Maybe so, but I still washed the dates I ate.

Besides being pastor for the English-speaking church and hospital chaplain, Wayne taught math and Bible to my eighth grade students. He also taught the nursing students Bible, had worship for the hospital workers every morning, made hospital visits, and worked with the newly appointed Iraqi mission president.

Shortly after arriving in Iraq, Wayne bought a four-door Dodge car that suited our needs. When the weather cooled in October, we decided to explore our new environs. On Sabbath or Sundays, several carloads of us would drive off the asphalt highways across the desert floor to inspect a Tell (a mound that covers an ancient city). We soon were hooked on the fascinating hobby of exploring Tells. We seldom found anything of value; desert Arabs and archaeologists had already absconded with those items. Still it was fan to imagine and question. Who of Noah's descendants lived there? What did they wear and eat? How soon after the flood did they build their community? Did they reverence the true God?

Most interesting among the Tells north of Baghdad were Khorsabad, Nimrud, Arbela (where Alexander defeated Darius in 331 B.C.), and Ninevah. The children wanted to investigate Ninevah because of their interest in the story of Jonah. Wayne used them as his excuse to spend the day there. He 'had to show them around" even though very little of old Ninevah was visible. Two thousand years of drifting sand had covered the remains. There were, however, depressions which indicated the places where archaeologists had dug.

"Children,—Wayne warned,—it is unsafe to walk over some spots—the unstable sand may let you drop between unseen buildings, and then filter in on top of you. So stay close to me."

Ninevah lies on the east side of the Tigris River, across from the modem city of Mosul. The ruins of the old walls form long, low hills of sand with gaps where the gates once stood. The total length of the wall was about 7 1/2 miles. It is estimated that about 160,000 people lived inside the walls. Many more people lived in the vicinity. One of the 15 gates is completely uncovered; winged bulls stand as sentinels on either side of the entrance.

If a person wants to see the treasure taken from old Ninevah, he/she must visit the museums of Europe, especially the British Museum. If someone wants to see the accuracy of the fulfillment of the prophecies of Nahum and Zephaniah, a walk across the heaps of dust covering the ruins is very convincing.

The reluctant prophet, Jonah, had given Ninevah his warning message about 810-782 B.C. Because they repented then, the Assyrians were given a reprieve of almost two more centuries. Then in 612 B.C., the Babylonians and Medes laid siege to the city and totally destroyed it. Two centuries after its destruction, Xenophan, who with his armed forces passed its ruins, could not even learn the name of the great metropolis that once flourished there.

Ninevah lay undisturbed for centuries. Modem archaeologists had a difficult time locating it. Finally, Layard and Rassam unearthed priceless treasures from Ninevah's formless heaps of earth and rubble. Ashurbanipal, the monarch who died only a few years before Ninevah's destruction, built a new palace which included a private library of 25,000 religious, scientific, and literary works. Scholars have learned more about the ancient world from these cuneiform tablets than from any other single discovery in the Bible lands.

South of Baghdad were other Tells such as Eridu, Erech, Borsippa, Nippur, Ur, Ctesiphon, and Babylon. Most of these were too far away for one day's excursion, but Babylon, which was only about 54 miles from Baghdad, was always a favorite site to visit. It wasn't a Tell since the archaeologists had excavated the ruins to street level. We became well acquainted with the ruins of Babylon since visitors always begged us to take them there.

Babylon is a ghost town of asphalt streets and fallen brick buildings. Archaeologists have excavated and reconstructed it to the extent that one can see the layout of the city. What a thrill it was to walk the same streets that Daniel's feet had trod during his years in Babylon. He had seen the same lion statues on the comers that named the streets. As prime minister of Babylon, Daniel was free to pass in and out of the public buildings and palaces. He probably avoided the ziggurat temple of the heathen god, Marduk. He knew the prophets had foretold the destruction of the world-famous Babylon, but could he have imagined it would look like this after 2,500 years?

Babylon was eerie in some ways—vultures flew overhead, dust devils swirled funnels of sand, and wind whistled through ancient brick walls. Jackals, hyenas, and wolves had dens in the ruins. Sometimes I saw animal footprints in the sand. Once I caught a glimpse of two jackals and heard the haunting, laughing cries of hyenas. Around the end of a wall and some distance away, I saw three hyenas fighting over a kill. The hair on the back of my neck stood at attention. Although they weren't likely to harm me, I quickly made my way to the car with the children in tow. Wayne captured the hyena dispute with his camera.

Every time I visited Babylon I was reminded of the words of Jeremiah 51:37, "Babylon shall become a heap of ruins, the haunt of jackals,…without inhabitant." And the words of Isaiah 13:20-22, "It (Babylon) will never be inhabited or dwelt in for generations, no Arab will pitch his tent there ... wild beasts will lie down there, and its houses will be full of howling creatures....Hyenas will cry in its towers, and jackals in the pleasant palace. "

Babylon truly was a "heap of ruins." However, it didn't become that way immediately after Cyrus the Mede conquered the city in 539 B.C. The Persians left the city mostly intact; they even made Babylon one of the capitals of their new empire. But the proud Babylonians kept rebelling against the tolerant Persians until King Xerxes punished them by destroying the palaces, temples, and walls in 480 B.C.

Some people still lived in Babylon when the young Greek, Alexander the Great, returned from his conquest of India and became ruler of the eastern and western kingdoms (about 331 B.C.). Babylon had its advantages: it was close to the Euphrates River so canals could bring water into the city; the irrigated plains produced an abundant supply of food; millions of brick could be salvaged from broken down buildings to construct new ones; and asphalt (which was used as mortar) was easily obtained from a pitch pool about 120 miles north of Babylon.

Since Babylon was near the center of the kingdoms he had conquered, Alexander decided to make it his capital. Records show that Alexander paid for thousands of man hours of labor to clear the site of the original tower of Babel. (Today the base of the Tower and the Babylonia of Nimrud, as well as the Babylon of the Amorite Dynasty and Hammurabi, are actually below the water level of Nebuchadnezzar's city). A cuneiform tablet describes the Babel Tower (ziggurat) as having a base of about 300 feet square and a height of 300 feet (equal to 30 stories). It was constructed of brick using asphalt as mortar. The tower rose skyward in seven progressively smaller stages. It was topped by an altar. Nebuchadnezzar kept the ziggurat in good repair during his reign and added a shrine to the god Marduk on top.

It was Alexander's fond ambition to build a monument for himself on top of the 300 foot base of Babel's tower, but before the workers had completely cleared the site, he died. On the banks of the Tigris River, his successor built Seleucia as his capitol using bricks from old Babylon. Bricks that were intended to build Alexander's monument, can now be found in the river dam of Hindiya, at the modem city of Hilla (three and a half miles south of Babylon), and in many other buildings in the area. Babylon has served as a brick quarry since Alexander's time.

There was always a guard on duty at the ruins of old Babylon. He carried a shotgun and claimed he had felled many of the four footed beasts in the vicinity. The guard seemed happy to have us as visitors because we spoke Arabic with him. He showed us buildings where nondescript animals were fashioned in relief on the brick walls. It must have been logical to Daniel that God represented the kingdoms of the world with strange combinations of beasts.

"When did they make the asphalt streets here in Babylon?" David asked.

"During Daniel's time or before," the guide told us. "Are you surprised to walk on asphalt streets that are 2,500 years old?"

"Yes," I answered, "I'm amazed!"

We walked down the street and entered Nebuchadnezzar's palace through a high arched doorway. The guide told us to note the immense size of one of the rooms which he claimed was the banquet room. I caught my breath. Could this be the banquet room in which Belshazzar defied the living God and served wine from the sacred vessels taken from the temple of Jerusalem? The room could easily accommodate the thousand lords and ladies the king invited for the banquet—the final feast before the Persians captured the city. I looked at the wall where the message "Mene, Mene, Tekel, Parsin" might have been written by a bloodless hand. I imagined the terrorized guests, their eyes riveted to the phenomenon, clinging to one another.

I pointed to a loose brick laying on the wall. "Could I have that?" I asked the guard.

"Why not.? Everyone in the region takes bricks from here," the guard laughed. "Now let me explain how the kings and wealthy people of Babylon cooled their dwellings. Servants drew water from a branch of the Tigris River that ran through the city, hoisted buckets of it onto the roof of the house, and dumped it into storage tanks. A copper pipe with holes punched in it rested on the edge of the roof right above the window. The window was covered with woven reed curtains. Whenever the king wanted the room to be cooled, the servant opened the spigot on the tank and water ran through the copper pipe. Water dripped from the holes onto the reed curtain. Then a servant stood outside the window and fanned the reed curtain. This sent moist air into the room and cooled it."

"How ingenious of someone," Wayne remarked. "Probably some engineer won the King's award for that idea."

"Now about the famous Hanging Gardens of Babylon," the guard continued. "Somewhere inside the palace area Nebuchadnezzar built a vaulted structure with a roof garden that became one of the Seven Wonders of the Ancient World. He also increased the size of Babylon until it was 10 miles in circumference. He built a double wall around it, but the Persians still got in by diverting the river water into a canal and walking under the river gates."

"Notice," the guard said, "that the inner bricks of the walls are of sundried brick while the facing bricks are of kiln brick or glazed tile. This was also true of the houses. They didn't have the fuel to fire all the bricks, so they put sun-dried brick between the inner and outer walls of their buildings."

Some of Nebuchadnezzar's city wall was still standing. It had been very high and thick. I wished I could have seen it when the outside of it was covered with blue and gold glazed tile. (The walls and gates of old Babylon are beautifully restored and can be seen in the Pergamum Museum of Berlin, Germany). The king covered the palaces with rosered glazed brick and the temples with white. The walls of Procession Street which went north to south were covered with varicolored lions in glazed brick relief. No wonder Nebuchadnezzar was proud of his magnificent city declaring, "Is not this the great Babylon which I have built?" Even the world acclaimed Babylon as one of the Seven Wonders.

Indeed, it was a thrill and a privilege to be living in Daniel's land!

CHAPTER 13
FINDING NEW FRIENDS

We had been in Iraq only a short time when a young an appeared at our Hospital Church one Sabbath. No one knew who he was nor from where he came. Our young boys knew HOW he came. "He drove up in a Land Rover, Mom! " David exclaimed in the tone of voice one would use to announce the arrival of an alien from outer space.

"Yeah, a LAND ROVER!" Paul Karmy emphasized, gazing in awe at the vehicle—not the being.

"I think he's a very important person," Buster concluded.

"All because of a LAND ROVER?" I asked. "I thought anyone could drive a Land Rover."

"Yeah, but none of us have 'em," Billy stated.

After church, the boys circled the Land Rover admiring the rusty, dusty piece of machinery while we curious adults plied the young man with questions. We learned he was Collin Mitchel from England. He had been hired by the Iraqi government to analyze the old irrigation systems, to determine the amount of chemicals left in the soil from years of irrigation, and to help them solve their present agricultural problems. He had secured this lucrative position because he was a geologist/engineer and was recommended by his school.

I was impressed with Collin's humble demeanor, his candor, and his English accent. He answered our questions politely, completely, but without a hint of pride. It was easy to see that he was well educated and cultured.

"And from what university did you graduate?" I asked casually.

"Oxford University in London," he answered.

I gasped. I had never known a graduate of Oxford. I had always believed that Oxford was the most prestigious university in the world only royalty, the elite, or the intelligentsias were privileged to go there. And to think, this young man in front of me was a graduate of that famous university! That knowledge left me speechless. Now I knew how the boys felt about the Land Rover.

Someone among our group had the presence of mind to invite Collin to eat potluck dinner with us. During the meal, we learned that he was a new convert to Adventism. He had attended an effort in London and was baptized even though he did not understand fully the doctrines of the Adventist church. Yet he had enough zeal to drive miles in from the desert to Baghdad to attend church. Since our English-speaking church group numbered less than 100 members, we were happy for any additions. We encouraged Collin to become a regular attendee. Wayne invited him to drive in from the desert on Friday evening and stay with us over the weekend.

We were pleased that Collin accepted our invitation. For the next eight months Collin arrived at our house every Friday afternoon. He showered off the desert dust while I put his clothes through the washing machine. We became very fond of this fascinating friend and looked forward to Friday nights, especially David, who felt "obligated" to ride in the Land Rover with him.

When I learned that a Danish couple, the Jensens, worked in the physiotherapy department of the hospital, I was anxious to meet them. My father was a native of Denmark, and I longed to hear Danish spoken again. (Not that I understood much of it). Nonetheless, Leif and Esther were happy to meet a fellow Dane and asked me to help them learn more English. They needed to speak English with their fellow workers and patients; therefore, it was important that they improve their English as soon as possible. We invited them to spend Friday evenings with Collin and us to study the Bible. The Jensens were natural linguists; they learned English very rapidly, while my Danish stagnated at the kindergarten level.

The Jensens invited Herbert Faimann, a 23-year-old Austrian patient of theirs, to attend the Friday night Bible studies at our house. Herbert had a most interesting story: After finishing his specialized education in Vienna, he was offered emloyment as a pastry chef at the Khyam Hotel, the most deluxe hotel in Iraq. For Herbert, this was like a fantasy come true—living in Ali Baba's Baghdad in a world-class hotel, meeting important dignitaries who patronized their restaurant, and exploring haunts of antiquity. It had been quite a fling until one night in February when flu-like symptoms forced Herbert to leave work early. Before going to bed, he drank a hot toddy, hoping it would also help his excruciating headache. In the morning, Herbert was feeling more miserable. When he got out of bed to take a shower, he noticed that his left arm was paralyzed. He went back to bed, hoping the paralysis would leave. But as the day went on, his symtoms became more serious and frightening. Soon his left side was paralyzed, and then his whole body. The Austrian hotel manager was alarmed at Herbert's rapidly deteriorating condition, and rushed him off to Dar Es Salaam Hospital. He was diagnosed as having a severe case of Bulbar Poliomyelitis. Since he was hardly able to breathe, Dr. Karmy did a tracheotomy on him. The hospital borrowed an iron lung from the Queen's Hospital. With its help, they were able to keep him alive. During his five-week recovery period, Noel read the Bible to Herbert and prayed with him. The Holy Spirit must have been working very actively because this faithful Bible worker did not know much German, and Herbert did not know much English. In spite of the linguistic barrier, some of the message got through to him. The love and devotion of the nursing staff witnessed to Herbert of God's love. After six weeks, Herbert went back to work but his left arm was permanently paralyzed.

By this time, Herbert had become attached to the hospital staff, and they to him. Jensens continued to give him physiotherapy and talk to him about God. The Holy Spirit instilled a desire in his heart to know more of the gospel. Jensens brought Herbert with them to our Bible study group.

Friday nights became the best night of the week for the eight of us. Our family and Collin used English Bibles, Herbert read from his German Bible, while the Jensens studied the Danish Bible. We were surprised how quickly they learned English through Bible study.

It was a very special experience with very special people. Collin learned what he had not acquired from the London effort.

Yet the meetings in England were the catalyst that sent him to look for Adventists when he got to Iraq. Herbert was not a religious person in Austria, but his illness put him in contact with Adventists in Iraq.[1] The Jensens were blessed spiritually as they perfected their English. As we drew near to one another, we drew nearer to our Lord.

Christmastime came, and I tried to find some kind of tree to decorate for the school children. I finally got a branch with fluffy greenery on it, stuffed it in a bucket, braced it with brick, and put bobbles and tinsel on it. It was the most pathetic Christmas tree one could imagine, but the presents under it tended to draw one's attention away from the "branch." The parents joined us for the Christmas party.

The children's Christmas program was scheduled to take place on Sunday night. Then disaster struck. On Saturday night the boys were playing hide-and-seek on the hospital compound. In a darkened area of the yard, Paul ran into something that cut a deep gash above his eye. The boys led Paul into the hospital and called for help. When they saw blood running down Paul's face and dripping onto his clothing, they turned ghastly pale. They fought to stay upright and keep down their suppers while Ronnalee went in and watched Dr. Karmy stitch up his son's cut. I should have known then that she would be a nurse.

We applied the vaudeville slogan—"the show must go on."

---

[1] Herbert was baptized the following May and has remained a faithful Christian. Today he manages a national cookie company in California.

Sunday night Paul was able to function. We simply pulled his shepherd's headgear down lower onto his face, and he said his fines like a regular trooper.

Living in Iraq at that time were hundreds of foreigners—oil workers, engineers, construction and agricultural advisors, and embassy personnel. Wayne became acquainted with many of them by sponsoring a Red Cross class (called the Red Crescent in Iraq) taught by the doctors and nursing staff of the hospital. This class drew many of the elite of the foreign segment to our hospital. Even the USSR ambassador and his daughter received Red Cross/Crescent diplomas.

That winter Wayne was impressed to hold evangelistic meetings for the English-speaking people of the city. We were pleased with the response—attendees were from many different countries. I was especially drawn to an English couple who came regularly. We soon became good friends. I shall call them Charles and Anne Gould.[2] They had a sweet six-year old daughter who loved to attend Sabbath School. (Their teenage son was away at school in England).

Early in the series, the Goulds invited us to their place for dinner. It was only when we entered their home that we realized they were people of means. Their home was beautifully and expensively furnished. The best of Persia's carpets covered the floors and original paintings lined the walls. Silver and gold objects, such as vases and statues, were tastefully placed about the rooms. I don't know why all this display of wealth should have astonished us. Anne always dressed exquisitely, and although we had no idea of the cost of jewelry, we should have known that large diamonds didn't come cheap.

The children joined their daughter in a separate room for their dinner. We were seated in the living room, enjoying a little pre-dinner chat, when a servant appeared with wine glasses on a silver tray. He opened the doors of a beautiful cabinet exposing many bottles of vintage

---

2   A pseudonym. Two years later we visited the Goulds in England. They lived modestly, but well. Their faith was rewarded as other family members joined them.

wines. There were at least 40 bottles from which we could choose our drink. What were we to do? We hadn't covered the health message in the evangelistic meetings as yet, so the Goulds were ignorant of our stand on alcohol and tobacco. Now it was the Gould's turn to suffer shock. They were amazed to learn that we did not drink wine before, during, or after our evening meals, or at any other time. This revelation flustered them; they didn't know how to properly set the mood for the evening. We tried to put them at ease as we sat down to eat without the benefit of the pre-dinner drink. Obviously, we came from two completely different societies. We felt we were eating with royalty while they could have viewed us as commoners. But they didn't. They were sincere seekers of Bible truth, and anyone who taught it was a prophet in their eyes. They were so easy to love.

We continued to surprise them by refusing coffee and tea. They were embarrassed to serve us plain water. Anne pressed the bell under the table and the butler appeared. He soon returned with fresh squeezed orange juice for us.

We had told them in advance that we were vegetarians. They didn't consider chicken and fish meat, so they set before us the next dilemma. We ate a little of the cornish hen they had fixed especially for us, and a sliver of imported Alaskan salmon. We felt that to eat was better than to offend.

The visit opened the way for an evening's Bible study on health. They accepted the idea completely. They didn't know how they were going handle it, but they were determined to become vegetarians. It was a BIG step for them to take all at once.

The next day they asked the servants to empty the liquor cabinet pour it all down the drain. Now the servants were completely baffled and hesitated to obey the order. They knew that wine was worth hundreds of dollars.

"Mr. and Mrs. Gould have gone crazy," one confided to another.

"Absolutely wasteful," another servant agreed.

Finding New Friends • 133

They begged the Goulds to let them sell it. The Goulds, however, believed that giving it to someone else was also wrong, so they insisted the liquors be dumped. The Goulds suspected that the servants absconded with some of the bottles, but they didn't try to press the point.

The Gould family made tremendous strides in their walk with Jesus. They accepted simplistic, Bible religion with the sincerity of Timothy. We worried how they would manage after they left our group. Anne was keeping the Sabbath, but Charles was still struggling with his work situation. The Goulds were scheduled to return to England in the spring. He forewarned his company of his intention to observe the Seventh-day Sabbath. They informed him that on the day he arrived back in England he would be fired if he failed to complete his contract.

When the Goulds left Iraq that spring, we felt our babes in faith, were going out to fight against the Goliaths of Philistia.

We received brief news bulletins from them frequently:

"We've kept every Sabbath so far and have worshipped with Adventists in every country we've driven through from Iraq to England. We're happy in Jesus."

"Charles has been fired from his job and cannot find work."

"Anne's parents refuse to move out of our house. We let them use it during the two years we were in Iraq. Our family is very opposed to our new religion and treat us like outcasts. "

"We were baptized Sabbath. It was the happiest day of our lives. Not even the bitter treatment of our parents and other relatives can drown our joy."

"We are having to live in a very small apartment. We cannot get our house back from Mrs. Gould's parents without a big fight."

"Our bank account is nearly exhausted ....

We prayed for the Goulds. We wondered how they could handle these horrendous trials. They had been accustomed to living like aristocracy. Now they were reduced to living like commoners in a cheap, poorly furnished, two-room apartment. Anne had sold her jewelry. They would soon be paupers with no money and no job. Their faith was surely being tested. Their family promised to return the house if the Goulds would give up their ridiculous religion. Charles was promised his job back with an increase in pay if he'd work two hours every Saturday. Few people face harder choices than Charles, but he stood firm.

Eventually Charles was offered a job with an Adventist institution. The Goulds adjusted to a scaled down living standard, and their son accepted their faith. Eventually, their families tolerated their religion and returned the house and some of their money. Through it all, their trust in God never wavered. That family must surely number among God's special people. What a joy and encouragement it was to have these Godly people as friends.

Another special family that came to the meetings were the Mandrechens. Mr. Mandrechen was Russian and his wife, Maria, was Assyrian. English was the common language for the family of five boys and two girls. (The oldest daughter was already working in America). The Mandrechens invited Wayne to give them private Bible studies in their home. It was easy to become attached to this lively, fun-loving family, and they soon became favorites in the church. Bible worker Noel Abdulmessiah, Wayne and I were just becoming acquainted with the Mandrechens when tragedy struck.

Wayne was in his chaplain's office one morning when a taxi screeched to a stop in the circular drive of the hospital. Alex and Teddy Mandrechen hopped out of the cab and called for a doctor to come examine their father who was lying on the back seat of the car. Dr. Dorothy Turner ran out the door, pressed her stethoscope to his chest, tried to find a pulse, then shook her head. He could not be revived. When the sons heard their father was dead, they threw themselves on the car's hood and wept bitterly. Mr. Mandrechen was not an old man. He had worked hard to support his family in spite of his heart ailment. Now his heart had failed him.

Wayne was shocked and sick at heart. Mr. Mandrechen, who had been raised with a communist philosphy, had just begun to show a genuine interest in Bible concepts. The family had mostly followed the Orthodox faith, but now they wanted to know more. Maria and daughter Nina were the most zealous Bible students, but truth did not escape teenage Alex and Teddy, either. After the funeral, they wanted to know what the Bible said about the fate of the dead. The family was relieved to know that death was only a sleep until the resurrection. They wanted to prepare themselves to meet their father and husband at the Second Coming of Jesus. Noel and Wayne spent many hours comforting the Mandrechens and helping them through their period of grief.

Earning a living became a big problem for the family. It was difficult for teenage Teddy and Alex to get work because, although they had been born in Iraq, they were considered foreigners by the Iraqis. Mother Maria had no professional, marketable skills. She was a refined, intelligent woman—above the mediocre drudgery of providing housecleaning services. She was willing to try, but the children knew she was needed at home to take care of the three younger boys. So, all the children earned a little money, pooled their resources, and managed to keep the family afloat. The following year, God opened a way for the whole family to move to the Middle East College hill in Lebanon. Concerned friends contributed money for the children's education. The Mandrechens were more new friends that would live in our memories forever.[3]

---

3   The Mandrechens eventually moved to the United States. They were, in a sense, refugees—people without a country. The boys all secured jobs and contributed to the economy of their adopted country. God blessed them.
Note: The incidents related in this chapter are what we personally experienced. Other visitors to the same places may have other impressions. The facts I used have been taken from various archaeological sources. Others may differ somewhat. I have chosen to relate the facts that seem most logical and accurate.

That spring Ken Vine, Bible teacher at Middle East College, came from Beirut for our Week of Prayer. He spoke to the church and my school children on last day events.

When the series was over, Ken wanted us to take him south to Ur of the Chaldees. Wayne hesitated a little because of the experience we had on our first trip to Ur.

"Let me tell you about THAT trip, and then see if you still want to go," Wayne told Ken. "Just south of Babylon we came across foot high water channels made to irrigate the rice fields. I slowed down for the bumps, but sometimes I didn't see them in time. Those times we flew to the ceiling, then landed with a crunch.

"Truck drivers hadn't warned us about the roads, but they had told us gruesome stories about desert wolves who killed man and beast. Drivers always carried loaded rifles and guns in the cab of their trucks. They said that if their truck broke down, a pack of hungry wolves would descend upon them. They would shoot them as fast as they could from the safety of their cab. The rule of the road was NEVER leave the cab at night, and never try to fix anything unless there was a friend standing guard. That was hard for us Americans to believe, but we found out later their story wasn't as exaggerated as we had thought. Truckers, who had left their cab to fix tires or make other repairs alone, were attacked and killed by wolves.

"Well," Wayne continued, "when we got to Ur we were thankful that the 1948 Ford had survived the bad roads and we had a chance to look over the city of Abraham and Sarah before it got dark. In Abraham's day Ur was a modem city on the Persian Gulf. Ships brought silk, spices, and other merchandise from India right to her gates. They had a zoo, a library, a banking system where men could write letters of credit and cash them at other cities in Chaldea. A fine irrigation system produced abundant food crops. Canals brought running water past the houses. With all the conveniences, it must have been hard for Sarah to leave Ur. On the other hand, the Chaldean practice of offering human sacrifices on the altar that topped the ziggurat must have repulsed Sarah and Abraham."

"You've only whet my appetite to see Ur," Ken smiled.

"But let me tell you what happened next," I said. "We had taken with us an American missionary, whom I'll call Adam, and a nurse from Turkey. Adam ridiculed the idea that wolves would be harmful to man. He almost had us convinced, too. About sundown, Adam, the children and I were completing our visit to the old library when I noticed fresh wolf tracks leading to a den under a clay library shelf braced at an angle against the wall. I pointed this out to Adam. He took one look and let out a yelp. Adam was out of there—I couldn't even see him for dust.

Dusk time is hunting time, and it was dusk. Our feet sprouted wings as we flew for the safety of the car. When we reached the car, Adam and the nurse were sitting in the car with the doors locked. I begged them to unlock the doors so we could get in. I finally convinced them that it wasn't necessary to lock the doors since wolves couldn't open car doors. Wayne joined us about then."

"Yeah," Wayne laughed, "I wanted to ask Adam why he fled from those 'harmless wolves,' but I tried to be kind about it. None of us wanted to spend the night at Ur. It was the Chaldean version of a Western ghost town—only this city had desert wolves thrown in for added terror. As we drove over the railroad tracks about two miles from Ur, we heard a crunch in the back end of the car.

"'What was THAT?' Adam asked, still shaking.

"I don't know. Let's get out and see, I suggested.

" 'I'm not getting out,' Adam said.

"So Midge and I got out with a flashlight and looked under the rear end. The springs had broken completely and dropped the car down on the axle. I took off the front bumper and braced it up, but that didn't work well. The weight of the car bent the bumper badly and we were about down to the axle again. We limped along over to the village by the river. They had no hotel so sent us back to the guest house at Ur Railroad Junction."

"GUEST HOUSE!" I sniffed, interrupting Wayne's story.

wouldn't call it a house nor put guests in it. In the shower were two small snakes sizing up a frog. Broken strands of rope were drawn across the wooden sides of the bed, which was their version of a box spring. There was no mattress. When I asked them about bedding, they explained 'you lay on coat.' The final straw, though, was the rat, the BIG FAT RAT, sitting defiantly on the post of the bed. I told Wayne, 'I'm not staying here.'"

"Actually, Midge said considerably more," Wayne teased.

"The nurse and Adam hadn't left the cu. So, I bedded the kids down on the floor in back, and I slept on the seat. Midge and the nurse slept in the front seat with Adam sandwiched between them. We got the car fixed the next day in the village, and drove on to Basra where we spent Sabbath with our believers. On the way back to Baghdad, an old man jumped out from a crowd in front of my car. He was hoping to get killed so his family could collect insurance money. He only broke his hip, but it was a sickening experience for me to hit a human."

"Well, Ken, that's it. Do you still want to go?" I asked.

"Absolutely," Ken affirmed. "Wild wolves couldn't hold me back."

"Then we'll go!" Wayne said.

The next morning, Dr. Dorothy Turner (whom we called DDT), Theo Williams (our laboratory technician), Ken, David, Ronnie, Wayne and I set off for Ur. We took with us four gallons of water, two five-gallon cans of gas, and lots of food. Since we had no room for suitcases, it was good we planned only a two-day trip.

The trip between Baghdad and Ur was fascinating. Turtles of all sizes cruised the road and banks of the Euphrates River. David begged his dad to miss them, but I'm sure Wayne crunched a few of them. At least the children didn't ask us to take a turtle for a pet'. They had outgrown turtle mania. Ronnie was captivated by the birds

Finding New Friends • 139

of all sizes and colors, and the mongoose killing poisonous snakes. We spotted several pairs of sleek wolves loping gracefully across the barren desert. They watched us, and even advanced towards us. This convinced me that the truckers were right.

We reached Ur by noon. While eating lunch, we noticed a Bedouin with his white headpiece whipping in the wind, race across the desert toward us on his chestnut-colored Arabian steed. The horse and rider appeared to be one unit, so well did the man sit his horse. They slid to a stop by our car. We greeted the man with the usual, "Salaam alaikum." (Peace to you). He responded with, "Wa alaikum salaam." (And upon you peace).

We offered him some food and water which he refused. We had forgotten that it was Ramadan, the month when the true Moslem neither eats nor drinks from sunup to sundown.

The Bedouin introduced himself as Ali and offered to be our guide. A mighty good guide he turned out to be! He had been a guard for the Sir Leonard Woolley archaeological dig 30 years earlier. In the most colorful language he told about the encounters they had with snakes, wild animals, and tribesmen. He recalled the accidents they had and discoveries they made in vivid detail. His stories correlated with Sir Leonard's book exactly, but Ali told it so much better. We were so spellbound by his recital that we almost forgot to translate for DDT and Theo, who didn't speak Arabic.

Thanks to Ali, this visit was much better than our first visit. We learned much from this very intelligent man. His memory was like a magnet, clinging to every detail. Had he been born in another place at another time, Ali could have been a Harvard professor.

From living in the desert, Ali had become very cautious. He was wary of snakes and wolves. Before we went around any building, he preceded us with his rifle aimed, ready to fire. He had encountered danger previously and had had to shoot and kill. He was willing to take us down into the tombs if Wayne shone his flashlight in all the tunnels and crevices first to make sure there wasn't some creature lurking in the shadows.

He showed us the tomb of one of the queens. When Sir Leonard uncovered this gruesome pit, they discovered many servants, horses, dishes, mirrors, make-up, food, and other items for the afterlife buried with her.

"I suppose they had to kill the servants, since they wouldn't just die naturally at the same time as the queen," I suggested.

"No, Madam," Ali said, "they buried them alive."

"ALIVE!" I fairly shouted. "How horrible! If I'd been a servant, as soon as I noticed the queen's health waning, I'd have fled from the palace."

"We believe they gave them some stupifying drink before they shoveled the dirt over them," Ali said. "Does that make you feel better?"

"No," I replied. "I'd have known the custom and wouldn't have slept for nights worrying about still being conscious while they covered me up."

"Being a servant to the queen or a temple prostitute were the most honorable positions available for women in Ur, " Ali stated.

"What choices!" I mumbled. "I see no honor in either of those jobs."

Then Ali took us down a very narrow street. With outstretched arms, I could almost touch the walls on either side. He brought us to the door of one house with a placard that read, "Abram, son of Nannur." (Nannur is another name for Terrah, the moon god). We walked through the door and an entrance which opened into a courtyard. Six or more rooms with covered walkways surrounded the square. Each room had a door and window facing the courtyard. The outer walls of the house were solid brick; therefore, the only access to the abode was through the courtyard entrance. This design was typical of all the houses up and down the narrow street.

"I like this house plan," I decided. "Sarah could be in her parlor, look across the courtyard, and see what the servants were doing in the kitchen. She must have had a firm belief in God to leave a modem city like Ur to go to Canaan and lead the life of a nomad—collecting sticks for fuel, carrying water from wells, and living in a goat's hair tent. She must have missed her nice brick house and the convenience of canal water running right past her house."

"A servant would have done the menial work. But are you sure this is the Biblical Abram's house?" Theo was skeptical.

"This, or one like it," Ali insisted. "All the houses in the wealthy residential area look almost alike."

Ali shared one last bit of information with us. "You know the Chaldeans were very intelligent people. They developed the clepsydra (the water clock), the sundial, the banking system, writing and geometry, and mapped out the heavens."

Theo and DDT had a little discussion about the Chaldean's contributions to the world. Theo thought he could do without the clocks, and DDT thought geometry was the curse of their inventive genius.

Then it was time to tip our guide and leave. We went to Ur Junction to show Ken the "guest house" that we hadn't used.

"It's worse than you said it was," Ken observed. "We can't stay here. Let's hurry to the next town north of here."

It was almost 9 P.M. before we reached Samawa. There we found an oriental khan—sometimes called a caravansary or inn. This building was established back in the days when traders drove their camel caravans 20 miles or more a day. The outside walls were solid brick, much like a fort. We rang the bell, and the gate man admitted us into the compound. After we finished the greetings and chitchat with the owner of the establishment, we rented three rooms, each with two beds. Ken and Theo took one room, Wayne and David another, and DDT, Ronnie, and I the third room. Each room had a door and a window opening to the courtyard.

We washed our hands with our water and ate supper.

In the middle of the courtyard was the drinking pool for the camels. Now it was filled with water for the convenience of the guests who wished to cleanse their feet, or any other body part, before retiring. We took advantage of that luxury and soaked our dusty, tired feet.

Theo went into his room to rest. "HELP!" he yelled. "I fractured my skull!"

"How? Where?" the rest of us questioned as we ran to his side'

I dropped my head on this poor excuse of a pillow," he complained. "How could I know it was like Jacob's rock?"

I laughed, thinking Theo was teasing us. I examined the three-foot long, 10-inch diameter pillow stuffed firmly with cotton. It was, indeed, almost as hard as a rock. None of us could use them.

Before retiring we asked directions to the toilet facilities. Stupid question! We could have followed the strong stench of urine wafting our way from across the courtyard.

Since it was a unisex bathroom, we gals had Wayne stand guard to give us some privacy. We tried to hold our breath to avoid becoming ill. The system used for flushing the toilets (holes in the floor) didn't clean away the spill-overs. We decided that in the morning we would leave early and use the hot, dry desert for our facilities. Then wash up with our water, eat breakfast, and head for home.

We returned to Baghdad that afternoon. We had driven over 500 miles in those two days, but had learned so much. It had been a journey into the past. We had visited the 4,000-year-old remains of Abraham's city and had slept in a 500-year-old Arab khan. It was a time to remember because it would never happen to us again, anywhere.

We had spent 10 months in Baghdad. They had been wonderful times. We had made so many new friends, friends we would never forget—Noel, Herbert, Collin, the Jensens, Mandrechens, Goulds, the school children, the Christian and Moslem hospital staff, the Iraqi Adventists, and others. How we would treasure those memories in the months to come! For though we did not know it, a period of separation and tragedy was soon to befall us.

CHAPTER 14

GOD WORKS OVERTIME

We had enjoyed living in Iraq for nearly a year—our church members were wonderful, our hospital personnel amiable, our work exciting, and our children were happy with their friends and school. We were comfortable and ready for another year. We did not sense the unrest that many Iraqis felt.

"Something is going to happen," they warned us. "We don't know exactly what, when, or how, but conditions are ripe for a revolution against the government."

We heard their concerns, but could hardly believe that a revolt was imminent. King Faisal was a friendly, ambitious young man in his early 20's. He was popular with his subjects and had their interest at heart. However, some of the hospital employees told us that the prime minister and the king's uncle were despised by many of the people because they were dishonest, immoral men.

Near the end of May, I was preparing for the eighth grade graduation of Jeannie Wagner and Bob Karmy. Kathleen Wagner and I were in charge of the flowers and decoration, so we drove out to one of Baghdad's nurseries to make some choices. On the way we came to a bottleneck in the street where some water lines were being repaired. As we started down the one-way street, we met King Faisal driving his convertable. He looked handsome and debonaire in his white suit and tie. His dark hair was slightly windblown; his smile was winsome, revealing a happy person. Why shouldn't he be pleased with life? He had everything going for him—he was young, healthy, educated, a king, and about to be married to a young lady in Turkey.

We stopped our car in deference to his royal highness, but he would have none of it. He stopped, backed up to a wide spot in the road, and waved us on. Kathleen and I were embarrassed but honored by this courteous young monarch. We exchanged smiles with King Faisal and waved as we passed.

"Was that really the king?" I asked Kathleen.

"I'm still a little choked," Kathleen admitted, "but it had to be. 11

"I just can't imagine him driving around the city without an escort, " I said. "An American president doesn't do that. I guess it proves how popular he is with his subjects and the trust he has in them. I know his act of courtesy has certainly endeared him to me."

We drove on to get our flowers, but the mental picture of the handsome young king had fastened itself in my memory forever.

Meanwhile, we had a special problem. Nine-year-old David's eyes were becoming more and more crossed. The eye specialist in Baghdad suggested surgery to correct the problem, but our mission doctors recommended caution.

"If they shorten the muscles in the eye too much," Dr. Joy (Louise Ubbink) warned, "he will have a problem for life."

We wrote to the division headquarters in Beirut. They suggested that we have David's eyes examined at Johns Hopkins Medical Center in Baltimore. We wrote to the director of that institution, and he very graciously responded that one of their specialists would see David whenever we could get there. We decided that David and I would fly to America for his eye exam sometime in June.

Wayne had had a baptismal class during the school year for those interested in joining the church. Four of the American children set their hearts on being baptized in the Jordan River. The parents agreed to make the pilgrimage from Baghdad to Jerusalem as soon as school was out.

During the last week in May, the Aldriches took the bus, David and I flew, and Wayne and Ronnalee rode with the Wagners to Palestine. We rendezvoused in Jerusalem.

Sabbath morning, May 31, we gathered at the Garden Tomb. (This place seems sacred because it so nearly fits the Biblical description of Joseph's new tomb. It even has a trough where the stone could be rolled, a garden and a winepress.)

After Sabbath School, we walked around enjoying the peace and the aura of sacredness that seemed to linger in this garden. Looking over the east wall we could see the hill covered with Moslem tombs. Some believe it is the site of Golgotha, while others say the Romans set the crosses by the roadsides to put fear into rebellious Jews. The actual site might be at the base of the cliff that has a skulllike formation. Since positive proof is lacking, we were satisfied that it was in this vicinity where Jesus was crucified. The thought always sent chills through me.

In the garden are many kinds of plants. While we were investigating the miniscule mustard seeds, the Arnold Peterson family from California came up to us and introduced themselves.

"Are you Seventh-day Adventists?" Mrs. Peterson inquired.

We assured them that we were.

"Is anyone among you a minister?" Dr. Peterson asked. We noted that his son had prodded him to ask this question.

"Yes," Wayne said. "I am a minister. We all live in Baghdad but came here to baptize our children in the Jordan River."

Young Donald fairly leaped into the air. "I knew it! I told you God would answer my prayer! All the time I have been secretly praying that I could be baptized in the Jordan River, but Dad said it wasn't likely that we would find a minister—that I shouldn't set my heart on it. I wasn't baptized with my friends because I prayed I could be baptized in the Jordan while we were on this trip."

I guess most of us got a little choked up then as we thought how miraculously God had answered Donald's prayers. God makes no mistakes in His timing. The Petersons were impressed to go to the Garden Tomb the first thing Sabbath morning. As they listened to our Sabbath School they sensed our Adventism. They were thrilled to chance upon fellow believers; we were equally pleased to meet them. The Petersons then joined us for the communion service.

We parents washed the feet of our children who were going to be baptized. Then it was time to serve the bread and the wine. We served the juice in the regular communion cups I had brought with me from Baghdad; but for the children who were going to be baptized, I bought special little pottery cups with the word "Jerusalem" and " 1958" inscribed below the design. I planned that this should be a lasting memento of the time and place they had chosen to publicly declare their faith in Jesus.

When I brought the cups out of the paper bag to fill with juice, lo and behold, there were FIVE Jerusalem pottery cups instead of the four I had ordered! How could this have happened? I'm a teacher. I can count to four. Of course, I gave the extra cup to Donald. That was a serendipity for him.

After sharing our picnic lunch with the Petersons, we squeezed 15 of us into two cars and drove down to the Jordan River. I pulled the baptismal robes that I had brought with me from Baghdad out of the plastic bag. To my amazement there were FIVE robes instead of four. How could I have miscounted? This was more than incredible. It was miraculous! By now we believed that God had a special care for Donald that went beyond reality. How marvelously He had worked to fulfill a young boy's secret desires! Perhaps none of us will ever forget how God provided a minister, a communion cup, a ride to the Jordan River, and a baptismal robe for a 12-year-old boy who believed in prayer.

Sunday, June 1, we separated. The others drove back to Baghdad while David and I flew to Vienna, Austria, to see Herbert, who was home on vacation. From there we went to the World's Fair in Brussells, Belgium. Our favorite spots were the Russian exhibit of Sputnik and the American Circlarama.

We left Europe via a four-motor Pan American plane to cross the Atlantic from Ireland to New York. There were only 12 passengers in the large plane meant to accommodate more than 80 persons. In a short time, all of us were acquainted and moved into seats where we could converse while we ate dinner. The two stewardesses showered us with food and drink. By 9 o'clock we were ready to go to sleep.

Halfway across the ocean we were caught in a horrendous wind storm. Our plane suddenly dropped in space, leaving us disoriented and ill. The wings of the plane quivered, and it seemed possible that they could snap off.

The stewardesses strapped themselves into their seats. Things spilled from the overhead storage bins and flew about the cabin. Everyone was paralyzed with fear.

I strapped David in tightly, prayed with him, and he dropped off to sleep.

"We're in a wicked storm," the voice of the captain crackled over the loud speaker. "We cannot turn around in this wind, and we're being blown off course."

"Oh, no!" We heard the voice of the co-pilot scream. "The motor on the right wing is on fire. God help us!" Then the P.A. system went dead.

We watched with agonizing fear as they activated the mechanism that shoots extinguishing fluid on the engine for just such an emergency. It worked! But now they had to turn off that engine.

"Ladies and gentlemen," came the captain's voice again, this time with a quiver in it, "we will be turning off the outer engine on the left wing to balance the thrust. If we crash, put on your life jackets and get into a life raft as quickly as possible. The water is very cold, and the icebergs below you are much larger than they look. Don't be alarmed."

"Don't be alarmed!" I thought to myself By the sound of his voice, he himself was alarmed. We were beyond alarm—we were cold and stiff with fright.

Sitting in the seat behind me was an American man who worked for ARAMCO (Arabian\American oil company) in Saudi Arabia. He poked me. "Lady, do you know how to pray?" he asked. "I'm scared as! I've been out of touch with God for so long, He doesn't even know who I am anymore."

"Yes, He knows you," I assured him. "God never forgets anyone, saint or sinner; but now is the time for you to know HIM. Confess your sins and prepare to meet Him. Remember, God loves you."

"But I don't know how to pray," he sobbed.

The roar of the engines fighting the storm made it almost impossible to communicate. I didn't dare leave my seat, so I turned my head in his direction and yelled as loudly as I could, "Begin with 'Dear God' and tell Him what is on your conscience. Then accept Him as God, Jesus as your Saviour, and believe they forgive. The thief on the cross made a last minute confession, and Jesus promised him eternal life."

"What thief? What cross? When was that?" he questioned.

"Wow! You really are out of touch with God! You don't even know the rudiments of Christianity. This is incredible!" I thought.

"Have you ever read a Bible?" I asked kindly.

"No, but I think I saw one in a hotel room once," he confessed. "My wife goes to church at Christmas, but I never saw a Bible around the house, I don't think."

"Now listen carefully, and I'll try to tell you about God and His plan for your salvation. We don't have time to waste." Then I tried to capsulate the entire message in the Bible for this guilt-ridden, fearful soul. After half an hour of yelling out a synopsis of Genesis to Revelation, my throat went hoarse, and I prayed. Others heard my effort. They said "amen" and cried. God had helped me testify of His everlasting love and His care for the people of planet Earth.

Eventually the wind died down, and we limped into Gander, New Foundland, with only two functioning engines. All of us cried and praised God when we touched the ground. None of us ever wanted to live through that hell again.

Even though it was the second week in June, it was cold. We wandered about the barren airport and snacked on food from the plane. But we remained shaken. After six hours, the mechanics believed they had repaired the plane's engines. We were reluctant to board the plane and would gladly have taken a bus, train, or car to New York had that been possible.

Our flight to New York was without incident. We all felt like kissing the U.S. soil when our feet touched term firma. I took the train directly to Washington D.C. where I met with the medical director of the General Conference. He set up an appointment for David at Johns Hopkins Medical Center. Two days later, a friend drove us to Baltimore where we met with two eye specialists. Dr. Joy was right surgery would have been disastrous. They taught David eye exercises that would strengthen the outer muscle of his left eye and gave us some medication and helpful advice. They did all this gratis. The savings we made by not having surgery in Baghdad paid for both of our air tickets. Even without the bonus of free eye care, however, the trip would have been worth it to save David's eyes.

Now we had time on our hands since we weren't delayed by a surgery and follow-up care. I bought train tickets to Kansas to see Wayne's mother and other relatives. In July we took a bus to South Dakota to be with my family for a few weeks. Letters from Wayne and Ronnalee were waiting for us:

Dear Midge & David,

"Today is June 4, and we're happy to be back in Baghdad.

When we were walking down a street in Amman, Jordan, we heard clapping and cheering. We ran to the curb and saw a police escort which was followed by King Hussein of Jordan driving his own convertible. He was waving to the people and we waved back. Seems that driving your own car is the custom of the royal cousins, King Faisal of Iraq and Hussein of Jordan. Sunday morning the Wagners and us drove up to Mt. Nebo. It was great! We saw Jerusalem, Bethlehem, and most of Palestine clearly. We had a flat tire there. Roads are too rough on vulcanized rubber. We filled up with gas in Amman, and then the car wouldn't start. We got a push from a tow truck. At Mufraq we filled up with gas without stopping the engine. At 3 P.M. we stopped on a hill in the desert and ate lunch. We pushed the car to the bottom of the hill, got it started again, and off we went. We didn't stop the motor again until we refueled at Rutba at 9 P.M. We had to have another push to get started. Forty miles west of Ramadi we lost our brakes. We examined the situation and discovered that the main leaf of the right rear spring had broken and dropped the body down on the exhaust pipe which smashed the brake fluid line. We limped home with no brakes at all. Good thing Iraq is flat. We were quite exhausted by the time we got to bed at 6 A.M. The next morning I got my car and pushed Bill's car to the garage. The mechanic discovered that both front springs and one rear spring were broken, the brake fluid line shot, the exhaust pipe in pieces, the body cut in some places, and the starter switch gone. Otherwise, Bill's car was in good shape.

Love, Wayne"

Ronnalee wrote: "Jeannie and I are busy cleaning the school and getting off your year-end school reports. I'm having fun helping Dad and Theo put in the P.A. system. I string the wires through the tunnels because Dad is too big to slip through them. Lots of love, Ronnie"

The next letter was mailed July 2, but didn't reach us for 10 days.

Wayne wrote: "We got your letter telling about your trip to Oberlin.... The P.A. system is a complete success. I go into patients' rooms and find them listening to the messages.

We also broadcast our hospital worships and the news to them.

I walked into one little boy's room, and he had on his head phones, staring straight ahead. The broadcast seemed to help him forget his pain. Hymn , character-building stories, and the reading of the Psalms seem to be especially appreciated by the patients.... Please bring me a white summer jacket, size 36/33 trousers, some shirts and new ties.... Plan to meet us at the Iranian Camp Meeting in Tehran July 24. . . . Love, Wayne. P.S. We really miss you. We've only recieved one letter from you. Please write more often."

What I couldn't understand was why they weren't getting my letters. I had written two from Europe and 10 in the states. Furthermore, this was only the second letter I received from them from June 4 to July 11. This wasn't like Wayne. Was something going awry with the postal system in Iraq? I was puzzled still further by the cable Wayne sent on July 12, asking me to please communicate more.

The message from Ronnalee read: "Jensens had a baby girl and is she ever cute! Aunt Kathleen let Jeannie and me make sack dresses out of green dotted swiss material. I cut the hole for the neck too big, but she patched it up by taking lots of tucks.... They had the graduation for seven nurses—Kathryn, Samira, Natiga, Widad, Susan, Shakay, and Yonova. Dr. Geraty gave a challenge, but no one answered it. Maybe that's the way it's supposed to be. The recorded music for the exit march ran out, so Dr. Wagner rewound it. It played for a little bit and then the machine started eating the tape, so they had to march out without music. . . . Are you going to be back by July 20 for my 12th birthday? Love, your oldest child Ronnie. "

-Yes, my Darling, I'll be there for your birthday," I said to myself as I laid down the letter. I had enjoyed my visit with Wayne's mother and my parents, but I missed Wayne and Ronnalee. I wanted to get back to Iraq.

I purchased everything anyone wanted and packed my suitcases. Early on the morning of July 14, my brother Julius took David and me to the Pan American Airlines office in Sioux Falls.

"What can I do for you this morning," the travel agent asked pleasantly.

"I want two reservations tomorrow for New York that will connect with a flight to Baghdad."

"Baghdad, Iraq?" he exploded, as if I was asking for a destination in outer space.

"Yes," I answered calmly.

"But you can't go there!" he exclaimed.

"Yes, I can," I insisted. I flipped open my passport. "Here is my Iraqi re-entry visa and my round-trip plane ticket."

The man shook his head. "Why do you want to go to Iraq?"

"I have a daughter and a husband there. I'm anxious to see them again."

The man put his elbow on the counter, and his hand on his head. "I hope you will see them again," he sighed. "Haven't you heard the news this morning?"

"No, we left the farm early and didn't turn on the car radio on the way into town," I said beginning to sense trouble. "Is there something wrong going on in Iraq?"

"Something TERRIBLE has happened over there. They've had a revolution and killed the king. Oh, you poor lady! I'm so sorry for your husband and daughter. I hope they are safe."

I nearly collapsed. I leaned against the counter.

"A revolution in Iraq? King Faisal DEAD?" I mumbled in disbelief. "Who would kill HIM?" The memory of a happy, handsome, courteous young king loomed up in my mind. He had been so vibrant; how could he be dead?

"Come on, Julius, take me to the newspaper office. I want to read what's coming in on the teletype from the United and Associated Presses. Having written for a newspaper, I know that more information comes in than is ever printed in newspapers. I've got to learn all I can about this unbelievable turn of events." Julius was stunned, too. Each of us was busy with our own thoughts and fears as we drove to the Sioux Falls Argus Leader office.

CHAPTER 15
REVOLT AND REVENGE

I jumped out of the car before it was fully parked and ran into the newspaper office.

"Please," I cried, "take me to the teletype machines. I want to read the information that's coming in over the wires about the Iraqi Revolution. My husband and daughter are there."

"Oh, no," the manager said sympathetically. "I'll warn you, it's not good news. But I don't think anyone knows for sure exactly what's happening. I suspect that some information leaking out is pure speculation and some is gruesome. Are you sure you want to read it?"

"Yes, please. I must know."

He led me to the back room where the teletype was reeling out information from the United Press. What I learned was very disturbing. Simply stated, Colonel Karim Kassim had led a successful military coup d'etat against the Iraqi government during the early morning hours of July 14. The rebels forcibly took control of all government offices and cut all communications, inside and outside of the country. Planes were grounded. Cars, buses, trains, and any other means of transportation were forbidden to leave or enter the country. Even movement within the country was forbidden. The king, his uncle, and other government leaders had been killed. Foreigners had been killed, and others were holed up in their embassies—if they could get there. Mobs had taken to the streets, looting, vandalizing, and committing other acts of violence. The military was having a difficult time trying to stem the tide of anarchy. People were told to stay home until Kassim, got his new government firmly established.

That was basically all the information the United Press had to divulge. They admitted that the news they had given the world had been smuggled out of the country during the first few hours of the revolution. No one knew who had done it or how it had been done.

The words, "Foreigners have been killed," jumped out at me. Our house was six blocks from the hospital. I feared that Wayne and Ronnalee might be caught in the melee before they had time to get to the safety of the hospital. Maybe the hospital wasn't a safe place, either. My mind skipped from one thought to another: Had the military or the mob occupied the hospital? Were my family and friends still alive? Or were they among the foreigners who had been killed? What a pity that the young king had been assassinated!

Then the machine began typing out more information, "The United States is sending Marines into Lebanon to secure the situation there. They fear the trouble in Iraq might spill over to neighboring countries. The Lebanese Moslems are dissatisfied with the Christian majority leaders. Israel is worried that Jordan and Syria will attack them."

I turned to Julius, "It looks like the whole Middle East is coming unglued. Let's go. I've had enough bad news for one day. It seems that the foreigners are stuck there—either dead or alive. I just hope Wayne and Ronnalee are safe. Sometimes it's easier to be in the thick of trouble when you KNOW what is going on than to be miles from it. My mind is imagining the worst."

As we drove home, I was praying for my family and friends in Iraq and Lebanon. I wondered how this revolt could erupt so suddenly. Then again, maybe it wasn't that sudden. Our Iraqi friends had told us that the country was ripe for a revolution. We just had been too content with the status quo to take them seriously. I hoped the coming of Jesus wouldn't catch us off guard as this revolution had done.

I called the General Conference and asked to speak with the person in charge of Middle East affairs.

"What do you know about the situation of our workers in Iraq?" I asked.

"Don't worry about them. They are perfectly safe," he assured me. "They've been taken to the Phoenicia Hotel."

"The PHOENICIA HOTEL?" I shouted. "The Phoenicia Hotel is in Beirut, Lebanon, not Iraq. According to the United Press no one can leave Iraq. Just how did they get over to Lebanon a distance of over 800 miles?"

"Just relax. I have definite word from the Middle East Division that they are in the Phoenicia Hotel," he insisted. "There must be a Phoenicia Hotel, in Baghdad."

"No there isn't!" I argued. "I know the country and the cities well. Maybe the missionaries in Lebanon are in the Phoenicia, but I want to know about the missionaries in Iraq. My husband and daughter are there. Please— -"

"I'm sorry," he interrupted. "I know they are safe in the Phoenicia Hotel. The division officers have assured us— -'

"But if there is no communication coming out of Iraq, how do the division men know where the Iraqi missionaries are?" I asked in frustration.

"I tell you the division men have assured us that they are in the Phoenicia Hotel." His answer was like a broken record.

"Thank you. When I hear where they are, I'll let you know so you can notify their family members here in America," I said and hung up. He wasn't hearing or believing me. He obviously did not understand the information the division officers had sent him. Talking further to him was futile.

I fell onto the davenport and wept in anguish. No one knew anything about Ronnie and Wayne. Julius and my parents tried to comfort me, but they were about as distressed as I was. I finally calmed down, remembering that we had gone through frightening times before. And during those times of danger, God had always been there. When we had faced certain death, He had opened doors of escape that stunned us. At this very moment, He knew where Ronnie, Wayne, and all of our overseas and Iraqi friends were. But I wanted to know where they were. I knew He would save them if it was His will, but I was impatient to know just what was happening to them. Were they dead or alive?

During the next few weeks I found solace in Bible reading and prayer. Yet I found myself vacillating between faith and fear. I turned on the T.V. to catch every news broadcast, but information was sketchy at best.

Three more times I contacted the General Conference Middle East representative, but he gave me the same old "Phoenicia Hotel" story, which indicated that he knew nothing about Iraq. I finally got so frustrated that I stopped calling him. I should have asked to talk to someone else at the General Conference who might have been more sympathetic or informative.

July 14, the day of the coup, the Sioux Falls Argus-Leader had taken a picture of David and me and splashed it on the second page of the newspaper. The caption read, "IRAQI REVOLT KEEPS FORMER S.D. WOMAN FROM FAMILY." I didn't realize then how important that contact would be for me within a few weeks.

July 20 was Ronnalee's 12th birthday. I went to the bedroom, took the gifts I bought for her out of my suitcase, and laid them on the bed German and Irish costume doffs, a skirt from the World's Fair in Brussels, a stamp album, and a new dress. I wondered if these presents would ever be delivered into the hands of my precious child. Oh, how I longed to be with Ronnie that day—to touch her, to hug and kiss her, to make and decorate her birthday cake, to watch her blow out the candies, to see the joy on her face as she opened her gifts. I fell on the bed. My pent-up emotions gave way to uncontrollable sobs. I fondled the gifts I had bought for Ronnie; I wished I knew if she were alive. I wondered WHAT foreigners had been killed. I was thankful Julius had taken David fishing so that he would not see his mother so distraught.

July 27 the T.V. news reported that the Iraqi government was allowing one Pan American plane a day into

Baghdad to evacuate American dependents to Rome. That gave me a ray of hope. I studied the pictures of the American evacuees as they got off the plane, but I couldn't see either Wayne or Ronnie among them.

July 30 1 received a letter from Wayne that was written July 17. He had sent it with someone who had smuggled it out of Iraq and had mailed it from Rome. Considering the fact that everyone and all luggage leaving Iraq was submitted to an intense search, it was amazing that this letter had not been confiscated. It was filled with more detailed information than I had gotten from any news source. Wayne wrote:

"My dear Midge and David, First of all, so far we are safe.

No doubt you've been listening to the news very closely these last few days. So have we. I'll tell you what I've learned from here. I knew nothing of the revolution when I drove to work on Monday morning, July 14, leaving Ronnie sleeping alone in the house. I hadn't heard the gunfire during the night because the air cooler makes so much noise it masks all sound. in the hospital lobby I found excited people gathered in little huddles, but I hurried to my office to prepare for worship. When the worship bell rang, hardly anyone came. About then, Noel Abdulmessiah, the Bible worker, came rushing into the chapel. She said, 'Have you heard? There's been a coup d'etat. The king, his uncle, and other leading officials have been killed. Turn on the radio so we can know what's happening.'

"Instead of the soft voice of a professional radio announcer, we heard the loud, harsh voice of an army drill sergeant saying, 'Go out in the street and celebrate. We now have the glorious People's Republic of Iraq. Last night we got rid of the foreign devils (meaning British and Americans) and the oppressive Iraqi government leaders. Now you can do as you please.'

"Immediately I drove home, got Ronnalee, and brought her to the hospital to be with the other Americans. Next Theo Williams and I drove to the closest station and filled the car with gas. I thought that if it was necessary to escape, a tank of gas would take us to the Iranian frontier. We decided to go down the street toward the city to see what was going on. That was stupid. After a few blocks we came to an intersection patrolled by the army. Soldiers laid on their stomachs holding machine guns pointed down the street. We made a quick U-turn and headed back to the hospital. It is providential that we got out of that situation.

"We stayed on the hospital compound the rest of that day. Young Iraqi hospital workers would catch a bus to town, look around, and then come back and give us an eyewitness report. They saw the body of the king's uncle, a man despised by the people, hung over Rashid Street, the main business part of town. People used it for target practice, and finally dismembered the arms, legs, and head. The newspaper ran gruesome pictures of it hanging like an animal carcass in a meat shop. One of our workers brought the dead man's little finger into my office. It was repulsive! Baghdad mobs get as violent and barbaric as American mobs. Most of the Iraqi people didn't like what was happening, but were helpless. The rebels had the guns. Many people were sad that the king was killed, even though they believed a change in the government was needed.

"The day of the revolution Dr. Wagner sought advice from the American Embassy, but they didn't know as much about the situation as we did. Knowing Arabic certainly helped me learn a lot about the situation. I listened to their conversations and passed the information on to the American counsel.

"Around the hospital all was quiet that day. Toward evening a lone Iraqi soldier was dispatched to patrol the hospital gate area. I don't know what he could have done if a mob had come—probably run and hide. That night the celebration turned into pandemonium and wholesale looting in the city. Megaphones and radios were employed to tell the people that a complete curfew had been called, and they must go home or be shot. Even so, it was 10 P.M. before the streets were cleared.

"The next day Noel told me what she knew about the revolution. It seems that Colonel Karim Kassim was in command of a number of Iraqi regiments patrolling the Iranian frontier. On July 13 he received orders to move all his troops to the Jordan or Syrian frontier to protect those countries against an Israeli invasion. That night he led a long column of trucks, tanks, cannons, and all types of military equipment toward Baghdad.

"Before reaching the capital, he called a halt to the procession, and invited all the officers to his side. 'Here are our orders,' he told them. 'We are to go to the Jordan-Israeli border and probably give our lives for another nation. Wouldn't it make more sense for us to stop in Baghdad and clean up the mess in our own government first?' Then he outlined what he had in mind and asked his officers if they were agreeable. He got their unanimous approval.

"Then Kassim proceeded to deliver his orders to the subordinates: 'Number 1, take your troops, capture and close the airport. Number 2, you and your troops will secure the central telephone building. Cut all telephone lines so no one can call anyone anywhere—including inside Iraq. Number 3, you and your regiment will take over the police station and the police duties. The regular policemen will take orders only from me. Number 4, you and your unit will man the radio station, but DON'T destroy it. I'll need it to broadcast my commands in the morning. Number 5, you'll secure the military base near Baghdad. Keep all soldiers and equipment on the base and wait for orders from me. Number 6, you'll occupy the entire military defense headquarters. Stop all communication going out until I send orders. Number 7, you'll capture the king, his uncle, the prime minister, and the other officials. They may be a On-eat in the future. We'll all strike at the same moment.'

"About 1:00 A.M. the police reportedly called the prime minister and asked what was going on since there were so many troops moving inside the city. Nuri Said responded, 'Don't worry about them. These are the troops I have ordered to move from the Iranian frontier to the borders of Jordan.' A few minutes later a group of soldiers entered his home forcibly, but he escaped. Two days later he was caught, dressed in a woman's black cloak with a veil covering his face. His disguise didn't work because his mannish-looking shoes protruded from under his street-length clothing. His captors persecuted and killed him.

"The king was staying with his uncle that night, and whether through intent or accident, he was shot as he stood on the balcony. Some say it was not Kassim's plan to have King Faisal killed. Rather, he intended to expel him from the country like the Egyptians had done to their King Farouk. King Faisal was still living when he entered the Royal Hospital, but bled to death since the doctors were afraid to give him medical treatment.

"As soon as I can, I will send this letter to you. I don't know how I'll get it out of the country. It is now three days since the revolution. This morning the embassy told us to be prepared to drive out through the Iranian border. This afternoon they revised their plans. Now they're trying to bring in planes to evacuate our American dependents as quickly as possible. A few hours later they may have a different idea. They're trying, but no one knows what the morrow will bring. Love you lots. Pray for us. Wayne"

This letter relieved my mind immensely. My family and friends were safe.

July 31 the manager of the Sioux Falls Argus-Leader phoned me. "I've got good news for you," he said jubilantly. "The American Embassy gives the list of the evacuees coming into Rome from Baghdad each day. Today they picked up the name of Ronnalee Olson who gave her home address as Colman, South Dakota. Your daughter is in Rome!"

I slumped into a chair. "Oh, that IS good news," I managed to say in spite of my shortness of breath and the lump in my throat. "Ronnalee's in Rome." After my brain absorbed the good news, my reason returned. "But, she's only 12 years old. Who, who is she with? Did they mention Wayne Olson?"

"No, they are only evacuating women and children—about 80 per day. I don't know who Ronnalee is with. We just receive the basic facts. United Press sends our newspaper the names of those who are from South Dakota. Ronnalee was the only person named from here."

"I see. Then Wayne didn't come out with her," I said, trying to disguise my disappointment. "I do hope Ronnie's not on her own in Rome."

"So do I," the man said kindly. "We know she's alive and in Rome. I don't think the American Embassy would leave her without adult care. By the way, do you have a picture of her along with a little story that we could run in the newspaper. Readers like stories that connect world events to hometown folks."

"Yes, I have a good picture of her. I'll mail it tomorrow along with a little information. But please, don't print anything unkind about the Iraqis. They are good people—as good as Americans. Derogatory statements about Iraqis will only bring trouble for the foreigners left in the country."

"I understand, and I promise I will use discretion in what we publish."

I called the General Conference Middle East representative and told him that United Press had informed me that Ronnalee Olson was in Rome. I hoped he'd know what other missionaries had come out of Iraq. If he could answer that question, then I could guess who Ronnie was with. He told me he only knew that English subjects had been evacuated from Lebanon to Rome.

"Good. Thank you," I answered somewhat relieved. "Then I know Ronnalee is in good hands if she is with some of them. But how would she know where to find them, or they her?"

"I don't know," he admitted. "I don't think she's in Rome."

Friday, August 8, 1 got a letter from Ronnalee mailed from Italy. My hands shook as I tore open the envelope. There was a short, typed letter from Wayne on onion-skin paper. This letter made me suspicious since it was worded so carefully. I could tell Wayne purposely skirted the political situation.

"July 27, Baghdad. Dearest Midge and David, I hope you are doing well. I'll bet David is having a good time on the farm with Uncle Julius. I'm not going to Iran, so we will save up our vacation for some future time when the family can be together.

"Ronnalee has been having a good time with the other kids on the compound. Dr. Joy (Louise Ubbink) had a nice birthday party for her son Buster and Ronnie—each child had a birthday cake. The kids played games on the lawn. Dick showed some motion pictures.... The new house will be finished sometime next month and then we'll move onto the compound. . . . Pauline Williams, little Chris and baby Larry left for Rome July 21. Ronnie is going with Kathleen, Billy, and Ruthie. They will wait in Rome for further word from the division committee as to what they should do next. It would cost $700 to send her to South Dakota from Rome. She will send you her address so you can write to her.

"The last letter I received from you arrived July 13. 1 hope mail starts moving freely soon. As far as this place is concerned, everything is quiet, but we don't know what will happen in the rest of the Middle East. The hospital is functioning but without as many patients. Ronnie will add more when she gets to Rome. Keep up your courage. Love, Wayne"

At the end of Wayne's letter Ronnie had written, "Florence, Italy, August 1. 1 smuggled Dad's letter and his slides out of Iraq with me. But since I was allowed only one small suitcase, or 20 pounds, I hardly have any clothes. Mrs. Vine is so sweet to me. She got me a towel and washcloth. I hadn't had a shower in three days. Kathleen (Wagner) got me some deodorant and powder, a dress and slip. The new government in Iraq say they are not communists and say they like us. But the Americans at the embassy have to stay put. It's like they're held hostage within the embassy, but they aren't being hurt. Last night I missed a step and really sprained my ankle. I'm just so tired. The day we landed in Rome, Aunt Kathleen, Billy, Ruthie, and I all slept in a hotel. The next day the mission gave us orders to come up here to Florence to the Adventist school. We came by train. They feed us mostly pasta. It would be nice to have some fruit. XOXOXO to the end of the world. Lovingly your closest relative, Ronnie."

When my brother read that letter he wanted to send Ronnie an airplane ticket immediately. I called the General Conference and asked them to expedite the matter, but they advised against it. They expected that we would be able to return to Iraq in a few weeks. They told me to go to Italy to be with Ronnalee and the other mission women evacuees from Iraq. I made immediate plans to do so.

Since our plane ride over had been so traumatic, neither David nor I wanted to get on a plane again. We took a train to Washington D.C. where an efficient General Conference travel agent got our round-trip air tickets to Iraq refunded and bought tickets for us on the S.S. Christeforo Columbo bound for Italy. We boarded the ship in New York and arrived 10 days later in Naples. I caught the first train out of Rome for Florence. It had been four months since I had seen Ronnalee. I could hardly wait to see her again.

Ernie Waring, Ronnie, and some of the others met David and me at the train station in Florence. I jumped off the train, took Ronnie in my arms, and we wept. Ronnie had been in Italy almost two months without either parent. She missed David and me, and was worried about her dad. She was drained emotionally.

Before we left the station for the school, I realized I was missing something. I had been so excited to get off the train and see my child that I left Wayne's good camera in the train compartment. I had guarded that camera so carefully the whole trip, how could I lose it now? I had taken many slides and they had turned out perfect. This was quite amazing considering that I had taken them all on the same setting. Before we left Jerusalem, Wayne had tried to teach me how to use his fancy camera. I have no technical skills, so I promptly forgot all his detailed instructions. I couldn't remember which gadget was for what, so I simply took the cover off the lens and shot all pictures at the setting Wayne used last during his instruction session. Since the slides turned out to be some of the best in our collection, I had no intention of telling Wayne how I had achieved my success. I just hoped he wouldn't ask me to set the speed, the focus, the light and all that stuff for him on his next pictures—if and when we ever got together again. Now I had lost the camera, and my secret was safe.

I despaired of ever finding the camera since there were so many rumors of pickpockets and bold thefts in Italy. However, Ernie thought I should at least make an attempt to retrieve it. We offered a little prayer and telephoned the next station. They phoned back in 30 minutes saying they had found the camera in compartment C, and that I could pick it up in the morning.

We went to the Adventist school (Istituto Avventista "Villa Aurora") for the night. It was fortunate I had arrived that night because the next morning the mission group was leaving for Rome. School was beginning and the Italian Adventists needed the rooms that our missionaries had occupied during August and September. If I'd been a day later, I don't know how I ever would have found them in Rome. I thanked God that His timing was perfect.

The next morning I dashed through the station, barely in time to catch the train to Bologna. There I picked up the camera, left a tip, ran back to the train leaving for Florence, and caught it as it was moving down the track. My leap onto the steps was more dangerous than I realized, but an attendant caught my hands and pulled me into the car. He shook his head and indicated that I was crazy to take such a risk. He was right, of course, but I couldn't explain to him that I had to catch that train in order to get to Florence in time to go with the group to Rome. When I sat down in my seat, I was out of breath, my body was shaking, and I knew that I had done a stupid thing.

I could have taken the next train. Ernie or someone of the group would have searched for me at the train station in Rome and re-united me with the group. But I hadn't thought of it soon enough.

In Florence, I had another near miss. The evacuee group was just boarding the train as I raced down the platform. I made it with a few seconds to spare, sunk into my seat, and tried to relax.

In the daylight I had a chance to look at the Baghdad group more carefully. Ronnie, the Wagners, and Williamses looked pale and tense. It was obvious that they were still going through trauma. They had lost weight due to a mostly pasta diet. Most of them had eggsized, green-and-yellow-pus-filled boils caused by their susceptibility to the Italian strain of staphylococcus.

Beside the problems they all shared, Ronnalee had been given 21 shots in the stomach for rabies. Wayne had sent a cable to Florence informing Ronnalee that our dog, Lizzie, had rabies. Lizzie had salivated on the gate, doors, and sidewalks of our place in Baghdad. Ronnie had tried to get her to eat, so had touched her often. After Ronnie was evacuated, Lizzie had slipped out from the gate and ran and ran until a policeman overtook her and shot her. Tests showed she had rabies.

Kathleen made sure Ronnie began rabies shots immediately. The first few days she took Ronnalee to the clinic. After that, Ronnalee usually went by herself. Ronnalee got tears in her eyes as she recalled her lonely treks to the clinic—how she walked down the hill, boarded a bus, got a transfer and boarded another bus. Then she sat in the clinic with 20 other patients waiting for their particular shots. She was the only one getting rabies shots.

"I was scared," she told me, her voice quivering. "I didn't know how the shots would affect me, or if I might get rabies. Every day I felt weaker. I tried to act brave in front of the other missionaries, but I was scared. I often cried myself to sleep at nights. I worried about dad in Baghdad and wondered when I would ever be re-united with you and Dave."

"Why didn't you tell one of the other missionaries about your fears and feelings?" I asked her as I held her close.

"Well, they all had their own children to care for. I believed I was an extra burden for them. I was the oldest of the kids, so I tried to repay them by baby-sitting the younger ones when the parents wanted to go somewhere."

"Good girt," I said as I squeezed her bony, little hand. "We appreciate what the missionaries did for you during those stressful days. God will see us through this. He's seen you through quite a bit in your 12 short years—malaria, skull fracture, and broken elbow, to name a few. Now you have survived the revolution, evacuation, and rabies shots. Soon you'll be as good as new again."

September 29 the Lebanese missionaries got clearance to return home. We would miss them—especially Ernie Waring. He had been a support for all the evacuees. The women and children jokingly called themselves "Ernie's harem" because he was the only man in the group. He had cared for everyone, even when he himself suffered a most painful carbuncle on his leg.

We Baghdad women and children were now on our own. We rented pensiones in Rome, snacked in our rooms, or ate in restaurants. I had been there only a few days before I knew it wasn't easy being an evacuee. What must the Wagners, Williamses and Ronnie feel like after two months?

Kathleen found a medical doctor who lanced our staphylococcus infections, gave us antibiotics, and tended to Baby Larry's dysentery. Besides our medical and food problems, we had to move every few days from one pensione to the next. The owners didn't like long-term residents with children—it might hurt their business, they said.

I don't think the division officers knew how difficult it was for us to keep six children, ranging in age from one to 12 years, in a city like Rome. The kids had almost nothing to do, and the confinement of hotel living made them restless. They weren't healthy, and restaurant food didn't agree with them. The division officers, however, were caught between a rock and a hard place. If they sent us back to the States, it might be demoralizing for our husbands who were trying to keep the hospital operating. If, as they supposed, we would be able to return to Baghdad in a few weeks, it would be costly to send us to America only to return us shortly to Baghdad. On the other hand, if they sent us to the states to live with relatives, they would save the rent and food money subsidies they gave us.

One day when almost everyone in our group was sick and crying, we went to the Adventist conference office, drew out our allowance money, and called Bob Osborn, the division treasurer in Beirut. I suggested to him that we rent a house with three bedrooms out in the country where the kids could have clean air, space to roam, and homecooked food. He thought it was a good idea and authorized the Italian office to advance us the money.

With money in hand, we three women took our six kids in tow and went to the American embassy. The American counsel was absolutely wonderful. He gave us addresses of vacation houses out by the sea. Since school had started, the Italians had come back to Rome, and most of the summer vacation houses were empty. We selected one that seemed good. The embassy secretary called the owner who agreed to rent it for the amount we could pay. Her son took us out to look over the property to see if it met our needs. It did. It had a bedroom for each family, and a living room, dining room, and kitchen that we could share. The owner supplied sheets, towels, pillows and blankets, gas and electricity. She arranged with a woman to do the household laundry on a weekly basis since we American women weren't used to doing sheets and towels by hand. However, each of us was responsible for our personal laundry.

We had spent only one week in Rome before the owner's son moved us to her house in Santa Marinella. Our rental was less than half a mile from the main road bus stop. We didn't mind the walk. The location was beautiful with plenty of "roaming room" for the kids. Furthermore, we were only one mile from a nice beach on the Mediterranean Sea. We found a man who would drive us in his horse and buggy to the beach for a reasonable fee. Almost every afternoon I took David, Billy, and Ronnie down to the beach. Sometimes all of us went. The kids loved riding in Tony's buggy with Napoleon at the traces. This became our regular afternoon activity.

The embassy also gave us shopping privileges in their commissary. We took advantage of that. American breakfast cereals took the fancy of our children, and they made us stock up. That wasn't such a brilliant idea. Carrying all those boxes plus other groceries on the bus to Santa Marinella was a hassle not to mention the difficulty with transfers around Rome in the packed, impossible-todescribe buses. I think the other passengers resented the space we took. I understood enough Italian to catch one man's remark, "Mamma mia, they shouldn't let haystacks with appendages onto the buses."

Every week we took the bus to Rome to get food and see sights. Every two weeks we got money from the conference office. We bought a few games and checked out books from the American Information Service. This filled our nights with pleasant activities. Still, we missed our husbands and fathers. Sometimes it was difficult to hold back the tears, but we mothers needed to present a brave front to our children.

The reigning Pope at that time was Pius the 12th. We decided it would be interesting to visit him at his summer home, Castle Gondolpho. One day we found all the right connections and got there. We took our place in back of the pious Catholics who stood in the courtyard waiting for the Pope's appearance. They had made their pilgrimages from Germany, France, and other places. We highly respected their devotion. They were a little disturbed by the presence of our American children who couldn't seem to remember to be deathly silent in the presence of "his holiness." Furthermore, our children objected to the term "his holiness. " "Only God is holy," they argued. We agreed and promised to discuss that later, outside the private courtyard of the pope's villa.

Suddenly all was deathly silent. The doors to the second floor balcony opened, and Pope Pius walked out in his beautiful pontifical robes. We caught our breath—he looked so regal against the backdrop of the ornate, old castle. (This was how I had envisioned the kings of England to look in the 17th century). He stretched out his arms in blessing, beckoning with his hands. The Catholic pilgrims cried and dropped to their knees in reverence. So did Billy. He was so anxious to do the right thing that he hadn't noticed the rest of us remained standing respectfully. Pope Pius looked disapprovingly in our direction, and I withered. I almost joined Billy. As soon as the
Pope finished chanting his blessings upon the faithful, we silently stole away. I don't think we were ever able to explain to the children's satisfaction why the pope was considered meritorious, so we just dropped the subject and told them to worship God as they always had.

It was only a few days later that I read in the Italian newspaper that the pope was seriously in. David wondered if we had caused the pope's heart ailment by not kneeling in his presence. I assured David we weren't to blame for that.

A few days later I read, EL PAPA MORTE. Now David worried that we were responsible for his death. I promised him that we had nothing to do with it. I hoped the world believed me more than David did.

The last day Pope Pius the 12th lay in state, we went to St. Peter's Square and stood in line with hundreds of other people to see his mortal body. When we reached the raised slab upon which his body rested, the odor of decomposition was evident in spite of the perfume they continually sprinkled on him and his bier. He was splendidly attired in his pontifical robes. Later that afternoon he would be transferred to a crypt prepared especially for him. What a contrast between the pope's passing and the death of our Savior. The pope was given a multi-day memorial service which was attended by thousands of adoring people; he was dressed as a king and had a tomb made especially for him. Jesus died a cruel, unnatural death, his naked body was wrapped in plain linen cloth, and he was buried in a borrowed tomb. Only two men and a few women attended his funeral. The dichotomy could go on. Jesus arose from the grave, was seen by many as He lived and worked on the earth 40 more days, and ascended bodily to heaven. For the pope, this would be different.

In October I decided to start school with the books I had brought with me from the States. Theo Williams had come to Santa Marinella to visit his family and had brought more books with him from Baghdad. I set up school every morning on the dining room table for Billy, Ronnie, and David. They weren't particularly interested in my zeal for their education, but they cooperated.

Theo's visit to Italy was a wonderful lift for all of us. He could speak without being censored and gave us an honest report. He said there had always been trouble somewhere in Iraq since the initial revolt. Most of the foreigners killed were done in the first day of the revolution. They had been dragged from the New Baghdad Hotel, driven to the radio station in an open army truck, and pulled apart by the mob. Then Theo proceeded to give us a detailed update of what had happened since the beginning—not necessarily in chronological order.

He said it was no longer safe for Germans, Americans, and Britishers to be on the streets. For example, a German engineer, who had been a demanding supervisor, was hung upside down from a tower. Americans (reporters, consultants, petroleum or embassy personnel) caught within the embassy couldn't leave except to get medical or therapy treatments at our hospital. Being cut off from communications and their families was hard on these men. Since most of them had no religious affiliation, they had nowhere to turn for solace. They couldn't see an end to the revolt or the revenge. This confinement drove some men up the wall. They began drinking excessively.

When the Americans came to the hospital for physical therapy, they habitually stopped at Wayne's office which was conveniently located near the front door. They wanted some spiritual encouragement and the latest news. Because Wayne spoke Arabic, the Iraqi hospital workers dropped in frequently to update him on the latest happenings. Wayne shared as much of this information as he deemed prudent. So when the Americans returned to the embassey, they shared their bit of news with their fellow confinees. This buoyed them up until the next visit.

A month after the revolution there had been a huge kerosene fire near the center of Baghdad. It had been a dry, hot August afternoon when one of the six tanks exploded into flames. Wayne had seen the smoke billowing high into the air and jumped into his car to go see what the excitement was all about. On the way, he met the Bible worker, Noel, and she flagged him down.

"Where are you going?" she asked suspiciously.

"To see what all the smoke is about," Wayne answered.

"NO! Don't do that! The radio reporters claim that the Americans and British started the fire to get revenge on the Iraqis. Iraqis now want to massacre you foreigners. Go back to the hospital immediately."

Noel got into the car, and the two sped back to the hospital. It was good Wayne had met Noel on the road—God's perfect timing again.

Later that afternoon the government asked the British Oil Refinery workers to help them put out the fire. One unit responded. But when they laid out their hose, the mob cut it up. Then they started attacking the British fire fighters. The captain ordered his men to jump in their trucks and get out of there as fast as they could.

One fire fighter, who had received a severe flash burn on his back, was inadvertently left behind. An Iraqi army officer offered to take him in the back of his jeep to the Iraqi Army Hospital. The Britisher knew better than to go there, but he needed to get away from the mob. When the jeep slowed down for a curve near our compound, the Britisher leaped from the truck and sought refuge and treatment in Dar Es Salaam Hospital. That night the mob went on a rampage. Revenge was insatiable. Government troops had to patrol the streets all night to keep a semblance of order.

We were spellbound with Theo's stories. He said that most recently the brother of the new Minister of Health led a counter revolution in Mosul, northern Iraq. About 3,000 people were killed in that fight Iraqis killed Iraqis. About that time Wayne was asked to perform a wedding ceremony in Mosul (across the river from old Ninevah).

"And, can you believe he went!" Theo smiled as he remembered. "Wayne and Behnam. Arshat, the Iraqi mission president, boarded the train to go north. They both knew foreigners had been forbidden to travel, but they counted on Wayne's Arabic accent to disguise him as a Lebanese and the help of the Lord. They were not connected with any political group, but Joe Blow on the street wouldn't know that. It was a calculated risk. When the army inspector came through the train, Wayne kept quiet. He spoke only enough Arabic to let the inspector know where he was going. A few minutes later he heard the inspector report to his superior, 'No foreigners aboard except that Lebanese back there.' On the way back to Baghdad their experience was similar. Later, as we considered that excursion, we all agreed it had been a perilous mission."

During those tense and uncertain days, Oder Vandeman, to everyone's amazement, arrived in Baghdad to photograph old Babylon. Somehow the outside world didn't seem to understand the potential dangers and tenuous political situation that existed in Iraq at that time. It was not a place for tourists nor photography. After many trips to government offices, Wayne finally secured permits guaranteeing Vandeman and company safe passage to Babylon. When Wayne asked if he might accompany Elder Vandeman, the security official said, "You don't need any special permit to travel you're Lebanese."

Wayne was shocked. He had fooled the intelligence agent, but he dare not try to fool the check-point patrols. It wasn't worth the risk. He then secured a bona fide travel permit.

Theo's visit ended, and he returned to Baghdad. I sent a gift with him for Wayne's birthday October 17. We exiles celebrated David's birthday October 18. 1 gave him the cowboy hat and belt Julius had sent with me, and ordered a cake. Next year maybe my men could celebrate their birthdays together as they had always done.

November 6 a cable from the division brethren advised us to move to Beirut. We would be much closer to Iraq and possible visits from our husbands. We were elated and flew to Beirut as soon as we could get booking. There the Karmy boys joined our school in exile.

Christmas Eve was a red-letter time for the Olsons— Wayne arrived from Baghdad and the family was re-united after almost seven months of separation. Basking in each other's love was the best Christmas gift God could have given us.

At -the January meetings, Elder Roger Wilcox, the new Middle East Division president, asked Wayne to be the division's ministerial secretary. Wayne accepted the position but thought he should remain in Iraq until the mission could replace him. He believed it would be demoralizing to the hospital staff to be left without a pastor.

I had emergency surgery for a strangulated hernia on January 7. A week later Wayne returned to Baghdad, and the rest of us began school again. I taught the children from my rocking chair at the house where we were camping for the duration.

In March we refugees returned to Baghdad. Conditions seemed a little improved, or so we thought. Besides, we ladies and children were really tired of living out of our suitcases in temporary quarters. After ten months, I wanted to get back to my own home, bed, and kitchen. I was especially anxious to be re-united with my clothes and washing machine.

While we were gone, the mission had built two new houses on the compound. In October Wayne had moved our belongings into one house, and the Karmys moved into the other. We really liked the new house, and it was nice living within a few yards of the Ubbinks and Wagners. The kids thought the situation was ideal—they only had to step outside their front door to have a yard full of playmates. Blessed innocents. They didn't realize that we had come back just in time to face a resurgence of trouble.

When we were in Italy, a baby boy had been born and left by his mother in our Dar Es Salaam Hospital. She was a sheik's daughter who had conceived the child out of wedlock. She knew her family would kill her for falling in love and fraternizing with a commoner. So she concealed her pregnancy under her robes, came to the hospital early, and had a Caesarian section to prove she had surgery for her "tumor." Now the hospital was left with an adorable baby boy.

When we returned to Baghdad in March, Anna Karmy decided to take the baby out of the nursery and give him more attention than the nurses had time to give him. She took him to her home and doted on him. Then Anna slipped in the bathtub and broke some ribs. She could no longer care for the baby, so she asked us to take him. When she saw how attached we became to the little guy, she suggested that we adopt him. Our whole family loved Danny Mark, and we couldn't bear to let him go to someone else. So we started the adoption process.

We hit many snags. The Iraqi in charge of children's services wanted to know if the child was born to Moslem parents. Of course, we knew he was. But then the kind gentleman figured a way around that objection. He decided that since the baby was born and left in a Christian hospital, he could as well be a Christian. Who could prove the point one way or the other? He promised us it would only be a matter of a month or two and the papers could be final. Meanwhile, the division brethren questioned the wisdom of our adopting an Iraqi child at this time. Suppose we would have to flee; would we be allowed to take him out of the country? The American counsel was also concerned about this matter. They were right, of course, but we had become so emotionally attached to Danny that we felt we couldn't give him up.

During the school hours, Danny stayed at the hospital nursery or with Wayne. After school, we'd pick him up and play with him. Danny really blossomed with the affection and attention we showered on him, proving Anna Karmy's theory a child needs a family and love. He was a sweet baby and laughed a lot. By the time he was five months old, we knew Danny was an intelligent child. He was definitely our boy! We hoped and prayed to get the adoption papers within a few weeks.

When the revolution first broke, there was concern about the future of the hospital. However, as time went on, the hospital staff began to feel confident that our institution was secure. Kassim and his men knew that Adventist missionaries were non-political people and were, therefore, no threat to his government. They allowed us to continue our humanitarian and Christian work.

Then there was a gradual shift to the left. The USSR was interested in the rich oil fields of Karkuk and was courting the favor of the new Iraqi republic. They pushed the new government to get rid of the British Petroleum Company and turn it over to them. Of course, that was like shifting a ball from one hand to the other, but the inexperienced Iraqi leaders didn't understand the shrewd deceit of politics. The fledgling government needed all the revenue it could generate and was confident that it could hold the reins of power against any foreign intruder. But the scheming communists were gradually maneuvering their way to take control. Westerners were hated. Some were attacked at their jobs sites, and businesses were surrounded at night and confiscated. Still our hospital seemed secure. We believed our workers were loyal because we were paying them much more than they could get working anywhere else. They had been content, maybe even proud, to be associated with Dar Es Salaam Hospital. But a rude awakening awaited us.

Every day the school children and I walked the block from the housing compound to the hospital compound. One day Buster Ubbink went ahead of us and was met by a mob on their way into the city. The nine-year-old was so frightened he scaled the wall and dropped onto the hospital grounds. The mob was probably not a threat to Buster, but he didn't know that. It was almost noon before he relaxed. The tense atmosphere surrounding us was not healthy for the children. They became nervous and unable to concentrate.

On the way to school, I heard men discussing the possibility of kidnapping Ann Ubbink and Ronnalee and selling them into someone's harem. That sent shivers through my soul. I couldn't imagine a worse fate for an American girl. Thank God, they decided the time wasn't quite right yet.

Even at home inside our housing complex, we began being harrassed. Shady characters defiantly climbed over the fence. The intruders were so brazen it was impossible to convince them that this was private property. "It's Iraqi property," they retorted belligerently. They took Ronnalee's bike and some of Danny's clothing. One day I looked up and saw a stranger walking around my living room examining the furniture. He wasn't embarrassed to be discovered nor in a hurry to leave. After that I kept my doors locked and an eye on the children.

At the hospital compound I noticed that the gardener and maintenance workers were opening the back gate of the hospital compound to admit men who did not work for the hospital. I soon discovered they were leaders of the local communist party and were organizing a labor union. Their shouts and clapping frightened the children. Ronnalee and I understood Arabic and knew what was going on but didn't want to tell them. When the children looked apprehensively at me, I tried to assure them that God would care for us. But every day I feared more for the children. We were in the back corner of the hospital compound within a stone's throw of the communist meetings.

When the children went out to play, two of the reprobates chanted, "Today they play; tomorrow we drink their blood." Ronnalee understood what they said, and it terrified the 12-year old. I made her promise not to tell the other children what the men said, but the kids seemed to sense danger, anyway. They didn't want to go out to play, so I let them have their recesses indoors.

I tried to tell my fellow Americans of the union's plans to take over the hospital, but no one except Wayne took me seriously. They reasoned that they had survived the revolution and things weren't worse than they had been. Perhaps they had built up an immunity or an acceptance of the unsettled conditions.

Then one day the chief laundry worker, whom I shall call Omar, appeared at a hospital staff meeting. When Dr. Karmy confronted him, the man replied that he represented the Union of Hospital Workers. By this time all the non-Christian workers had joined the union, and gradually some of the Christians were pressured into uniting with the traitors. Omar was asked to leave the meeting. He did, but he swore revenge on Dr. Karmy. He reported to the government that Karmy, our chief surgeon, was an imperialist spy. The accusation was so absolutely absurd that we didn't suppose any normal person would believe him. Furthermore, Omar, the traitor, was neither intelligent nor honest.

Easter Sunday the children were outside playing games when a rickety army jeep drove into the housing compound. The kids froze in their places as they watched four shabbilydressed men toting guns go to Dr. Karmy's house. They arrested Karmy and forced him into their jeep. Dr. Karmy was born a Palestinian Arab Christian, but he was also a naturalized American citizen. Karmy protested that he had surgery scheduled for 1 P.M. and begged them to wait until he finished that emergency. But they wouldn't listen to his pleas. They didn't care if the patient died.

Dr. Wagner and Mr. Ubbink jumped in a car, went to the American Embassy, and reported the incident. They promised to notify Dr. Wagner if they heard anything. Since this answer indicated that the Embassy had lost their clout with the Iraqi government, Wagner and Ubbink drove to the Central Prison.

Dr. Wagner walked into the dismal area and, as he looked down a long hall, saw Dr. Karmy sitting on a chair. (Because he was a doctor, Karmy received preferential treatment). On a lower, subterranean level, Dr. Wagner saw hundreds of political prisoners. He knew that many of them would be killed. Wagner was determined that Karmy would not be another statistic.

Dr. Karmy was next taken to the Criminal Investigation Division. Wagner and Ubbink followed him into the building. There Dr. Karmy was officially accused of being a tool in the hands of American Imperialists and was told he had to leave the country within 24 hours. Then the inquisitor looked up and saw Dr. Wagner. "Who are YOU?" he asked.

"I'm a friend of Dr. Karmy's," Dr. Wagner replied.

"How did you get in here?"

"I just walked in," Dr Wagner said in his casual manner.

"Well, get out of here quick!" the officer said nervously. "Don't worry about Karmy. We'll send him to immigration headquarters. You can meet him there in about two hours."

About the same time Dr. Karmy was arrested, Ayoub Azar, our hospital's pharmacist from Jordan, was taken from his home. It was interesting that the Iraqis chose two men of Arab descent to accuse as spies. This was Omar's way of taking revenge on Dr. Karmy for asking him to leave the hospital staff meeting. We never were quite sure how they concluded that Mr. Azar was a threat.

Wagner and Ubbink worked simultaneously on both cases to free the men.

Dr. Wagner and Mr. Ubbink got to Immigration before Karmy. Wagner was happy to discover that the director was a friend. He promised Wagner that if Karmy had to leave, he'd make certain Karmy was treated well. Wagner hoped for more. His wish became a reality when the sergeant walked in. Dr. Wagner had operated on the sergeant's father. The father desperately needed a blood transfusion, but none of the family or friends would submit to a blood draw. In desperation, Kathleen Wagner, whose blood was a match, gave her blood to save the life of the sergeant's father. The Wagners' loving care was about to pay off for Karmy.

An immigration officer came out swearing, handed Dr. Wagner a paper and told him to sign it. Wagner signed it then asked, "What did I sign?"

"It's a receipt for Karmy. Take him home, and we'll call him when we want him," the irritated officer answered.

The men came home to the compound late that night, but everyone was still very much awake. We'd done a lot of worrying and praying. We were very relieved to see Karmy and Azar return with Wagner and Ubbink. However, Azar and Karmy and their families would have to leave the country soon. We suspected this was just the beginning of the exodus.

Now we saw clearly what was happening—Iraq had become a police state. The peace and security in Iraq was shattered. Everyone was spying on one another. Innocent school children were asked to report what their parents were saying about the new regime. Their account often sent their fathers off to prison. Some days school children were forced to march down the streets in 100 degree temperatures shouting the glory of the new government. Some of them fainted from the heat and/or lack of water.

Neighbors reported on neighbors, and relatives reported on relatives. False accusations became one way of getting revenge on someone you didn't like. The prisons were so full of alleged "political enemies" that the government started bricking-in windows of factories and school buildings to house the ever increasing number of prisoners. Military courts were clogged with cases that there would never be time to try. Innocent people were executed. How could this be happening in Iraq? The country had educated, intelligent people who could have run the governmen effectively, efficiently, and justly. Perhaps putting an end to the monarchy was necessary, but THIS? The revolt had turned into an insatiable desire for revenge, and many innocent people were caught in the wake. It was with trepidation in our hearts that we watched the Karmys and the Azars leave. For us, too, we knew it was only a matter of time.

CHAPTER 16
DEATH OF A HOSPITAL AND THE AFTERMATH

During the next few weeks, many Western technicians and specialized workers were asked to leave the country. They were replaced by men from the USSR or communist satellite countries. This was a clear switch from monarchy to communism. Kassim had lost control; his "Iraqi democracy" had collapsed.

Our premonitions told us to prepare for an "exodus." We knew our telephone lines were being tapped, our mail censored, and our actions recorded. Besides the gardener, laundry worker, janitor and housekeeping spies, strangers would pace the hallways day after day. What they hoped to learn about us was a puzzle to everyone. Other than the fact that we carried a Western passport, they could have nothing against us nor any reason to fear us. We were not interested in politics—either of their country or ours.

We became increasingly uneasy. The very atmosphere dripped with ominousness. A Catholic priest, Father Patrick, and missionaries from other church groups sought refuge with us at Dar Es Salaam. The staff stepped up the instruction for the nursing class so they could graduate early if necessary.

One day the inevitable finale began. An Arabic newspaper published a ridiculous story, which in essence said that our hospital was a tool for the imperialist countries and the American government; therefore, the Iraqi government was taking over Dar Es Salaam. We were shocked with this news as no one had approached the hospital administration about the matter. Dr. Wagner, Dick Ubbink, and others protested the false propaganda and asked that they print a retraction. This idea was met with cool indifference.

The next week more lies were fed the public. Three newspapers published a release that claimed the Iraqi government had financed our hospital and, therefore, it rightfully belonged to them. Nothing could be further from the truth. The General Conference had funded the institution to the tune of $1.5 million dollars. Only $5,000 had come from local members; the government of Iraq had never invested one penny in Dar Es Salaam. Furthermore, up until the last year when the hospital finally became self-supporting, the mission had subsidized its operation. The legal documents that proved our complete ownership of the hospital were in the hands of the government officials, but they had no intention of revealing the facts. The situation was frustrating. We knew we had lost our case and our hospital. The final days had come.

I held little Danny, the Iraqi baby we hoped to adopt, and cried. Our whole family had learned to love him, and we worried that we would be forced to give him up. At six months old, he was adorable. We tried to expedite Danny's adoption papers. The social services director tried to help us get Danny, but the government wouldn't let an American family take an Iraqi boy child out of the country. We pleaded with the American Embassy to intervene, but since all westerners were "personas non grata," they couldn't help us, either.

The day came all too soon when we were forced to take our baby to the Iraqi social services and leave him there. I sent his clothes, bottles, and toys with him. It was a funeral for us—a final separation from our Danny. Only parents who have lost a baby can understand the grief. I sold the crib and chest that I had kept since David and Ronnie were babies. There would be no more babies in our home again.

We wondered what happened to our healthy, happy little boy. When we could stand it no longer, Wayne went down to the social services director and inquired. He told Wayne that before we took Danny to them, he had arranged for a childless lawyer and his wife to adopt him. That was some comfort to us. Danny would be loved and cared for by someone who needed the joy of having a baby boy. Events were happening so fast around us that we had little time to mourn our loss.

The last Sunday of May dawned cloudy and foreboding. This was not normal for sunny Baghdad; but then, this was not happing to be a normal day. Apprehension enveloped me like a dark mist. Why did I feel like I was suspended in space? Was I missing Danny? Did I fear for my other children and the future? My sixth sense told me that something calamitous was about to happen.

little swirls of dust rose and fell as I walked down the oleander-and palm-tree-lined pathway to the chapel. There I met with the other ladies who had agreed to decorate the chapel for the nurses' graduation exercises. The nursing students were excited and giggly as they practiced marching. Ordinarily this would be the normal pre-graduation scene, but today I just kept waiting for the moment of doom to strike.

At ten o'clock "the call" came. With the exception of the Jensens and us, the name of every foreign hospital worker was on the blacklist and was asked to leave the country within 24 hours. With a hospital full of patients, this was an utterly preposterous, insane request. There was no way the staff could push bum victims, new surgical patients, those on life supports, and others out of the hospital in one day. The staff needed time to transfer the patients to other hospitals and doctors. The administration pleaded with the authorities to use mercy and common sense in making their demands. At last the officials relented and granted a reprieve of two more weeks.

As negotiations were going on between the hospital administration and the government officials, we at the compound were praying. Dar Es Salaam Hospital was dying, and we were mourning its death. In two weeks,—it would be no more. It also meant the death of our hospital "family"; we would be scattered in different directions.

There was little enthusiasm for the graduation program that Sunday night. The nursing students had reached a milestone in their lives, and we tried to savor the moment; but our minds were occupied with the heartbreak of losing the hospital. After the students received their diplomas, we hugged one another and cried. Since most of the graduates were from other Middle East countries, they would not stay on to work at Dar Es Salaam.

We tried to inject a bit of jocularity into the reception, but it didn't work. The wonderful food prepared by Mr. Aldrich and his crew sat mostly untouched. No one had any appetite for food except the little boys; they polished off quite a meal. Perhaps no one slept that night, either, except the young lads who had their tummies full of goodies.

The next day plans for closing the hospital were outlined, and specific work assignments were given to the entire staff. We ladies packed or sold our earthly possessions, while the men worked with the patients or packed equipment to send to our hospital in Benghazi, Libya. The older children looked after the little ones, worked in the kitchen, or ran errands. We brought our food supplies to the hospital kitchen where the meals were prepared for the whole group. This saved time for everyone. No lady had to take time out to prepare meals, and the men didn't have to go home to eat. We became a commune, and we liked it.

After a few days the big exodus began—14 Dar Es Salaam nurses and Dr. Dorothy Turner flew out of Baghdad. We wept as we parted, never knowing if we would ever meet again on this earth. These weren't just fellow workers; they were family. Every few days other workers left. There were tears shed at each parting, but we didn't have time to wallow in grief. There was much work left to be done. Only our confidence that God was in control kept us going.

Since the children's games were packed or sold, they entertained themselves playing "hospital." The "doctor" of the hour would take the "patients" to surgery, then push him/her to a room on a gurney. "Nurses" would feed the "patients" and push others about in wheel chairs. No children ever had more fun "running" a 65-bed hospital. Probably, no other children ever had a big hospital in which to play. There were four children ages two to four years old, who cooperated beautifully with the six older children, ages 10 to 13. The kids seemed to handle the situation very well. Their buoyant spirits helped us cope.

Wayne transferred his Bible study students to Noel. He and Theo Williams packed the public address system they had installed the preceding July and shipped it to our new Adventist Center in Beirut. New laboratory and surgical equipment that had just arrived at Dar Es Salaam, and that Dr. Wagner planned to transfer to our Adventist hospital in Libya, was intercepted by the Iraqi government. They refused to let it leave the country. The doctors transferred or dismissed patients. In two weeks the work was done. The night before the hospital was given over to the government, those of us who were left gathered outside the hospital compound. All the lights in the hospital were turned on as they normally were, and we gazed with sorrow upon our beloved Dar Es Salaam (door of peace) Hospital. Nevermore would there be Christian worships in the chapel. Nevermore would nurses and doctors pray with their patients. Nevermore would we head those halls or enjoy visiting with our friends in the cafeteria.

Then someone manned the switch box and turned off all the lights. The hospital was left in utter darkness. Symbolically, our hospital died when the lights went out. Many wonderful memories died with it. Chains and padlocks were placed on the gates—the "door to peace" was closed. Solemnly we wound our way down the oleander-andpalm-tree-lined path that led to our houses. No one spoke; our hearts were too heavy for words. It was difficult to fall asleep that night. We kept remembering what had been and was no more.

About that time Bob Osborn, treasurer for Middle East Division, arrived on the scene, representing the interests of the division and the General Conference. He was not about to let the Iraqi Government confiscate our property worth over a million and a half dollars without remuneration. Along with Dr. Wagner and Dick Ubbink, he camped on the steps of various government offices. Our men bargained, cajoled, deliberated, presented papers and contracts, and persisted on getting a fair settlement. Long after all we foreigners left the country, Bob Osborn continued to plague the Iraqi government to get a fair return on our investment in Dar Es Salaam. He finally negotiated a settlement which wasn't completely satisfactory, but it paid the mission about 50% of the original investment. That was a lot better than the government's original nothing. I don't think the government expected to tangle with the persistence of our men.

Wayne, as ministerial secretary of Middle East Division, needed to go to Iran as quickly as possible for their camp meeting. We decided to go together and make it a family vacation. What was left of our household goods had already been shipped to Beirut where we would set up our next home on the division compound. We secured visas for Iran and left in a taxi for the border, about 60 miles away. Since our names had not been on the blacklist, we assumed we were free to travel out of Iraq by car. Every few miles soldiers stopped our taxi. When they discovered us passengers were "dangerous imperialists," the soldiers made us get out of the taxi, frisked us, opened all our suitcases, and emptied the contents. They found nothing questionable among our belongings. Since they couldn't find our names on their blacklist either, they were obliged to let us go. This happened seven times in 60 miles. Because of these delays, we arrived at the border at siesta time, instead of 10 A.M.

The soldiers at the border barracks were more than suspicious Americans fleeing to their enemy country, Iran? They suspected that we had some ulterior motives. We wondered what they were trying to prove since there was no evidence. Finally, a young private decided that Wayne was on their blacklist under an assumed name and was wanted for spy operations in Iraq. The private couldn't prove it, but he couldn't read, either.

Wayne laughed, "Even if I had the craftiness to be a spy, I wouldn't have the guts to do it."

I didn't think it was funny at all. They wanted me to leave Wayne in jail and go to Iran on my own. I refused to budge and insisted that I stay right there until their commander came.

About 3 P.M. the man in charge of the frontier post came walking into the barracks. He was an intelligent young man and very literate.

"Well, well, what have we here?" he asked pleasantly. "Wayne Olson? You and your family, I presume, are coming from Baghdad? What did you do there?"

"I was chaplain of the Dar Es Salaam Hospital, and

"Oh, I'm glad to meet you, Mr. Olson. I have all the respect in the world for Dar Es Salaam. They saved my brother's life. We love you people, and," he whispered to Wayne, "most of us citizens are very sorry to see you leave our country. I don't know what the leaders are thinking.

Sometimes, I feel sorry for Kassim. He's got himself in a jam.

He surrounded himself with impetuous (he used a strong word here). They're ignorantly selling us out to the communists, and we can't do a thing to stop them. They kill anyone who opposes their insane ideas. I'm sorry this young idiot (referring to the private) has detained you.

He's an example of some of the mental midgets with whom we are dealing these days."

Now I smiled. I knew we had met a friend.

The commander called the private back into the room and in a loud voice said, "Please get this family some lemonade to drink. They need to be refreshed after sitting in this shed for three hours. They are good people—the best."

The private who had been so haughty only moments before, now hung his head in disgrace. I was reminded of the powerhappy Haman who was also humiliated by his superior when he was forced to lead Mordecai's horse through the streets giving honor to his enemy. Now our tormentor was serving us; yet, I pitied him.

The commander called a taxi, and we were on our way again. The taxi driver was very nice and took us as close to the border as was legally possible. Then he apologized that we would have to walk the last two miles. The temperature was over 110 degrees in the shade, but on the desert road there was no shade. The asphalt was so hot it was sticky. Wayne and I carried our four suitcases, while Ronnie and David each carried two pieces of hand luggage. We had gone only a few yards when an Iraqi tribesman came dashing down a sand dune headed straight for us. We didn't have time to get frightened before he greeted us.

"Good day, friends. Let me help you, " he offered pleasantly. The winsome smile that cracked his sun-tanned face made us feel very comfortable with him.

He trotted down the road at a pace that, in the intense heat, was difficult for us to follow. When he got too far ahead of us, he'd set the suitcases down and rest. A fourth mile from the border, he handed us the suitcases and said, "Iraqi go no farther. "

We thanked this good Samaritan and offered him the rest of our Iraqi money. He protested saying that he hadn't done the favor for tips. When we told him that we were leaving the country permanently, and that the money would be no good to us anywhere else, he graciously accepted our offer. Then he waved to us and disappeared.

"Now that's the Iraqi people I know," Wayne said as he picked up his burden. "This new government and the people running it are a different breed."

We trudged slowly up the hill toward the Iranian border. We stopped and drained our gallon water jug. Before we reached the Iranian border, two men ran down to meet us and carried the four heavy suitcases. Wayne and I then relieved the children of their burdens. Soon we crossed the border and were in Iranian territory. The whole atmosphere seemed miraculously changed. We had left a country where the citizens were tense and distrustful; now we entered a country where the people were relaxed and happy.

The Iranians welcomed us to their country by signs and smiles. We had a communication problem—we spoke Arabic, and they spoke Farsi. They offered us tea and pop. They led us to a beautiful ceramic swimming pool and in sign language invited us to remove our shoes and coot our feet in the water. In no time we had our sandals off and were dangling our feet in the warm water.

Now that we were out of Iraq and rested, we became hungry. We took out our lunch and ate it while we cooled our burning feet. One Iranian man spoke some Arabic. Wayne told him that we needed a taxi to take us to the nearest town. He called for a taxi. Since it was an Iranian holiday, the car didn't arrive until evening. We loaded our luggage and took off for the nearest village. The Iranians were a happy, carefree lot and sang as they rode along on the bumper of our cab. When we got to the village, we learned there was no hotel there. The villagers obligingly found a truck driver who was taking a load of cucumbers over to Kermanshah where there were hotels. Ronnalee and I crawled up into the cab with the driver, while Wayne and David bundled up and rode in the back of the truck with some Iranians. They serenaded us all the way.

It was past 9 P.M. when we arrived in Kermanshah. The truck driver finally found a third-class hotel that had a room to rent and I do mean THIRD-CLASS. I was suspicious of the cleanliness of the sheets, but with only a 15-watt light bulb dangling from the ceiling it was too dark to examine the beds. We were so tired, we simply crawled into bed. Never mind that the bed was too hard and smelled. Never mind the lack of warm water and showers. Never mind the heat and mosquitos. It was so good to be out of the turmoil of Iraq that anything else verged on utopia. We sighed with relief, relaxed, and slept the sleep of tired souls longing for peace. Our Iranian Odyssey had begun.

POSTSCRIPT:

The Iraqi government invited eight USSR doctors to take the place of our four American doctors and occupy our homes. Those doctors used primitive medicine such as leeches for bleeding and enemas for every ailment. They didn't know how to operate some of the modem equipment we had to leave behind. Our Iraqi nurses were forced to stay on and work at the hospital. It was distressing for them to follow orders that were antiquated. They did their best, however, to cooperate. (They even cared for Karim Kassim when an attempt was made on his life). Possibly, the USSR didn't send their best doctors to Iraq, supposing that Iraqi medicine was behind the times. It must have been shocking for them to come into a modem country like Iraq with large houses, electrical appliances, private cars, swimming pools, tropical gardens, and lots of fruit and vegetables. They were disappointed that we hadn't left our houses furnished, but we were happy we had sold our possessions and pocketed the money. We all lost financially, but the mission gave us a replacement allowance which helped.

CHAPTER 17
IRANIAN ODYSSEY

Early the next morning we were awakened by the flies and the activity in the street below us. Vendors were hawking their wares; cars and buses were honking. Everyone else was shouting orders. I never heard such bedlam. I thought it would be fun to go down and shout some orders myself.

I opened a suitcase and took out clean clothes for the children and me. There was no tub or shower available but there was a wash basin in the toilet room. However, the basin was so filthy I hated to use it. I found a rag and soap and mustered up enough of my Danish determination to scrub through the layers of dirt. We took spit baths in cool water and felt partially civilized by the time we donned clean clothes. Then I looked at the beds in which we had slept. The sheets were made of red and white plaid cloth made thicker by dirt. I don't know how many truckers had slept in them before we did, but the proprietor of the hotel told me (with a bit of pride) that he always had the sheets washed twice a month. After that, even my sponge bath didn't seem sufficient to cleanse my body. But we never developed any skin disease or sickness from our night spent on dirty plaid sheets. Maybe I just have a fetish about clean laundry.

After eating breakfast, we hunted for the bus station to get transportation to the next place on our map. We had no special agenda; we simply wanted to see as much of Iran as possible in the time we had. At the station the man threw up his hands and pointed to the clock. What he was telling us was that the bus we wanted had left town at 4 A.M. We didn't want to stay there until the next morning's bus, so Wayne scouted around for a taxi that would take us to Hamadan. Hiring taxis was getting expensive.

We didn't regret being in a private cab on this leg of our journey, however, because the road passed by the famous Behistun Rock. We wanted to spend time there, and the taxi driver was willing to let us do that. In a bus we'd have just whizzed by the Rock, leaving us with only a passing glance at one of the world's greatest archaeological discoveries. Darius the Great was responsible for having three languages (Persian, Elamite, and Babylonian) inscribed on the face of this granite cliff. This proved to be the key for deciphering all cuneiform writing which was used in Persia, Assyria, and Babylon.

Henry Rawlinson spent four years copying the entire inscription. In order to do so, he had to hang off the cliff in a basket. He spent more time in a basket than the Easter bunny. It took him 20 more years to decipher the script. His contribution to archaeology was invaluable because he made it possible for linguists to translate many ancient manuscripts from civilizations that existed hundreds of years earlier.

While at the Behistun Rock, we met some English soldiers. Since our next stop was Hamadan, we asked them if they knew of a good hotel in that town. "Oh, sure," one answered. "I hear that the Blue Alley Hotel is a jolly good spot. "

"Thanks for your help," Wayne said shaking his hand. (I don't know why men do that - shake hands for no reason that I can figure out.) When the men were gone Wayne said to me, "Midge, don't you think 'Blue Alley' is a queer name for an Iranian hotel?"

I did, but we couldn't argue with free information.

We got to Hamadan in time to look around the town that in Biblical times was called Ecbatana. The city of 250,000 people is located in the Western Iranian mountains at an elevation of 6,000 feet. In the days of Esther and Mordecai (470's B.C.) the Achaemenian dynasty of Persian kings had their summer palace in Ecbatana. The ancient town is buried beneath Hamadan, so nothing of archaeological interest is visible. Clandestine diggings will frequently turn up some artifact of antiquity. To us, it was important that Queen Esther and Mordecai had lived and died here. Their bodies were entombed in a memorial building. This fact has been authenticated by authorities.

I was disappointed that the Iranians hadn't fancied-up the tomb on the outside. It was just drab brick and mortar. Many important Iranian buildings are tastefully and artistically covered with ceramic tile. Maybe Esther and Mordecai don't mean much to Iranians, so they haven't beautified their tombs.

Early that evening we started hunting for the Blue Alley Hotel. The taxi driver cruised the town, but no one had heard of such a place. Hamadan had some very swanky hotels, supposedly run by the Shah. We would have enjoyed the luxury, but our limited funds checked our desires.

Finally, a helpful soul suggested that we go to the Presbyterian Mission on the edge of town to see what they might advise. When we got to their home, they welcomed us with open arms. "Go no farther," they insisted. "Come in and stay with us for the night. Our home makes a fine hotel and restaurant, and a laundromat, too, if you need it."

We accepted their kind invitation, and, after a good dinner and showers, spent the evening telling them about our last year in Iraq. They had heard many stories and knew that some of their missionaries had taken shelter at Dar Es Salaam. They wanted to return the favor and hear first-hand information about the revolution. We had a good Christian fellowship with these Protestant missionaries and thanked God for leading us to them. We were still in the process of unwinding from the last tense days in Iraq, and these were good people with whom we could comfortably unwind.

When we asked our new friends about the Blue Alley Hotel, they laughed, "Those Englishmen twisted the Persian words around until they heard 'Blue Alley' instead of 'Abu Ali'." We all thought that was pretty funny.

Early the next morning our friends wakened us, fed us a good breakfast, and took us to the bus station. That day we got our introduction to the hazards of riding Iranian buses. Our driver was a jolly fellow and very friendly. He frequently turned around and talked to people behind him while cruising down a very narrow, two-lane highway at an incredible speed. If he happened to be riding the center of the road when he met a car, the car simply swerved off on the rocky shoulder, and we went merrily on our way. Did I say WE? No, I meant the driver and his Iranian passengers were merry. The Olsons were bug-eyed and gasping for air most of the time.

"Maybe we should just close our eyes. That way we won't see the moment of death," I lamented.

"Oh, I think we'll - - -," Wayne began just as we hit a huge bump in the road. We flew to the unpadded ceiling of the bus and banged our heads hard enough to develop knots that added to our stature. Fortunately, the driver managed to hang onto the wheel and kept the vehicle on course. We savored THAT blessing.

"What were you saying?" I asked Wayne as I checked my spinal column.

"I was going to say that I thought we'd make it all right, and not to worry. But I've changed my mind. Go ahead and worry. " Wayne rubbed his head. "Maybe I have a concussion, but I think I'll still be able to preach at camp meeting if I can just retrieve my briefcase with my sermon notes."

The other passengers were very obliging. No one dared leave his seat, but the people on the aisle passed Wayne's brief case up to him.

At noon we suddenly came to a screeching stop in the middle of nowhere. Dust billowed so thick around us that we couldn't see what had happened. We knew everyone was leaving the bus, but we didn't know why. We decided to get off, too. Everyone filed into an opening in a structure. We had no idea what it was but were fascinated by the way they had cut open 100-gallon drums, unrolled the metal, and fastened it together to make walls for a

– whatever. They used very little wood. Some parts of the wall were dabbed with clay. Then they covered the whole "whatever" with a thatched roof. We thought that was very ingenious of people who live in a desert area where wood is scarce. As soon as we entered the "whatever," we, knew it was a roadside cafe.

David was hungry so we sat down at a table. There were no menus so we waited for further information. When you can't speak the language you feel like a blubbering idiot, and probably act like one, too.

Soon a waiter appeared at our table. "You want eat?" he asked.

"Yes," Wayne answered. "May we see the menu?"

"Huh! Menu?" he asked.

"Yes, what can we order? We're vegetarians," I informed him. Now that was a stupid statement that ought to be recorded in the annals of "Lame Brain." If the man could speak only a few words of English, he certainly wouldn't know the word "vegetarian."

"You want eat?" he began all over again, trying to be patient with us.

"Yes," Wayne said emphatically in a louder voice. Why is it that when we try to communicate with someone who doesn't speak our language, we think they will miraculously understand if we talk louder?

"Good," the man smiled, obviously relieved that we understood each other. Maybe he knew what we were talking about, but we certainly didn't. He went over to the stove and came back with four plates heaped with white rice, a glob of melting sheep's butter, a white pita bread, and some white radishes.

"How fitting," I remarked. "White food for ghostly white people who are scared to death to get back on that bus."

David downed his food and ate some of Ronnie's and mine. Wayne's appetite was diminished, but he ate anyway. The food was tasty, but with our stomach in knots from fright, it was difficult to eat. It seems that in the roadside cafes they serve one dish, and one dish only rice. It's a "stop-gap" until the evening meal when Iranians eat well.

When we got outside, I saw them rinsing the dishes in the irrigation ditch that ran in front of the cafe. Why hadn't I noticed that when I entered the establishment? Now I had something else to worry about.

"Aw, don't be so squeamish," Wayne advised. "That food was steaming hot when they put it on our plates. The heat killed all the microbes and worm eggs - -"

"Enough. Don't tell me about another organism!" I interrupted.

"Someone probably took a bath and watered their buffalo in the water up stream," Wayne continued with an impish grin.

"If you don't stop," I warned him, "you'll see what I ate."

He stopped, and we boarded the bus again. We flew down the road in the same reckless fashion as before. This time the bus driver's friend caught up with us. The two buses careened down the road, side by side, while the drivers chatted and passed cucumbers and melon slices back and forth through the open windows.

"OHHH," Wayne groaned. "And I thought it couldn't get any worse!"

Just then we saw a bus coming our way. We held our breath and prayed. We hoped that one of the drivers would give way to the oncoming vehicle, but they stayed side by side. We braced ourselves for the inevitable three-bus crash. At the last minute, the on-coming bus simply pulled off onto the desert floor and waved congenially. The amazing thing was that no one, except us, considered it a miracle.

"Wow! " Wayne said as he exhaled explosively. "Who knows who should give? What are the rules of the road? It stymies my reason. An American bus driver would have cracked up by now - both his vehicle and his nerves."

"You look a bit distraught, yourself, Wayne," I giggled nervously. "In fact, if you clinch your jaw any tighter, you'll be wearing dentures."

We were greatly relieved when we reached Tehran that night. Other than shredded nerves and filthy clothes, we were still intact. We took a taxi out to the mission where we were greeted by Bob Skinner, mission president, and his wife Gladys. Our kids struck up an immediate friendship with the Skinner children.

Camp meeting was held a few miles out of Tehran at the Adventist secondary school. The setting was pastoral and peaceful. God's spirit seemed to touch each of us with His love. At the closing meeting, several candidates were baptized in the swimming pool.

Wayne needed to go on to Isfahan to visit some of the members there. Gladys suggested that I go with him, but leave Ronnie and David with her. The kids thought this was a scathingly brilliant idea. They welcomed the invitation and settled in at the Skinners for four glorious days.

Wayne and I boarded the bus for all points south. (I couldn't believe we would take another bus, but that was the only transportation available). Either this bus driver was more cautious than the first one, or we had adapted to Iranian travel. We enjoyed the people and the country, but the straight, unpadded seats and the pitted roads were hard on the anatomy.

We were quite excited as we approached Qom, the holy city of the Shiite Moslems where Ali, one of the great Moslem leaders, is revered. In the distance we could see the goldcovered dome of the mosque glistening in the sun. What a picture!

The bus drove within half a block of the mosque. Guards would not allow us off the bus. Further, they requested that we take no pictures of their sacred building. We respected their desire and admired the tenacity with which they adhered to one of the tenets of their faith not to make idols or pictures of anything in the heavens or the earth. From the bus we marveled at the beauty of the ceramic-tiled, goldendomed mosque. I was sorry we couldn't photograph it.

That night we were at Isfahan, 315 miles south of Tehran. We spent a few days with our members there and were inspired by their faithfulness. I think they were more of a blessing to us than we were to them.

Persepolis, the winter palace of King Darius the Great, was only 315 miles away. The temptation to see this place moved us to bus on down to Shiraz, and then take a taxi out to the site. The sculptured walls and staircase leading up to the palace were beautifully and perfectly etched. The whole palace remains are so incredible that I could not possibly find words to describe them. It is a must-see-tobelieve place. The detail is absolutely amazing. The pincurls on the men's beards and even the cuticles on their fingernails were carved precisely.

Across the valley from the palace and city of Persepolis are the tombs of the kings. Caves were excavated in the high stone cliff for that purpose. They were not easily accessible. I never thought I'd make it up the shaky ladder to enter the tombs, but I did. In the tomb of King Darius the Great there were seven sarcophagi which held members of his immediate family. Now that is real family togetherness!

That night Wayne and I went out to the airport at Shiraz. I use the word "airport" loosely because there was no building, just a tent set up by the side of a landing strip. We purchased tickets at the tent, climbed into the six-passenger plane, and landed in Tehran a few hours later. I would not have been willing to fly in that plane had it not been for the bus experiences. The words "risk," "danger," and their synomyms had taken on a whole new meaning since we had experienced travel in Iran. Any mode of transportation seemed perilous. The poly-knit dress I had worn on the buses had holes worn across the shoulders where my back had jiggled back and forth and up and down on the unpadded seat backs. I tossed that dress along with Wayne's holey shirt in Gladys's garbage can when I got back to Tehran. That made two less things to pack.

The Caspian Sea area in northern Iran was next on our agenda. Taking another bus was our only option. It went through the beautiful Alborz Mountains. Along the way we passed fields of grain. Higher up were the grazing lands. Near the top even trees struggled to grow. In the distance we saw Mt. Demavand, towering 18,386 feet high. That is about 1,584 feet higher than Mt. Ararat in Turkey. Worldwide there are 46 taller mountains, but Mt. Demavand looked quite spectacular.

I kept my eyes on the upper slopes because it was too frightening to watch the road. The steep, hairpin curves, which had no railings to stop run-away vehicles, kept my blood pressure in the danger zone and my heart racing for an attack. There were places where only oneway traffic was possible. I wondered if it might be safer back on the desert with two buses driving side by side.

The journey up the mountains and down to the Caspian Sea (2,000 feet below sea level) took nine hours. Considering the extremely steep roads, the over-heated motor, the two flat tires, and the motor repairs, that was probably good time.

I We swam in the Caspian Sea. It was wonderful - clear, clean, warm, and no undertows or waves. The next day we took a taxi back to Tehran for the weekend.

Our vacation time was nearly over, so we needed to head for home. We decided to go overland through northwest Iran, eastern Turkey, then south through Syria to Lebanon. Monday we rode an all-night train bound for Tabriz. The accommodations were super. We had a compartment for six people. Wayne stashed the suitcases on the floor making two beds for the children; then he and I stretched out on the padded bench seats on either side. Ah, what luxury!

It was not difficult to find a nice hotel in Tabriz. After settling in, we looked up the few church members. They were as happy to see fellow believers as we were to see them. Wayne spoke at their evening prayer meeting, and I talked to them the next day at their Dorcas meeting. Then it was on to Turkey.

Our bus had generator trouble along the way; consequently, we didn't arrive at the border until 1:30 A.M. There was only one, very expensive, and not-so-nice hotel there, but we needed some rest. Another bus had arrived before us, and the passengers had occupied all the rooms. Finally, the manager herded 14 of us women and children into a room with eight single beds. Ronnalee and I occupied one bed, and David slept on the floor. I didn't stay awake to see how the other 11 people made out with the seven remaining beds.

Two Englishmen invited Wayne up to their two-bed room. One man went out to his jeep, got his sleeping bag, laid down on the floor, and gave Wayne his bed. God bless those Englishmen.

We awakened early the next morning because the customs officials had told us to be ready for inspection by eight o'clock.

Unfortunately, they processed the people on the other bus first.

While we waited, we wandered over the soft, grass-covered hillsides looking at the interesting flora. In the distance we could see snow-capped Mt. Ararat. Just the name "Ararat" inspires a sense of awe in Bible Christians. It is there where

God parked Noah's ark. Possibly it is still there, buried in the glaciers and snows of Mt. Ararat. The story of the flood and the destru ction of the world by water is one of the greatest stories recorded in Biblical history. It is interesting that most civilizations also have written their versions of a worldwide flood.

Wayne had a lot of time on his hands that day - the numerous pictures we have of Mt. Ararat testifies of his boredom. When he got too frustrated with the apathetic customs officials, he took another picture of Ararat.

By 4 P.M. we had passed the Iranian and Turkish customs and were on our way again. Our bus arrived in Erzurum, the first large Turkish city, at 3 A.M. No innkeeper is in a very good mood that time of the morning, but one hotel manager answered Wayne's persistent knock. He allowed us to sleep in the lobby that night.

Ile next morning we rented a room in the hotel. The manager cleared the large Turkish bath of other customers and rented it to our family for an hour. We donned our swimming suits and enjoyed the best cleansing possible. We found good food in a nearby shop, then ate and slept. In the late afternoon we heard music and singing. From our window we saw an interesting wedding procession made up of about 50 horse-drawn carriages. It was a glimpse of what had been in America in the late 1800s - a live picture of years gone by.

That night we left Erzurum on the train for Kayseri. We came to a jolting halt about 2 A.M. Two freight trains had crashed into each other. Animals and splintered boxcars littered the tracks. Fortunately, our conductor had been able to stop before causing further damage. Nine dead men had been pulled from the wreckage and lay along the side of the tracks. It was a pitiful sight - one that filled us with horror and sympathy. There was nothing we could do to help anyone. Men shot the animals that were still living but were injured too badly to save. A crew had come out from Kayseri to clear the tracks, but the task was overwhelming.

The railroad company solved the passengers' problem by sending another train out from Kayseri. We carried our luggage a mile around the wreckage and boarded the other train. We met the passengers from Kayseri going to Erzurum doing the same thing in reverse. It was quite a time-consuming transfer.

I A few hours later we arrived in Kayseri. There was one compelling interest in that area - the early Christian settlement of Cappadocia (mentioned in Acts 2:9 and I Peter 1: 1). A taxi took us to these unique conical formations. Huge rocks, shaped like an up-side down ice cream cone, rise out of Goreme Valley. Through the centuries, people have hollowed out the rock and made their homes in the cones. We were awed by the maze of cones, windows, and fairy chimneys built directly into the malleable rock. Beneath these fanciful shapes lie even more wonders: underground chambers and an entire village. Residents fashioned homes, storerooms, and churches in the rock, connecting it with a labyrinth of passageways.

We climbed the rocks to visit some of the early Christian churches. I was surprised at the frequent use of the cross and frescoes which represented the life of Christ or the apostles. These churches are preserved for antiquity, but there are few, if any, Christians in the area today. The citizens of this part of east-central Turkey are mostly Moslems.

One family invited us into their home to see how they lived. The entryway on ground level led into their living room, dining room, and kitchen area. Going up the rock-hewn steps to the next level were bedrooms. Stiff higher in the cone was a small bedroom and storage area. The rock floors were covered with Turkish carpets, and the window shades were hand woven. I saw no glass or bars across the windows. I wondered how they dared raise their children in these rock high-rises. I asked the mother if she tethered her crawling baby to some brace. She just smiled and shrugged her shoulders. Obviously, Turkish children are a lot smarter about danger at a younger age than American kids.

On the way back to Kayseri that evening, we knew there was something wrong with our taxi driver. He seemed to have no control of his vehicle. He raced one minute and came to a screeching halt the next. He claimed there were monsters in the middle of the road and he had to avoid them. What we didn't know until then was that while he waited for us to explore Cappadocia, he had been smoking hashish. He was really on a high and had us scared to death. When he stopped and got out to smoke another joint, Wayne jumped into the driver's seat and refused to budge. There was a struggle between the men, but Wayne finally convinced him that there would be no pay unless he let Wayne drive us back to Kayseri. The driver finally crawled in the passenger seat and promptly went to sleep while Wayne drove us back to our hotel.

A train took us from Kayseri to Aleppo, Syria. Then we rode in a limousine with three other passengers to Lebanon. It was a relief to be "home" again.

Our Iranian Odyssey had been quite an adventure. Had we known what we would encounter, I think we might have flown from Baghdad to Beirut like our sensible fellow missionaries had done. But then, we wouldn't have had those exceptional family memories.

Note: In this chapter I relate the conditions of Iraq, Iran, and Turkey as they were at the time of this narrative. Roads, transportation, hotels, governments, and everything in general has changed with the times.

CHAPTER 18

ON THE DAMASCUS ROAD

"It's good to be back in Lebanon," I sighed. "Iraq was great, but the revolution changed all that. Now to set up housekeeping again."

"Well, we don't want to get too many things," Wayne admonished. "We leave for furlough next year."

"I know. We'll just get the bare essentials. It was sad that we had to sell our furniture in Baghdad. I especially wanted to keep the cedar chest you gave me."

"Yes. Cherished heirlooms are gone forever," Wayne sighed. "We've lost material things, but we're safe and together. Tomorrow we'll begin again."

Wayne found a dependable four-door Opel Rekord (a German Chevy), which gave us wheels. We went to garage sales and purchased used beds, dressers, a stove, and a refrigerator. Since Keoughs were on furlough, we were assigned their house for the year. They left bookcases, table, and chairs for us to use. After unpacking our kettles, dishes, and bedding, we were back in the business of living.

Elders Schubert, Chafic Srour, and Wayne finished the division ministerial meetings on Wednesday night. After the meeting Ben and Margaret Mondics, missionaries from Turkey, came up to me. "We've got a proposal. We'd like to take our twin boys, Bill and Bob, down to Jordan and Israel before we go home. We'll pay for your gas if you will take us?"

"Whoa! You've taken me completely by surprise. Ah, I always like going to Jordan, but 1, ah, don't think its possible on the spur of the moment. Wayne, Elder Schubert, and Chafic are flying there tomorrow. Wayne is performing the marriage ceremony for our dear friends, Herbert Faimann and Widad Meshni, on Sunday. I'd surely like go to their wedding, but I think it's impossible to get a trip ticket (permit to drive the car out of Lebanon) and a Lebanese re-entry visa in a day. Plus, since we have to drive through Syria to get to Jordan, we have to have visas for both countries. We're talking two days per visa. We only have tomorrow in which to do it. If we don't leave Friday, it's useless to go. I couldn't be at the wedding, and you can't catch your plane back to Turkey."

"Right," Ben agreed. "My family can get Lebanese re-entry visas in Jordan since we aren't residents here. All we need is Syrian and Jordanian visas. But you and your children, well, ah, let's be at the embassies at eight in the morning and see what you can do about visas."

"We can give it a shot, but I'm skeptical," I said.

Thursday morning, Ben, Margaret, the twins and I were at Jordanian Embassy when they opened. "Since you're so short of time, why don't you just get your Jordanian visa at the border. It shouldn't take long," the consul suggested.

"Good! We hurdled that one in a hurry, "I said to Ben as we left. "Now to the Syrian embassy. Are you praying?"

"For the last 12 hours I haven't let God forget my desires," Ben assured me.

At the Syrian Embassy they said they would give us an emergency visa. It would take only 24 hours. "But," I argued, "we have to leave in the morning. I still have to get my Lebanese re-entry visa."

"Well, then, go to the Lebanese Surete General for your reentry visa now and bribe them into giving it to you this morning. Then come back to us, and we'll have your visa ready early tomorrow morning," the man suggested.

I thanked him but left disheartened; I knew I had come to an impasse. No one gets a re-entry visa in less than 48 hours. It never had happened before, and it wouldn't happen now. But the Mondics's urged me to try, anyway.

At the Surete General's office, I dropped my passport on the counter. "Fill out these papers," the bored officer monotoned. "Leave your passport, and we'll give you a re-entry visa. Come back to pick it up Saturday mom . . . ." Then the man's attitude changed abruptly. "Wait a minute! Why are you asking for a re-entry visa? You have a multiple re-entry visa in your passport. "

I couldn't believe it. "I, I do?" I squeaked, completely stunned. "Whwhere? "

"Right here. Written in plain French and Arabic. " He pointed to a page.

"Oh, yeah! " I choked, pretending to be knowledgable. Taking the passport, I turned it right-side up, and scanned the page. "It's there somewhere," I mumbled under my breath as I tried to read the Arabic script. (Though I spoke Arabic, I read it poorly).

"But it expires next Wednesday night," he warned.

"Oh, sure," I laughed nervously. I hoped my pretensions weren't too obvious. "No problem. We'll be back before then. It's good my kids are on my passport so they don't need separate visas."

We dashed back to the Syrian Embassy, left our passports, and planned to leave early the next morning. I would risk getting a trip ticket at the border.

Friday morning we were at the Syrian embassy as soon as they opened. The Syrians had filled a whole page of my passport with such beautiful stamps that it left my young stamp collectors drooling. I warned them NOT TO TOUCH THE STAMPS.

Things had moved so miraculously, we hadn't expected to hit a snag. The Syrians observed that they had filled the last page in Ben Mondics's passport; therefore, he had to go to the American Embassy to get official pages added. We were impatient with the delay, but in two hours we would learn that God had a reason for this. Ibis half hour delay would put us just where God wanted us at the precise moment.

Our little Opel was bulging as we headed for Damascus. Ben, Margaret, and I squeezed into the front seat, while the four children (David, 11, Bill and Bob, 12, and Ronnalee, 13) were squashed but happy in the back seat.

Three suitcases, a gallon water jug, and a lunch box filled the small trunk.

Our spirits soared as we cruised over the Lebanon range of mountains, through the Baka Valley, and up into the AntiLebanon Mountains. A lively conversation in the front seat competed with jokes and games from the back seat.

"First border stop," I called out. Ben and I lined up to get our passport and customs check while Margaret fed the children sandwiches and orange pop. We breezed through the Lebanon border formalities in half an hour.

Ten minutes down the road we came to the Syrian check post. "Pray that I can get a trip ticket here, or we'll have to turn back," I cautioned the group.

The officer in charge was the epitome of kindness. While he did our passport and customs check, a subordinate helped me with the trip ticket formalities. I nearly panicked when they asked me to drive the Opel up onto a ramp built for the wide wheel base of the American cars. I had plenty of advice from Ben, our three boys, and the customs officials as I inched the Opel's wheels just a little over the inside edge of the ramp. I was afraid the raising and lowering of the lift might jiggle the Opel off the ramp, but it didn't.

Half an hour later we were counting our blessings as we drove up through the steep, barren Anti-Lebanon Mountains. The narrow road with hairpin curves had no railing. It was scary. I was glad to be on the mountain side of the road. As we rounded a steep curve near the crest of the mountain, the road was swarming with people. A few women were screaming, crying, and wandering aimlessly on the highway. I pulled over and stopped the car.

"What's wrong?" I asked.

"Accident! Bad accident!" a pale-faced woman mumbled as she turned from the dreadful scene below.

We jumped out of the car to see for ourselves what had happened. Halfway down the mountain lay the wreckage of a green bus. It had rolled three times as it catapulted over the cliff. The top was smashed down to such an extent that it would be difficult to extricate the passengers. Scattered down the hillside were bed rolls, suitcases, canteens, pieces of metal, broken glass, and, worst of all, broken and bleeding bodies. I turned my face from the gruesome scene and told the children to get back in the car. As the dust settled where the bus rested, it was evident that only a few large boulders on a wide, grape terrace kept the bus from plunging down into the canyon. A woman's cry broke the frozen silence, "For God's sake, help them!"

Strong farmers jumped down the terraces to carry up the victims that had fallen from the bus windows. Gently, each farmer picked up a mangled body and struggled up the rugged slope with his burden. The effort took superhuman strength. In a short time, three broken and bleeding young men lay by the side of the road. I was repulsed by the sight; blood and suffering humanity always made me nauseous and/or faint. But these victims needed my help. I couldn't pass out now. I never thought I would ever practice my First Aid lessons, but I prayed that God would help me use them now. I asked for wisdom and strength.

We were the first car on the scene. Now we were impressed that God had delayed us in Beirut just long enough to give us this mission. We couldn't fail Him or the injured.

I leaned over one youth whose leg was badly torn just below the knee. I told Ben to put pressure on his groin to slow down the bleeding. I went to the next man. He was spitting blood, and complained of pain in his chest. His short, laborious breaths indicated that some of his ribs were broken. Not being a doctor or a nurse, I had no idea what was causing the bleeding.

Just then a businessman and his friend drove up beside me. "Anything I can do to help, Doctora?" he asked anxiously.

"Yes. Put this man in the front seat with you, but don't let him bend over. He's got broken ribs and internal bleeding. Have your friend sit in the back seat with this other victim and apply pressure to his groin. Ben will show you how. Take them to the hospital in Damascus. Then tell the staff to send out as many ambulances as they can. We need a lot of help here."

"Yes, Doctors," he said as he hurried to follow my directives. "But Damascus is 15 miles away. It will be an hour before they get here."

"I know. Do it anyway. By the way, I'm not a doctor," I called to him as he sped off down the road.

Margaret came up to where I knelt by the third person. "Midge, the children are getting too upset by the sight of torn flesh and blooddrenched bodies. We five will walk on down the road. When you and Ben get finished, just pick us up on your way into Damascus."

"Sure. Good plan," I agreed, hardly aware of what she'd said.

Another car stopped. Ben and the farmers put three victims with multiple cuts and head lacerations into that car. I told the driver to get them to the hospital as quickly as possible and send back ambulances.

A farmer dragged a sixth man to my side. "What's wrong with him, Doctora?" he asked, confident that I could pronounce a diagnosis.

"I'm not sure; probably a skull fracture. His one pupil is dilated, he's semi-conscious, he's bleeding from the ear. Oh, dear," I agonized. "I don't know. I'm NOT a doctor. Just lay him down in the back seat of the car that just stopped over there and have them rush him to the hospital."

They laid the seventh victim beside me. He was dead. Where his head was crushed, there was matter oozing out between the cracks. The sight almost sent me into shock. Ben prayed, "Lord, help Midge to keep going."

Someone covered the dead man with a cloak and pulled him away from the main flow of traffic. God filled me with a surge of energy and grit, making it possible for me to continue.

After the hillside had been cleared of bodies, the most difficult rescue effort began. The farmers had to go down three terraces to the overturned bus to try to extricate the bodies still inside. They needed a crane to lift the bus; they needed stretchers to carry the victims and trained personnel to care for them. But all they had was their own strength, and Ben and me.

"Just bring up the living people for now," I advised. "When we've done what we can to save them, then lay the dead by the side of the road for the hearse to pick up later."

"Does anyone know why the bus went off the road or who these people are?" Ben asked the first alert young man brought up from the bus.

"We are Boy Scout youth leaders from Egypt," he answered in short gasps. "We were on our way (gasp) to join other young men from various Middle East countries (gasp) in a mountain camp for a Today training session." He paused and winced with pain. "We met two cars racing side by side up the mountain. (gasp) Our driver pulled onto the shoulder of the road, and (gasp) it was soft, and we went over the edge. The cars never stopped."

"Rest, my friend," I said as I patted his shoulder. "You may have some broken ribs. Don't move more than needed or bend over."

The next car stopped, let out their passengers, and took our friend and two of his buddies to the hospital. I learned that all of the trainees were 18 to 20 years of age. What a pity that some of them could be maimed for life!

As I passed from one unfortunate youth to the next, I felt God was beside me, telling me what to say and do. My first aid course had not prepared me for this trauma, neither had I inherited medical skills. I needed courage, wisdom, and strength, and God supplied it.

Everyone that came along was willing to help. People produced towels, scarves, or tore their clothing in strips for bandages, tourniquets, and slings. Ben got out our jug and gave the victims sips of water.

Feverishly we worked to help the twenty-two live victims. Among them we believed there were two with broken backs, four with concussions, three with broken ribs, some with broken arms or legs, and all of them had multiple cuts and bruises. I never asked for the death toll, but I believe there were just two.

Ben and I examined the last victim—a plumpish youth from Cairo. He was the worst off of all the trainees. He was bleeding from his ears and mouth, his dilated pupils indicated a head injury, his legs were broken, his lips were purple, and he was numb all over. He was in and out of consciousness. Someone brought a blanket and wrapped him in it.

"Don't move him," I told the farmers. "He needs to be moved by ambulance."

At last the roadside was cleared of victims. The groans and cries had ceased. I looked at the farmers who had done such noble work. They were blood-stained, dusty, damp with perspiration, and exhausted. Ben and I were, too. Sad smiles and tears mingled as we hugged one another. An emotional bond of unity and respect had developed among us as we worked together to rescue and save the lives of our fellow men. Our gruesome task was done, and we had done our best.

I turned to Ben. "My knees are saluting one another. I feel sick all over. I can't drive that car."

"You have to, Midge," Ben answered calmly. "You're the only one insured to do so. You did great! Now pull yourself together. We'd better get going. Margaret and the children have been walking for almost two hours."

"Hey," shouted an anxious farmer, "who's the owner of this car? He'd better get these patients to Damascus right away. The Doctora said this man has a broken back, leg, and head, and that I wasn't supposed to move him. But I got desperate because he's unconscious most of the time. I finally got him propped up in the back seat. And the guy in the middle hasn't opened his eyes yet. Tell the Doctora to come check him out before he dies."

"God have mercy!" I cried as adrenalin raced through my drained body. There, sitting half alive in the back seat of my car, were the last three victims. All of them needed to be moved by ambulance, but no ambulance ever came.

Moving them again might prove fatal. I jumped in the car, and we sped down the road. We stopped when we got to Margaret and the four children.

"Keep walking," Ben told them. "We'll be back for you. We got three seriously injured boys in the back seat."

On our way in to the city we stopped at the Boy Scout Headquarters and told them about the accident. The International Commissioner of the Boy Scouts of Syria and Egypt was shaken by the news. He drove behind us to the hospital.

The plumpish Egyptian youth cried out, "Oh, my mother, I love you. I want to see you again. Doctora, tell me will I see my mother again?"

I parried the question. He was in critical condition and would probably die. "Is your mother near here?"

"She's in—Egypt," the youth panted. "Pray—Allah. You, Christian—me, Moslem."

Ben turned around, reached over the back of the seat, and put his hand on the youth's arm. He prayed for God to spare his life so he could see his mother again. Then the young man lapsed into unconsciousness.

As I swung into the hospital gate, attendants directed me to the emergency door. I stopped the car and jumped out. "Take the man in the back right corner first," I called to the whitecloaked stretcher bearers. "Careful how you handle him—he's got a broken back or neck, skull fracture, and other injuries."

A young intern ran over to me. "Please come in, Doctora, and help us with the wounded. We're overwhelmed. The chief begs you to—"

"Please, I'm NOT a doctor or even a nurse. I'm a Seventhday Adventist missionary teacher from Beirut," I stated, wanting to set the record straight.

"But you diagnosed every case right. How?"

"Not me!" I pleaded. "God was in charge. He impressed us what to do to save lives. Now we really must go. We left Ben's wife and four children out on the Damascus Road. We must go back and find them."

"Of course. But come back. This is your hospital, Madam," the intern said as he squeezed my hand.

"Thank you," I responded. I was never so happy to be called "Madam." At last I had convinced someone I was not a doctor.

I swung the car around and out the hospital gate. We were just leaving the city and starting up the mountain when we met a green Vaxhall blinking its lights. Waving hands protruded from every window.

"Someone wants us to stop," Ben observed.

We stopped. Margaret and the kids piled out of the Vaxhall and joined us. Their faces were flushed from the noon-tide heat. They were exhausted and famished for water and food. Even before we thanked the driver, the children had the trunk open. They polished off the rest of the food, but they had to wait for water until we could fill the jug.

As we drove back to Damascus, Ben gave Margaret an account of our experience. He ended up with the story of the Egyptian boy he had prayed for. "Let's stop at the hospital and see if he's going to make it," Margaret said soberly.

Back at the hospital, Ben filled the jug and watered the "camels" while Margaret and I went into the hospital. The chief surgeon invited me in to see the unconscious Egyptian boy.

"He L46 of the doctora, his mother, and the preacher. But I don't think his prayers will be answered," the doctor said sadly. "I believe all the other boys will heal. There may have been fatalities if you had not been on the scene rendering first aid. The first hour is so important. I can't believe you're not a doctor."

"I'm a teacher, and Ben is a preacher. But we are well acquainted with the Great Physician. We believe God detained us in Beirut long enough to fulfill the mission He had for us to do on the Damascus Road. HE was the doctor."

As I walked down the corridor, I saw accident victims on every examining table and hospital bed. They called to me, "Please come see me, Doctora", or "Thank you for helping me, Doctora. "

I stopped briefly to speak and pray with everyone. The Boy Scout Commissioner joined me. He took my name and address,* and I promised to send him the information he wanted about Jesus and Seventh-day Adventist Christians.

We left the hospital feeling happy that 21 youth would recover. But tears stung my eyes as I thought of the Egyptian youth who would not see his mother again on this earth.

We headed south out of the city on the Damascus Road. Somewhere along this country road, Jesus appeared to Saul. Jesus had been preciously close to us that day on the Damascus Road, too. Had anyone seen Jesus in us?

Two weeks later I received a letter from Ibrahim Zakaria, the Boy Scout Commissioner, thanking me for services rendered August 21, 1959. 1 cherish the letter because it's a reminder of how God touched me on the Damascus Road.

CHAPTER 19

GOOD SAMARITANS

The sun had set before we checked into the hotel in Jerusalem where Wayne and the ministers were staying. I had called Wayne Thursday night to reserve rooms for us. He was getting worried when darkness engulfed the city and we hadn't arrived. While we ate supper, we told the men about our experience on the Damascus Road. Before retiring, we prayed for the accident victims—especially, the Egyptian boy.

Sabbath was a pleasant day spent with our believers and visiting special places such as the Garden Tomb, the Temple Mount, the Garden of Gethsemane, Antonia's Tower, and the Home of Caiaphas. Visits to these sites where Jesus suffered and died filled me with unfathomable gratitude.

As I knelt 'neath the old olive trees, I felt I could almost touch my Saviour. I knew He had been in the Garden of Gethsemne long ago, and I knew He was there with me now. The children enjoyed the blessing, as well.

Sunday morning we completed our tour of Jerusalem; the afternoon was reserved for Herbert and Widad's wedding. The pleasure of attending a Middle East wedding in Ramallah (Ramah) cannot be equaled. The happy bride was dressed in the latest fashion, while her aunt was beautifully clothed in her national dress. I fingered her headdress with gold coins sewn onto its edge. "Auntie," I said, "what is the value of the gold coins on your headpiece?"

"Oh, I don't know. Maybe three thousand dollars," she answered casually.

I gasped. "Aren't you afraid to walk on the streets with that on your head?"

She grinned mischievously. "This isn't Chicago, you know. No thugs here."

This witty little woman didn't miss a beat. My fascination with her was exceeded only by the radiant bride Widad, a nurse trained in our Dar Es Salaam, and the groom Herbert, the Austrian pastry chef from Baghdad. (Wayne had studied with Herbert and had baptized him that spring. That made him a special brother.)

The blond groom looked handsome in his dark suit. Widad was resplendent in her white, delicately fashioned bridal gown. Her brown eyes sparkled with pleasure as I pulled some of her dark curls around her veil. They were an attractive, wellmatched couple. Although Wayne was late getting to the church, he was honored to perform their wedding.

Family and friends crowded into the local Protestant church for the quiet, unhurried, personal wedding ceremony. The focus was on the bride and groom, and the sacred occasion. There were no pompous frills, elaborate decorations, or a host of attendants. The simplicity of the ceremony, the love exuded by the couple, and the fresh-cut flower decorations lent dignity to the event.

After hugs and kisses of congratulation to the newlyweds and the family, we enjoyed a lovely reception.

Since Herbert had to leave Baghdad like the rest of us, Middle East College had employed him to start a bakery and pastry department. We looked forward to living near each other on the college hill.

Monday we toured Bethany, Bethlehem and Hebron, then left for Qumran and the Dead Sea Caves. We took the old Jericho road through the Wilderness of Judea.

"Boy, I can just imagine thieves hiding behind those huge boulders and jumping out at unsuspecting travelers," Bob said.

"Yeah," Ronnie agreed, "especially since you can't see what's around the next corner."

"Is this where the Good Samaritan helped the thief?" Bill began.

"Not the thief!" Bob laughed. "He helped the man that the thief had—-"

"I know. Don't act so superior!" Bill sniffed.

"Boys, settle down," Margaret advised. "Yes, the Good Samaritan helped the man on this road. Now stop arguing and just enjoy the Biblical history you are seeing."

We reached Qumran at noon. The air was so dry it seemed to crack in the 105 degree temperature. Although it was blistering hot, we doggedly explored the site. We earned the deep sunburns we got. We medicated them, and then, during the next few days, peeled off skin.

We all craved water, and we drank until the liquid sloshed around in our stomachs. Food was not tempting to anyone except the three boys who wolfed down peanut butter sandwiches and bananas.

"Are we going to the Jordan River now?" David asked as we road along.

"Sure," Ronnie answered. "Don't you remember this desolate, dusty, disgusting country? Even the boulders shrivel up in this heat."

"Mom, she's not telling the truth, is she? Rocks can't shrivel, can they?" David questioned.

"I don't think so, but the plants have given up," I observed. "Look over there where only brown stems are—-—WAIT! What's that? Looks like clothing."

"Where? WHERE?" everyone asked. The gang was coming back to life.

I stopped and pointed to the spot. "There! To the right of that big rock down there."

Ben jumped out and ran down the incline to investigate. "It's clothes alright, but there's a man in them. " Ben yelled back as he bent over the man to take his pulse. "He's alive, but not responsive. I wonder what he's doing out here?"

The man came to briefly, and Ben helped him to the car. "Wasser, ach mein Gutt, wasser," the blond German pleaded as his eyes rolled back in his head.

I I grabbed the jug from the trunk, filled the lid with water, and handed it to Ben. "He's dehydrated but don't give him much water at a time."

"I know," Ben said. "I'll just give him sips."

As soon as the man tasted the water, he grabbed the lid forcible. In his wild effort to satisfy his thirst, he spilled half of it.

"Nein!" I scolded. "Klein wasser. Langsamer werden."

"What are you trying to tell him?" Margaret questioned.

"That's probably what he'd like to know, " I laughed, embarrassed at my feeble attempt to speak a little German. 'I was trying to tell him, 'No, just a little water. Slow down., But he may have understood me to say 'I'm an alien from Mars.' See the way he's looking at me? I wished my mother would have taught me her native tongue! It surely would come in handy now."

"Ach, mehr wasser, " the man begged.

"He's asking for more water," I said, pleased that I understood some German.

"I understood him," Ben said. (I think Ben had a German background.) "Just put a few ounces in the lid. He's hard to control like a wild animal fighting for his life. If we resuscitate him, we should probably take him to Jericho."

"And leave him in an inn? Just like the good Samaritan," Ronnie added.

"Hey, then we'd be good Samaritans, too. Right?" questioned Bill.

"I guess," Margaret murmured, reluctant to assume the tide.

After 20 minutes the German had emptied the jug. He still was dehydrated but had become lucid. We learned that he was one of 20 theology students from a Lutheran seminary in Germany who had come to spend a few weeks in the Holy Land. The boys were attempting to do it on a shoestring eating cheap food, hitchhiking their way around or walking, sleeping in hostels, and accepting any hospitality offered to them.

The young man we'd happened upon had walked out to Qumran alone that morning without taking either food or water with him. No car had come along to give him a ride, so he was attempting to get back to Jericho on his own steam. With no food or water in his system, he had gotten dehydrated, become disoriented, and collapsed in the wilderness. Maybe he had suffered a heat stroke. We didn't know. We only knew we had a helpless young man on our hands.

"It seems that rescuing men has become our calling. But what do we do now?" Margaret asked. "The car is crowded and it's too hot for us to walk to Jericho."

"He'll die if we leave him here. It's so insufferably hot," Ben reasoned. "There may not be another car along for some time. There weren't any visitors in Qumran except us. Midge, let's do this. I'll ride on the right fender so you can see to drive, and we'll put the young man beside Margaret."

That was the best, and only, solution under the circumstances. With Ben on the fender, and the German gesticulating that he wanted food and more water, we were off for Jericho. We took him to a little outdoor cafe in Jericho. In the spirit of the "Good Samaritan," I paid for his food, water, and pop. We stayed with him until we felt he had recovered sufficiently. Then I gave him a lecture about going anywhere alone, taking along water and food at all times, and using better judgment. I don't know if he understood a word I said, but it made me feel better to ladle out advice. I thought I did a pretty good job of acting out my words, too. He kissed my hands as we left. Though he may not have understood my words, he understood our loving care and appreciated it.

"Well," Ben sighed. "Are we going to get to the Jordan River today, or will we come upon another emergency?"

"Impossible!" Margaret said. "I've never been on a trip when I've come upon so many people in desperate need. It was providential that you saw him, Midge, or

I think he would have died. This trip has been a unique experience, but I can now do without any more pitiful travelers."

"Me, too!" I agreed, breathing a sigh.

"I'm going swimming in the Jordan River," Bob shouted excitedly.

"Yeah," the other three kids crooned, their eyes sparkling.

"No, you won't," I said firmly.

Groans from the back seat indicated the childrens' disappointment, but I was adamant. The Jordan River isn't a dangerous place to swim in the summer, but it's too muddy to see where you're swimming. Besides, they didn't have their swimming suits along, and I didn't want the kids sitting on the seats in wet clothes.

When we got to the place where many churches do their baptizing, we got out to look around. The Orthodox had a little shack and a boat that they used to take pilgrims out in the river. There a priest would dip up water and pour it over the heads of

the candidates. Down stream a little from this spot is where Wayne baptized Ronnie and her friends. Though not very wide, the Jordan gets deep within eight feet of the bank. Wayne always had to be careful to stay near the edge of the river.

We walked back upstream beyond the Orthodox boat ramp. We could hear people laughing and yelling to one another. Around a loop in the river, three German young men were having a great time splashing and swimming in the Jordan.

David looked accusingly at me, "Their mother didn't keep them from swimming in the Jordan. They're having fun."

I ignored his complaint. I watched one youth climb a tree by the edge of the river and scoot himself out on an overhanging branch. I knew he was going to dive; I also knew it was dangerous to do so. The guys had stirred up the mud so much that it made it impossible for him to see where treacherous rocks may lay just beneath the surface.

"Nein, Nein," I yelled. "Felsen! Don't dive. You can't see the rocks in the muddy water. DON'T DI—- -"

He waved to me and plunged head first into the river. About a foot beneath the surface of the water, his head must have hit something because his body just doubled up and fell over. When he didn't come up, I screamed, "Someone call the Orthodox to come here with their boat. QUICK!"

The boys were off like a shot. Ronnie ran after them. She could explain the urgency to the Orthodox in Arabic, and she understood the risk of delay.

The two swimming companions didn't notice that their friend was in danger until they heard me yell and point. They panicked when he surfaced and saw blood streaming down his face. "Catch him. Hold his head above the wasser. Kopf above wasser," I screamed, lifting my arms and pulling up on my own head. I hoped they'd get the idea from my pantomime, but they just froze.

I ran along the bank following his body as it floated down stream. He lifted his head out of the water occasionally which indicated to me that he wasn't drowning. He was bleeding profusely and seemed stunned. I worried that he might have broken his neck or back.

Somewhere between the tree and the boat dock, a priest and

his helper rowed toward us. I pointed to the body in the river. They drew their boat up broadside to the man. I shuddered as they grabbed him by the head first, then arms and body, and rolled him into their boat. If his neck or back wasn't broken already, they gave him a second chance to get that injury. Ben, Margaret, and I ran along the bank as the boat drifted downstream to the Orthodox church's little shack. The men pulled up to the dock and unloaded their catch. I closed my eyes and shuddered, "Good grief! I can't believe their emergency care!"

"Well," Ben drawled, "he's heavy, and it isn't easy getting someone out of the water. Let's go and assess the damage."

They dragged the German up on the shore and pumped his chest. Obviously he wasn't waterlogged, but he did have a deep gash across the top of his head.

"Do you have any disinfectant," I asked the priest in Arabic.

"Sure," he said as he went into the shed. He came out with a bottle of Arak, an alcoholic beverage which may be 80 proof. The assistant puffed open the wound while the priest poured on the Arak. The German came to with a start. He screamed with pain, kicked his legs, and flailed his arms.

"Well, I guess his neck and back aren't broken," I said candidly. "He has great movement."

"Not necessarily," Ben disagreed. "That treatment could bring one back from the grave. I think Arak poured into a cut would make one move regardless of any spinal injuries."

The priest and his assistant gave the German another shot of Amok in his wound. "Be sure we got out all the mud and germs," they smiled, satisfied with their work.

"Have mercy," I pleaded. "This man is in tremendous pain. We'll take it from here." Ben and I moved to the side of the German. Margaret ran and got the towel from the lunch box and put pressure on his head. The man shivered and groaned in pain. The two companions stood beside us, wide-eyed, observing our first aid treatment. They were worried, but thankful someone was caring for their friend. "Gute! Franke schon! " they said, cheering us on. They said more but I didn't understand their hurried, nervous speech.

"He needs some stitches," Ben observed.

"I'd say he needs quite a few stitches," I agreed. "The cut is at least six inches long."

"Well, have at it, Doctora," Ben grinned.

"Stop the nonsense, Ben," I laughed. "You know I don't have my medical bag with me. So, I won't be sewing him up."

We discussed the problem and decided we could take him to Jericho, find a hospital, and pay for his keep. The poor man was wet, bloody, and muddy, but Margaret sat bravely beside him and held the towel on his head. Ben was relegated to ride on the right front fender again.

We couldn't find a hospital in Jericho at that time, but we were directed to a clinic. The nurse in charge was a "takecharge person." The German youth was afraid of her, and so was I. He held tightly to my hand and started calling me "mein mutter." When he went into the emergency room, we were still clinging to each other. I pitied the youth. He couldn't speak Arabic or English. He acted as if he was in enemy territory, and he wanted me there to protect him. He was willing to do anything I suggested. In a mirror, I showed him the cut in his head. Through signs, I demonstrated how it was opening wider with the swelling, and that it needed to be sewed up. He nodded approval.

The nurse gave me a scissors to cut his hair next to the wound while she got other things ready. The German and I both gulped when the nurse appeared with a regular sewing needle and thick thread. She didn't use gloves or disinfect the thread. I insisted that she run the thread through alcohol. Then she started sewing. I winced with each stitch, while my German boy screamed with pain. My heart ached for him. It was cruel and unusual treatment. He squeezed my hand harder and harder until I suspected my bones were crushed. But I couldn't blame him. No one should have to endure the surgery without Novocain or other pain killers.

At last she was done. She covered the wound with iodine and slapped on a bandage. I asked for some pain pills, and she gave him aspirin. We bought him some soda and a sandwich. I put him on a service taxi going to Jerusalem and paid the driver a little extra to deliver him to his hostel. Then we hugged each other and said goodbye.

I dropped into the driver's seat and held my head in my hands. "This can't be happening!" But when I looked at the blood on my hands, I knew it was true. "This has been the most amazing trip. Everywhere we go we have to rescue someone. "

"True, but maybe God is trying to teach us that our neighbor is anyone who needs our help," Margaret commented.

"I truly believe that," I agreed. "It's a good feeling to know that we've helped someone in need. But this is draining for me. I think I'll just stay off the roads and in my hotel room tomorrow."

"But the hotel manager could fall down the—" Ronnie began.

"Ronnie, don't even think it! There has to be an end to this."

"Oh, I think this has been an exciting trip!" Bill exclaimed.

"Yeah, we've been Good Samaritans," David bragged.

We were weary and quiet as we drove back to Jerusalem and our hotel. Even Good Samaritans needed to relax at the end of a very unusual, but rewarding, day.

NOTE: We left for Beirut on Wednesday. We stopped in Damascus to see our Egyptian boy. We shed a few tears when we learned that he had died. He would not see his mother again, but it would be wonderful if we could see him in heaven.

CHAPTER 20
THE UNEXPECTED

Wayne was gone most of the time, traveling in various Middle East countries for the division ministerial department. School began for the children and me the last of September. Izella Stuivenga taught grades one through four[1] in the mornings, while I instructed the older children.[2] In the afternoon Izella had them all. I was happy to work only half days because I wasn't feeling well.

The first of October a few mission families went down to the sea for the last swim of the season. One of the men thought it was great sport to dunk some of us women. When we objected, a husband ordered the dunker to leave his wife alone. But Wayne wasn't there to protect me. Before I could get out of the water, the dunker caught me and kept me under too long. I struggled to come up for air, but he didn't release me long enough to catch a breath. I was sure I was going to die, but my attacker didn't seem concerned. My last thoughts as I passed out was "this death is so easy."

Ronnie and the lifeguard noticed me floating face down in the water. She panicked when the lifeguard pulled me out of the water limp as a rag. He laid me on the beach and administered artificial respiration. I coughed up the water clogging the air passage. It felt so good to breath again, but I still needed the lifeguard's help for a few more minutes. As I regained consciousness, I knew my children were on their knees beside me, praying and crying.

---

1 In the lower grades were: Jacque and Patsy Gott, Billy Waring, Gorm Hansen, and Eddie McGhee.
2 In the upper grades were: Larry Fund, Mary Gammon, Tommy Gott, Vivian Hakimian, Annette McGhee, David and Ronnalee Olson, and Dick and Ken Osborn (they left during the year).

When I sat up, the lifeguard was happy that I had recovered, but he was so angry with the senseless act that he went to beat up the dunker. The dunker couldn't be found. He'd gotten in his car and sneaked away.

The children and I were shaken, but thankful for an alert, capable lifeguard. I went home, thinking I was none the worse for wear. However, for the next few months, I had occasional nightmares when I'd leap out of bed, gasping for air.

I continued to feel ill and lose weight, but thought it might be related to the near drowning incident. When Wayne got home in November, he insisted that I go to Dr. Susan at the American University Hospital of Beirut. After a thorough examination, she informed me that I was pregnant.

"PREGNANT!" I shouted in dismay. "I thought I knew about pregnancies since I've had two children. This sickness doesn't fit my previous experiences. This is so, so unexpected."

"Well, you'll probably recognize the experience of giving birth to the baby when it arrives in May," she laughed.

Wayne, the children, and I were thrilled that we'd have a baby in the house again. We had wanted another child, but had given up hope. The loss of Danny, our Iraqi baby, was still a painful memory. One we'd never forget. Perhaps another baby would assuage those emotions to some extent.

Ed McGhee and family had arrived from the states that year. As a musician, he was anxious to organize a band. Many of us bought instruments and learned to play. Ronnie used Wayne's old trumpet, David got a new clarinet, and I got a saxophone. It was a good thing Violet Wilcox, the Osborns, the McGhees, Violet Wentland, and Izella were already skilled musicians, because they made our December concert sound almost good. They'd have sounded even better without us beginners, but we were glad to be part of the band.

Tuesday morning, May 3, our little blond bundle of joy arrived. Ronnie and David named her Rebecca Gay, but we called her "Bekki." That name seemed more suited to a little girl.

The following Monday, the older children came up to the house for their classes. Bekki was only six days old, and I didn't feel up to going down to the school just yet. I had already missed three school days, and my absence put an extra stress on Izella.

The children got involved with the baby, and it was hard to keep them concentrating on their school work. Most of them took turns holding and feeding her.

The next week I went to the school building to teach. We put Bekki in Ronnie's old doll buggy and took her with us. I had sold all my baby things in Baghdad because we never thought we'd ever need them again. Fortunately, the mission ladies gave Bekki a shower, and among the gifts was a bassinet.

Every morning, the children wheeled Bekki to school in the doll buggy. Our house was only 200 feet from the school so it was easy to send Ronnie or David home for bottles and other necessities. Having a baby at school was a learning experience for the children which they seemed to enjoy. Whoever had his/her schoolwork done could hold or feed the baby. Bekki was a happy baby and never cried, so she probably gave the children a wrong impression about babies and parenting. But why shouldn't she be content? Did any baby ever have so many willing baby sitters and loving care?"

One noon David pushed the buggy down to the division office to get the mail. (The office was within a few hundred feet of the school and our home). He and Wayne met and walked home together. While we were eating dinner, it suddenly dawned on us that the baby and buggy weren't in the house.

"My goodness!" David exclaimed. "I plum forgot her down at the office."

He ran down to the office and found the buggy and baby at the back door, just where he had left her. She was asleep, enjoying the fresh air.

The Nolte family had moved while we were in Baghdad, and we missed Max and Roger. But others joined our ranks.

Vivian Hakimian, an Orthodox Armenian girl from Beirut, registered for the eighth grade. Her father, who owned the Ford garage in town, was a man of means. Every morning a chauffeur drove her to school in an expensive car. If the younger boys were not impressed with Vivian, they were with the car. David and others would wait, rather conspicuously, for Vivian just to's ee what car she was riding in that day. A few times she even arrived in a limousine. That gave her notability in David's mind. But Vivian was a down-to-earth person, and she never flaunted her privileged rank.

During the middle of the school year, Vivian became very interested in the prophecies we studied in Bible class. It was my privilege to study the Bible in depth with her. Each week we studied some new facet of Bible prophecy. By graduation time, she had decided to become an Adventist.[3]

Graduation for Mary Gammon, Vivian Hakimian, and Ronnie was the grand finale for our closing school program. It was a happy, yet sad occasion for me. Ronnie had stepped up another rung on the ladder to adulthood. Soon she would be off to academy, college, and marriage. It pained me to think of her leaving our home. But I had to accept this since I could not slow or hasten time.

In July we left on our second furlough, driving our new Mercedes-Benz through Syria, Turkey, Bulgaria, and Yugoslavia. The diesel car was a lemon. In Belgrade the car wouldn't go into reverse, so Wayne tried to park where he

---

3   Though she wasn't baptized at that time, she went on to Middle East College and joined the church. Vivian came to the states, completed pre-medical training and went on to get her medical degree at Loma Linda University. She brought all of her family to America. Eventually, all of them joined the church. She and her husband were medical missionaries in Central America for a while.

wouldn't have to back up. Whenever we stopped, people gathered around the shiny, black Mercedes to admire the vehicle they could never afford. When David, Ronnie, and I had to get out and push it backwards, they were agape. One man tried to help the "stupid American" by showing Wayne that, if he'd just shift gears correctly, the car would go into reverse.

The gears got worse; Wayne could only get it to go in high gear. Now we had to stop on hills. We spent three days in Venice getting it fixed. Then we went on through Austria, Switzerland, Germany, Denmark, Norway, Sweden, Belgium, Holland, and England. We put our car on a boat in England and sailed to Montreal.

The Canadians questioned the veracity of Bekki's Lebanese birth certificate. We read the Arabic script to them, but they were still suspicious. They suspected that since David and Ronnie were older children (about 12 and 14), we had kidnapped this baby to sell in the United States. Since it was time for her bottle and change of diapers, I jokingly told them to keep her. Finally, I opened my passport and pointed out that all three children were pictured with me. Somehow they had missed this evidence when they inspected the passport earlier. They let us take Bekki and proceed to enter the United States.

After a hurried visit to our families in the Middle West and the West Coast, we settled down in Berrien Springs for the school year. Wayne walked to his classes, Ronnalee and David rode their bikes to school, and I just stayed home and enjoyed caring for the home and mothering our little gift from God.

The year had held a lot of unexpected experiences. It always does. But the best unexpected event of the year was getting Bekki. She was the unexpected gift we could keep.

CHAPTER 21

THE EMPTY NEST

The year spent at Berrien Springs passed quickly. School, sermons, talks and programs in churches of many denominations kept us busy. It was time to pack and return to Beirut. We visited our parents again. When I saw my mother's condition, I was reluctant to leave her. She had had a minor stroke.

"Now, Midge," Mom chided in her slurred speech, "we raised you to serve God. Your staying in the states won't change my condition. I have seven other children here, but there's only one of you to go back to your field of service. Go with my blessing. If we don't see each other again, we'll have a family reunion in heaven.

We held each other and wept. I knew I would not see her again alive on this earth John Thompson, my nephew, drove us to Montreal to board the freighter, the S.S. Utrecht. Three weeks later we were back in Beirut. We moved onto the Division compound as soon as a house became available. Wayne continued his work as division ministerial secretary. I agreed to teach a few classes at the college prep school.

The work assignments were very satisfactory. But two weeks after our arrival, we had to send Ronnalee to school in India (5,000 miles away). Our family had bonded more closely than some. Our children were our life, and we were theirs. So parting with Ronnie was a big sacrifice.

Ronnie had just turned 15, and I felt she was really too young to be so far from us. 'Me Middle East Division and the Southern Asia Division had collaborated to have one academy for missionaries' children at Vincent Hill in northern India. We sent our children there to support the school, but it was a great price to pay emotionally. They were gone for nine months, March to November. That's a long time for teenage children to be separated from their parents. Especially since phone communication was primative in the early 1960s. (I never was able to contact the children by telephone at their school during the years they spent there).

While Eileen Lesher, who had come up from Egypt, and Ronnie got their Indian visas and cholera shots, my spirits sagged. Leshers must also have had some misgivings.

Wayne cabled the Southern Asia Division notifying them of the girls' arrival time. They cabled back that someone would meet the girls at the New Delhi Airport and drive them up to Mussoorie. Then they would "walk" the girls down to the school.

"WALK?" I questioned. "Why don't they just put them in a taxi?"

We learned then that the school was in the Himalayan Mountains Where roads and cars weren't priorities. In fact, porters would be hired to carry the girls' suitcases and bedrolls down to the school. Vincent Hill was owned and operated by the church as a school and a summer retreat for missionaries.

I got some consolation from the last bit of information. Since I had never seen the place, I had visions of it being a modernized summer resort area like those in Lebanon. However, as Ronnie would inform us later, its primitive facilities provided only the bare necessities. They had hot water only on Tuesday evenings and Friday afternoons. The rats and mice contended with the students for possession of the territory.

Many tears were shed as we put the girls on Air India. They would be gone from July 26 until Thanksgiving. Distance and communication made the four months seem like an eternity. As we parted, Ronnie clung to me for a moment, almost ,begging me not to send her away. Yet, Ronnie was an adventurous child, and part of her wanted to go to India.

True to their word, the Southern Asia Division had the Browns meet the girls at the airport and drive them to Mussoorie. The girls feasted their eyes on the undulating foothills of the Himalayan Mountain range, an Edenic scene.

They arrived at Mussoorie after dark, hired porters to carry their luggage, and began the two-mile walk to the school. Using flashlights, they picked their way through the jungle trail and down the other side. The girls were unfamiliar with the turf, which was scary. Worse yet, the Browns entertained them with stories of vicious tigers and leopards who preyed on man and beast. Behind every tree and bush, Ronnie and Eileen expected a lurking tiger to pounce on them.

They were relieved to come to the school's gate at last. Ronnie was thrilled when she saw her old pal from Baghdad days, Jeannie Wagner, waiting for her. They always had great times together. Now they would share a room and the India experience.

The next morning, Ronnie was still in slumberland when a siren blew. She leaped out of bed and headed for the exit. Jeannie ran after her. "Where you going in your pajamas?"

"I'm out of here," Ronnie panted. "Hear the fire siren?"

"It's not a fire. It's just the wake-up call, " Jeannie laughed.

Ronnie was on the verge of collapse. "WAKE-UP, you say? It scared me out of my hide! Couldn't they find something—something less alarming than that? A bell, for instance. I'm still shaking."

But Ronnie soon got used to the siren and all other phases of life at Vincent Hill School. The kids loved their principal, Mr. Merle Manley. He instinctively understood the needs of teenagers and children some as young as eight. The students formed a family unit of sorts. The teachers tried to help the lonely kids through the "homesick period." Friday nights Ronnie missed the closeness our family always shared at the beginning hours of the Sabbath. Other than that, I don't think Ronnie was all that lonesome. Her letters were always upbeat. She worked at the laundry, enjoyed her classes, hiked in the hills, skated and played, and dated schoolmates.

Ronnie, had no complaints until she twisted her knee in November. The nurse wrapped her knee with an ace bandage, but her misery was constant. After a few days it was time for the kids to return home. She was carried in a dandee (like a canoe with four men carrying it on poles) up to Mussoorie to ride the bus to New Delhi.

In Beirut, we took her to an orthopedic specialist. He believed her injury was caused by a congenital weakness in her knee joints. He expected she would outgrow it.

By Christmas, Ronnie's leg was as good as new. She participated in the missionaries traditional New Year's expedition to the high, snowclad mountains. There we slid down the slopes on anything we could find that would work as a sled—dish pans, trays, plastic, whatever. Bekki was almost two then, and she decided snow was the best stuff God created.

The end of February was time to send the children back to Vincent Hill.—This would be a nine-month stint for the kids. Just before time to leave, Ronnie's knee cap slipped off again. We had to keep her home. She finished her sophomore year through home study and by taking a few classes at the secondary section of Middle East College.

In March we went to Jordan and Israel for Easter. There, residents and pilgrims memorialize every aspect of the season by re-enacting the last week of Jesus life. On Palm Sunday, thousands of pilgrims marched the route of Jesus' Triumphal Entry from Bethphage to Jerusalem. A high ranking church official rode a donkey, and palm branches were scattered on the path

We had several free days in which to explore Palestine. Thursday evening the priests met in front of the Church of the Holy Sepulchre, washed one another's feet, and partook of bread and wine. Communion was served to the common people, too, but we didn't partake of the wine because it was the real thing. At the Garden of Gethsemane, we prayed beneath the old olive trees.

Together our family rededicated our lives to the One who had suffered tremendous anguish there.

Friday morning we assembled at Antonia's Tower. With pilgrims from all over the world, we walked the Via Dolorosa, stopping at the 14 stations of the cross. We joined Father O'Brian's English-speaking group. It was so crowded and hot that one lady fainted. She simply fell against the people beside her—there was no space for her to fall to the ground. Since there was no water available, some men fanned her, took her by the arms, and dragged her along with the crowd. Eventually, she recovered and exited to the shade of a side street.

Sabbath morning -we wended our way through a narrow street in old Jerusalem to meet with Adventist believers in a house that was over a thousand years old. That afternoon Wayne baptized David in the Jordan River. Besides the presence of God, several Adventist families joined us for this sacred rite.

Sunday at the Garden Tomb, we commemorated the resurrection of Jesus at the Sunrise Easter Service. After we left, five other large groups had services there.

On our way home, we noticed the hills of Judea were covered with red poppies, pink cyclamens, white daisies, and yellow and purple spring flowers. The landscape appeared like a huge Persian carpet.

Spring warmed into summer. June 18 arrived, and it was time for Ronnalee, Don Oster, and Malcolm Russell to leave for school at Vincent Hill. We celebrated Ronnie's 16th birthday a month early. I sent four gifts with her (one from each of us at home) to open in India on July 20.

I spent the summer reading through the Koran for Jim Russell's college Bible class. I wrote a paper on salvation as taught in the Koran. Until then I hadn't realized the beauty and simplicity of salvation through Christ as compared to those religions that teach one must earn his way to heaven.

David started the eighth grade that fall. At five foot eight, he was stretching into a man. He was delighted that, for the first time in his life, he had a man teacher, Harold Johnson.

Since Eileen Lesher had health problems that would be exacerbated by the cool, damp climate of Mussoorie, she was obliged to stay home and take correspondence lessons. I was asked to tutor her. Each morning Eileen came to our house to study. If for any reason she skipped a day, Bekki got all bent out of shape. She loved Eileen and became quite possessive of her.

Bekki had an ideal play situation. Living on the compound were Joni and Greg Anderson and Leonard, Allan, and Kenny Darnell. Bekki only had to go outside to find a playmate. Sometimes the Jensen and Brauer children joined the preschool crew. Though Bekki was our "caboose" she was never lonely.

The telegram I had been dreading came: MOTHER DIED OCTOBER 24. When a loved one dies, that's the worst time to be overseas. The air ticket was prohibitively expensive. Beside that deterrent, I couldn't have gotten to South Dakota in time for the funeral. For a few days I didn't want to see anyone. I had to do my mourning alone, silently. I wanted to remember everything about my mother—from my earliest recollection of her telling me Bible stories and rocking me to sleep, until the day I left her in the summer of 1961. Though I know she wanted me near, she unselfishly encouraged me to return to the mission field. What a wonderful counselor and friend she had been! What a loving spiritual guide! I would miss seeing her when I returned home. Not being at her funeral meant no closure for me. I knew my Dad would miss her dreadfully. I hoped he would live until I got back home again.

Ronnie wrote from India that her knee cap had slipped off again. The nurse sent her in a dandee to a small Protestant Hospital in Mussoorie. The doctor put a hip-to-ankle cast on her leg. The cast was too tight for the edematous knee, so Ronnie took charge of her case. She chiseled on her cast until she had loosened it enough to improve circulation.

Vacation time arrived, and Ronnie was again carried back up the mountain and down to the bus. When she arrived home, we were alarmed at the purplish hue of her leg and foot. Ronnie had noticed the numbness. At the American University Hospital a specialist examined her and exclaimed, "Dear me! It's a good thing she loosened the cast or she'd have lost that leg. She needs corrective surgery."

We had planned to go to Egypt for ten days during Christmas. Ronnie was determined that her knee wouldn't stop her from that excursion. Ronnie, David, and I boarded a boat for Alexandria where we would meet Wayne. We left Bekki with the Leshers because she was too young for the grueling schedule we had planned. We covered the country thoroughly, seeing Aswan and the High Dam, the Valley of the Kings, Luxor, Thebes, Cairo, and Mt. Sinai. We also visited church members in upper Egypt. The children enjoyed their geography lesson, but we were anxious to get back home and see Bekki. I don't think she missed us much because she often wanted to go spend the night with Eileen.

Ronnie had knee surgery in January. She suffered excruciating pain because the doctor had to move the tendon and bone from one side of her knee and insert it into a hole on the other side of the knee. Stretching the muscle across the knee would supposedly keep the knee cap in place, but it also caused much pain. A week later we took her home with the admonition to be alert for any changes.

The second day, Ronnie's leg and foot suddenly swelled to double in size. The leg turned cold and blue, and started going into spasms. We rushed her to the hospital. The doctor removed her cast releasing the pressure. Her recovery was slow and painful. Since her medical problem was congenital, it was likely she'd be plagued with this weakness the rest of her life. But Ronnie was unconcerned, "Hey, I'll take a small measure of precaution, but I'm still going to skate, hike, climb mountains, and do everything that anyone else does. When I have knee trouble, I'll just live with it. Don't worry, Mom."

When it was time to return to Vincent Hill in March, Ronnie was still hobbling around. I had misgivings about her leaving, but Ronnie wanted to get back to Vincent Hill to finish her junior year. (Ronnie would have made a good mailman—no adversity could keep this effervescent, optimistic girl down). Besides, Ronnie had a lot of good friends at school. She held school offices and she loved her work assistant to the dean and laundry student supervisor. Maybe she thought the school couldn't operate without her.

Bill McGhee, a strapping young man in Ronnie's class at Vincent Hill, had moved to the college hill with his missionary parents. He gallantly offered to "look after her" on the trip. It was another sad parting at the airport, but we were relieved that Bill would be with her all the way.

David and Larry Fund graduated from the eighth grade in June. In July, David, Bekki and I flew to India where David would begin his freshman year at Vincent Hill School. Soon after our plane reached its flying altitude, Bekki insisted that we get off the plane. We were flying too high to suit her. I tried to explain that the drop of 20,000 feet was a bit risky, but this bit of sage information didn't register in the mind of the threeyear-old. When we got off the plane in New Delhi, Bekki believed she had willed it so and had proved her point.

The train took us to Derha Dun, and then by bus to Mussoorie. We strained our necks to catch our first glimpse of
Ronnie. She was smiling as we stepped off the bus and fen into each other's arms. A porter was hired to transport our baggage up the mountain and down the other side to the school. When we arrived, I was surprised at the primitive conditions of the school. But then, India in general was not as wealthy or modern as the Middle East. During the three weeks I was in Mussoorie, I can't

remember having a warm shower. But the people were nice, and the location was beautiful.

Bekki and I stayed in the infirmary between the girls and boys dormitories. Ronnie was assistant to the dean, but came down and stayed with us when she could. One night when Ronnie, Bekki and I walked down the hill, we saw tigers close to the path. Tigers or leopards had disposed of a number of pets on campus, and I supposed they weren't partial to dog meat. I was reading a book about man-eating tigers by Jim Corbett. It stimulated my fears and imagination.

As I looked at the feeble door and windows of my cabin, I realized that even Bekki could probably break them down with a push. Ronnie laughed at my fears. "Oh, Mom, if God could protect Daniel from the lions, a few tigers should be no problem for Him."

I felt ashamed. I had taught her to have faith in God; now she demonstrated it for me. We talked and then slept in peace, knowing we were safe in the hollow of God's hand.

David and Ronnie's faces were awash with tears as our bus pulled out for Derha Dun. It was monsoon season, and the bus leaked. We had to put up our umbrella in the bus to keep the rain off. The ride overnight on the train from Derha Dun to New Delhi was comfortable, but our suitcase had become soaked. The Langes met us and took us home. I spent the day drying out our clothes.

When I got home and opened my mail, I was disturbed by a sympathy card I received from my high school friend, Hilda Nebben. This meant someone in my family had died, but she didn't indicate who. She had attended the funeral so that narrowed the field down to Dad, Julius, or Dorothy. I'd gotten a letter from Dorothy dated July 5 saying that Dad was in the hospital, but I didn't understand that his illness was serious. I wrote to him from India.

I couldn't rest; I wrote home begging for an immediate answer. I tried to be careful how I worded the letter. What if Hilda had our family mixed up with another Thompson.

The middle of August, I finally got a letter from home. Dad had died July 22. 1 was angry. Why hadn't someone sent me a telegram? I understood that they were mourning Dad's demise, but I was his child, too. I deserved to know. I grieved over my father's death for weeks. I felt akin to him—his jolly nature, his optimism, the twinkle in his blue eyes when he laughed. I had hoped he would live until I got home from the mission field. Now both of my parents were gone.

I felt lonely. Wayne was off to Iran on mission business, and Ronnie and David were in India. Except for little Bekki, I was left with an empty nest.

I was happy when November came and the nest was full again. Ronnie and David were home for the winter break. We enjoyed a great reunion!

One night we asked Ronnie, who would be graduating from Vincent Hill in June, about her college plans. She was shocked that we should ask. "Why, I'm going to Middle East College, of course."

"No, Ronnie, for the nurse's course or medicine, you'll need to go to America," we told her. "You'll be with your aunts and cousins there."

"But they are paper relatives. I know them only from letters. My aunts and cousins are right here—the Middle East friends, the missionaries and their kids. I grew up here. This is my home. I don't want to go to America alone," she insisted.

We made up our minds then to return to America; at least until David and Ronnie finished college. The children returned to India in March. We promised Ronnie we would somehow get to India for her high school graduation.

During the next few months we disposed of property and packed mementos to send to the states. I prayed that we could be located near schools where the children could stay close to home for just a few more years. Or at least, until I could hurdle the empty nest syndrome.

CHAPTER 22

GOODBYE, MIDDLE EAST

We were torn between our desire to stay in the Middle East and our need to take Ronnie to the United States, a foreign country to her. Wayne gave the division notice that we would be going on permanent return that summer. In March, Wayne accepted Glenn Davenport's invitation to be Bible teacher for the 1964-65 school year at Campion Academy in Colorado.

The next few months were busy. Wayne finished an effort at the new Beirut Center and visited the churches in the various countries of the Middle East. In his spare time, he fixed up our Volkswagen microbus for camping. He turned the first bench seat around so that its back was against the front seat. That way he had room to put a fold-down table between the two back seats. He fastened a roll-up awning to the roof and made food boxes that would slide under the seats. He attached a hose and shower head to a five gallon can so we could fill it, set it on top of the bus, and take showers. I sewed curtains that could be pulled around the windows for privacy. The Volkswagen was ready to roll.

I sold or packed our belongings and finished my classes at Middle East College Academy. June 23, Wayne, Bekki, and I left for Tehran. We easily drove the 1,000 miles and were on time for the Iran Campmeeting, June 25 to July 4.

Our next engagement was Ronnie's graduation exercises in India. We'd promised her we would be there. On Sunday, the Osters started off for India in their fast American Valiant, and we in our slow German Volkswagen microbus. They left visual messages along the way such as a corn flakes box sitting in the wilderness of eastern Iran.

Once we left Kerman, we followed a gravel trail through gullies, hills, and desert floor. The "road" was nothing more than a swath the width of the road grader that had plowed it.

Dust from oncoming vehicles billowed in the air for miles. The tell-tale dust clouds made it easy for wayside robbers to pick off their victims. However, most of the vehicles using that road were trucks, and they often traveled in caravans. It was a long, hazardous trip to make, but parents take risks to accommodate their children.

Our route took us through southeast Iran, Pakistan, western India, and then on north to Mussoorie, a distance of about 2,500 miles. Other than going through a sandstorm and monsoon rains and plowing through ripples of sand and flooded roads, the trip was almost without incident. A few times we had to ford rivers. We passed Osters somewhere when their lower Valiant conked out in a water-filled dip. Our higher microbus made it through fine. Whenever we met a truck or an ox cart, or needed to avoid hitting people or animals, we had to move to the shoulder of the one-lane road. We spent a lot of time keeping the left wheels on the asphalt and the right wheels hop-scotching on the shoulder. The streets of Indian towns are incredibly crowded, and cars have to inch their way through the mass of humanity.

The trip took a little more than four long days of driving. We got to Vincent Hill on Thursday, in time for the weekend events. Sunday Ted Torkelson gave the graduation address, the students received their diplomas, and the excitement was over.

We spent a few extra days in India going to the jungle to see elephants work, monkeys play, and other forms of wildlife. We visited the Taj Mahal, one of today's seven wonders of the world (in my estimation), then we headed west to Pakistan. We studied the map. It looked as if a side road through Pakistan would shorten the trip considerably. Ten miles into the country, the road, which was terrible from the start, deteriorated into a bumpy, rugged trail.

"I think we should turn around, Wayne," I suggested. "We're going to lose a wheel in the ruts."

"Maybe the road will improve." Wayne said. "This Swede is determined to drive on. Be optimistic; be courageous."

Soon we met a horde of wild-looking mountain men pointing big guns at us. They didn't shoot, but they didn't smile, either. Wayne, supposing we had invaded enemy territory, turned around as fast as he could and drove back on the bumpy, rugged trail to the "main" road.

"Am I to conclude that those men were able to alter your Swedish determination, your optimism, and your courage?" I asked smugly. "Ken Oster warned us to stay on the beaten trail. We've wasted two hours on this detour."

Wayne never got ruffled or upset. "Well, just think what we have seen a part of the country few tourists ever see."

The children and I had a dozen retorts to that statement, but who could argue his point. Few tourists ever attempt to drive from Beirut to India, either. Most people have more common sense (or, if you want to be kind in your assessment, think of us as being adventurous). Undoubtedly, missionaries and journalists test their guardian angel's protective services more than the average person. Perhaps they even plead with God not to assign them a missionary or a journalist.

We had wasted so much time on the "short cut" that we had to camp at a military outpost in Pakistan. Wayne and David slept under the awning, Bekki on the front seat, and Ronnie and I stretched out on the two back seats. We slept with our clothes on even though the temperature hovered at the sweating point. It made Ronnie and me nervous to have Pakistani soldiers stare in the window at us. I discreetly closed the curtains, thus eliminating their entertainment. The next day we took off through the Pakistani desert again. Sand drifts are worst than snow drifts to plow through. Driving was hard; riding wasn't good, either. Too frequently we were air borne. Going up was bad, but coming down was worse. "Can't you keep the car on the road, Daddy?" four-year-old Bekki asked. She was tired of being jostled about and wanted her dad to get on a ROAD.

We were thankful when we finally reached the Pakistani and Iranian borders. It took us far too long to get through both check posts. Since we didn't feel comfortable staying in Zahedan, we decided to gas up and go on. Besides, we wanted to get to Kerman for Sabbath.

"There's bandits out there," Iranian truck drivers warned us. "To be safe, we travel in caravans and carry rifles. Haven't you heard about the Americans that were stopped by bandits a while back?"

As a matter of fact, I had. I read about it in an American journal. The men had been killed, the women were taken into a harem, and the car was dismantled. One woman finally escaped and told her harrowing story. Even so, we decided to proceed. Sometimes we Christians do take unnecessary risks, and hold God responsible to deliver us from our unwise choices.

It was Friday evening July 17 when we left Zahedan. Wayne was exhausted. He and David slept on the back seats, and Bekki rested on a sleeping bag on the floor between them. As I drove, Ronnie regaled me with stories of her school year. About nine o'clock, I seemed to hear a voice saying, "You are going to meet three men. DON'T STOP."

Goose bumps peppered my body. I turned to Ronnie. "Wh-what did you just say?"

"Oh, I was telling about the things I bought from a Tibetan lady and " Ronnie rambled on.

I wasn't listening. An eerie feeling seized me. Shivers rippled through my body. I felt certain God was trying to tell me something. "You will soon meet three men. DON'T STOP." My heart went into overdrive as I watched for three men.

Fifteen minutes later we came up a steep rise. As I started down the hill my lights shone on three men standing on the road at the bottom of the hill! How specific had been the message I received—three men!

"DON'T STOP! " I remembered the warning given me and raced the car toward the men. In a moment my eyes took in the scene. The men were dressed in khaki clothing which blended with the sandy road. The two men on the left held shotguns with shiny brass decorations on the stock. The man on the right waved a large white cloth with one hand. In the other, he held a dagger.

I stepped on the gas and headed straight for them. "Oh, God, please save us," I said aloud. At the last second, the men, knowing I wasn't going to stop, jumped to the sides of the road. I drove between them. One man raised his gun and shot at my head. I saw the flash and heard the zing of the shot. And I kept going. The wheels of the microbus spun in the gravel as I tried to speed up the next hill. I knew we weren't going fast enough to avoid getting hit by more blasts from the guns, but I prayed. Oh, how I prayed! So did Ronnie.

But there was no second shot. We crested the hill and kept moving. I drove dangerously fast up the hills and down the dips, sliding around the curves. I worried that there may be more bandits farther up the road. I didn't dare stop. I should have remembered and believed the voice that said there were "three men," and we'd just passed them. But adrenalin was pumping through my body, making my fear almost irrational.

Ronnie, young but full of faith, began to quote snatches of Psalms 91. "He that dwells in the secret place of the Most High, shall abide under the shadow of the Almighty. I will say of the Lord, 'He is my refuge and my fortress; my God, in Him I will trust.'—He shall cover you with His feathers, and under His wings you shall take refuge."

I joined Ronnie. "You shall not be afraid of the terror by night.... He shall give His angels charge over you to keep you in all your ways."

Our shaky voices blended as we half cried, half sang, "Under Ms wings, I am safely abiding, though the night deepen and tempests are wild. Still I can trust Him, I know He will keep me. He has redeemed me, and I am His child."

"Mom, are you hurt?" Ronnie asked, worried because the shot was aimed at me.

"I don't think so. I feel nothing except I'm trembling."

"Then we really were under God's wings. How else could we have escaped? God must have re-directed the bullet, Ronnie said in reverent awe.

"He did," I said hoarsely, realizing that God had just delivered us miraculously. "I'm shaking too badly to drive on, Ronnie. Wake up your dad. He'll have to take over."

Ronnie leaned over the back seat. "Dad, DAD, wake up!" But Wayne never stirred. What a fright we had then. We supposed the shot that had missed me had hit his head and killed him.

"Shake him, Ronnie. Shake him!" I cried.

She turned around and shook Wayne vigorously.

"Wh-what, wh-where, ah, I'm sloe—" Wayne mumbled incoherently.

"Oh, God," I prayed. "Please don't let him be hurt!"

Ronnie tried again. She shook him. "Dad, are you alright?

"Sleepy," he murmured as he turned over.

"You have to wake up now and drive," I said. "We've been shot at. "

This brought Wayne to an upright position. "Are you sure?"

"Yes! I'm shaking too badly to drive on this rugged, gravel trail. I feel too weak to keep the car under control. I can't even see well right now. I'm afraid I'll miss a curve and crash us on the boulders. Please! I need you to crawl up here and take the wheel."

Wayne was wide awake and not injured. He crawled over the back of my seat, I slid over, he put his foot on the accelerator, and we continued down the road without ever stopping. Ronnie and I told Wayne our harrowing story. When the lights of Kerman came into view, we sighed with relief. Our nerves were shattered.

We drove into the courtyard of the inn, and truck drivers gathered around us. "Driving kind of late, eh?" "Did you come over the road from Zahedan alone?" "At night without a gun?"

"Yes," Wayne answered. "And my wife says three bandits shot at us when she didn't stop."

The men looked questioningly at Wayne. "Your WIFE was driving?"

"Yes. She was driving then. I was sleeping in the back seat and didn't hear anything."

"You Americans are crazy. You're lucky you got away," was their response.

"God delivered us," Wayne said reverently.

"Yes, yes," they agreed- "Allah is great!"

We spent Sabbath in Kerman, and drove on to Tehran on Sunday. Monday was Ronnie's 18th birthday. Joe Warda, a good friend and student of ours from Middle East College, invited us to celebrate the event at his home. His family had prepared a feast, and Ronnie had the most beautiful birthday cake of her life.

The next day, we said farewell to Iran. That was the beginning of our goodbyes to the Middle East. Joe rode back to Beirut with us since he was scheduled to fly to Lincoln, Nebraska, to attend Union College. When we got to Baghdad, we couldn't resist driving past the hospital. It was a bitter/sweet experience. It brought back many happy memories, yet it was sad to see how Dar Es Salaam Hospital had deteriorated in five short years. "Goodbye, Iraq."

We drove through Jordan and Syria. It was sad to think that we might never see these lands again. We hoped to return in eight years, but since life is tenuous, we knew something could prevent us from fulfilling these desires.

Leaving Lebanon on July 29 was the hardest leave-taking of all. As we drove out the gate of the division compound for the last time, the goodbyes and best wishes of our fellow workers and friends made the parting more difficult.

Driving through Lebanon, Syria, and Turkey, we tried to concentrate on the positive—that returning to the states for a few years was the right decision. It was goodbye Middle East, and hello America.

Note: After completing a tour of Europe, we landed in New York August 26. Two months later we had purchased and settled into a home in Loveland, Colorado. David stayed at home and attended Campion Academy. Ronnie was only 500 miles away at Union College. After 18 years in the Middle East, we had to adjust to the American way of life. It was nice, but the Middle East countries and people would always have a big piece of our hearts.

Epilogue

A REVIEW OF THE NEXT THIRTY YEARS

Bekki missed the freedom of the mission compound and her friends. The second year we were at Campion Academy, my sister, Gladys, called from Idaho to say that Ronda, a four-year-old girl staying temporarily with my sister, Jean, needed a home. We told her we weren't interested in taking a child again unless we could adopt her permanently. We didn't want another heartbreak like we had with Danny. They brought Ronda to Colorado, she was a beautiful child, and we loved her the minute we saw her. She and Bekki were close in age, and they became immediate pals. The next year Ronda Lynn was ours legally adopted.

We lived in Colorado for seven years and loved every minute of it. Wayne taught Bible at Campion and worked on his Ed.D. I taught in the H.M.S. Richards Elementary School and worked on degrees in library science, English, and social studies. While David completed his secondary education, he enjoyed his horse, Honey. The girls had Tiny, a Shetland pony, and a poodle they named Renee.

Joy and sorrow mingled during the summer of 1968. Ronnalee married Kermit Netteburg, and our saintly mother Ada Olson, the last of our parents, passed away.

In 1971, Wayne became principal of Sunnydale Academy in Missouri. Over the next six years, I seemed to inherit all the jobs no one else wanted. To save the academy money, I worked full-time for half-time pay, and Wayne and Laurel Otto graded the academy's circle drive and did other heavy physical tasks. Wayne's pay for this was slipped discs. When he could no longer move, he had back surgery.

David graduated from Union College, married Cathy Hartman, and began his ministry in the Missouri Conference in 1972. 1 was devastated when my sister, Dorothy, died. She was like my second mother. For me, it was like a triple funeral since I was not present to say a last farewell to Mom and Dad. This funeral helped me complete the closure.

Our first grandchild, Charity, was born to Kermit and Ronnie on July 16, 1973. Grandmas Vernice and Midge wore signs that read, "We gave to Charity. " After a few weeks, however, Ronnie and Kermit took our little darling away to Andrews University at Berrien Springs, Michigan, where Kermit taught in the Communications department. Two years later Kristin Angel was born.

In 1975, Middle East College called Wayne to work in the Bible department and me to teach English. We requested a delay until Wayne could finish his doctoral dissertation. By the the time Wayne finished his degree, unsettled conditions in Lebanon made it impossible for us to get visas. So we missed the chance to return to our beloved Lebanon.

We moved from Sunnydale to work at Battle Creek Academy the fall of 1977. We were happy that we'd be close to Ronnie and family. Our excitement was short-lived, however, because they moved to Minneapolis so Kermit could complete his doctoral degree. So once again our family headed in different directions.

The first year at Battle Creek I taught eighth grade, then moved into the academy as English and library science teacher. Wayne taught academy Bible classes for a year and then became the associate pastor of Battle Creek Tabernacle Church. (Both of us kept these positions until our retirement).

Bekki returned to Sunnydale to graduate with her class, and Wayne and I earned additional degrees. The summer of 1978, Ronda, Bekki, Wayne, and I celebrated our accomplishments by taking a 21-day Eastern Airlines special. We had a splendiforous time on the Virgin Islands, Puerto Rico, Jamaica, and Mexico. Bekki entered the nursing program at Andrews University that fall, and Ronda graduated from Battle Creek Academy the following spring.

Bekki married Scott Gardner in March, 1982. That summer I had my 11th surgery. The previous autumn I had slipped on the wet floor of a shopping mall, threw my shoulder out of its socket, and tore the muscle cuff. Physical therapy was of no benefit, so an orthopedic surgeon tried to staple the muscle back on top of my shoulder. Since the accident occurred almost a year prior to surgery, stretching the degenerated muscles caused excruciating pain. The situation was worsened when the hospital nurses, failing to follow doctor's orders, got me up to go to the bathroom. They also failed to support my weakened arm which dropped to my side and tore loose the newly stapled muscles. The next few days were an eternity of unmitigated, incessant pain. The damage had been done, and I was left with a permanent disability. My right arm is without strength, and I still suffer pain. But, thank God, I still have an arm, and my hand works well.

Wayne and I were blessed with wonderful children:

Ronnalee completed her B.S. in nursing at Union College in the spring of 1968. That summer she married Kermit Netteburg. They worked in Colorado, Iowa, and Andrews University, Berrien Springs, Michigan. Charity was born to them in 1973, Kristin in 1975, and Olen in 1979. Kermit earned his Ph.D. in communications from the University of Minnesota. They left Andrews for the Columbia Union where Kermit served as Communications Secretary for five years. They returned to Andrews University in 1991. Kermit is currently in charge of student enrollment there. Since 1977, Ronnalee continued nursing in hospitals, primarily in the O.B. departments. She has an M.S. in nursing and is currently teaching at Andrews University.

David graduated from Campion Academy in 1967, and from Union College in 1972. He married Cathy Hartman and together they worked in the ministry in the St. Louis, Missouri area. David earned an M.Div. from Andrews University in 1975, and Cathy received her M.A. in English. They returned to work in Missouri until 1979 when David accepted a position in the Illinois Conference treasury department in Chicago. Hans was born in 1977 and Heidi in 1980. In 1985 they relocated to Cyprus. David served as assistant treasurer of the Middle East Union, and Cathy worked in the mission school and office. They returned to the United States in 1992.

Bekki finished Sunnydale Academy in 1978, and went to Andrews to get her B.S. in nursing. She married Scott Gardner, a medical student, in 1982. While Scott completed his M.D. she worked in the oncology department at Loma Linda Medical Center. In 1985 they moved to Kettering, Ohio, for Scott's residency program. Bekki worked in the coronary heart department. Jonathan was born in 1989 and Lindsay in 1990. They moved to Oregon where Scott does general surgery in the Tillamook County General Hospital.

Ronda graduated from Battle Creek Academy in 1979. She went to Andrews University and Union College. She worked in the office of Pioneer Seed Company in Des Moines, Iowa, then moved to Boise, Idaho to manage a health club. In 1992 a swelling in her nasal cavity made it difficult for her to breathe. After numerous doctors' visits, xrays, and a CT scan, she learned she had an egg-sized, cancerous tumor. A nine-hour surgery at Oregon Health and Science University removed most of the adenoid cystic tumor. Her recovery was long and difficult since they had to remove part of her skull and shrink her brain to do the surgery. She began her 30 radiation treatments in February. Then she went to Iowa to see friends. When she was able to go back to work, she got employment at Americomp. She is currently working in Denver, Colorado, in the office of HunterDouglas Window Dressings.

In 1983 Wayne and I yearned to return to the Middle East and celebrate Christmas. Scott, Bekki, and twenty-eight of our friends from Battle Creek enjoyed fifteen wonderful days in Egypt, Jordan, and Israel. For Wayne and 1, it was a special thrill to be back in the land where we could see old friends and hear Arabic spoken again. We enjoyed that first tour so much we returned the following Christmas with Ronnie, Kermit, Charity, and twenty-nine others. We added Greece and Sinai to our itinerary. Wayne's greatest pleasure was baptizing Charity in the Jordan River, as he had her mother 26 years earlier. It was a moving serendipity enjoyed by our entire group.

The summer of 1984 our children gave us a 40th wedding anniversary celebration. Ronnie explained, "Mom and Dad, your older brothers and sisters may not be alive for your 50th anniversary. We'll celebrate now while they can still join us." (We could not have guessed then that Wayne was the one who would not be there for our 50th anniversary). Ronda was married after our anniversary celebration. Our three daughters and Cathy donned their wedding dresses that day and posed for a "brides picture." It was a memorable family gathering.

We had a wonderful life in Battle Creek. We became so fond of the people there that it became a toss-up as to which was our favorite place, Battle Creek or the Middle East. We worked long and hard in Battle Creek, but the friendships we developed helped us through the next few trying years. Dr. Im discovered a lump in my breast and performed a mastectomy on July 11, 1985. In the hospital I cried out in anguish, "God, why have you deserted me now? I prayed the lump would prove benign. It was cancer. Then I prayed that it would not have spread. It invaded a lymph node. Then I prayed I wouldn't need chemotherapy. Now chemo is recommended. May I ask you two favors? Please don't let me get sick from the chemo and extend my life a few more years. You've given me a wonderful, exciting, satisfying life, but I don't want it to end yet."

God granted my request. In August, I began school as usual. Every other Friday after school I went to the hospital for an hour-long chemo injection. Sitting in the room with many other cancer patients, I forced myself to concentrate on the GUIDEPOST magazine because the groans and vomiting of other patients made me upset.

I was never sick from chemo, I never took medicine for nausea, and I never missed a day of work. I drove myself home after treatment, reviewed the Sabbath School lesson, and taught my Sabbath School class the next morning. God's strength is made perfect in weakness.

A few weeks after my surgery, David and family left for Cyprus where he would be Assistant Treasurer for the Middle East Union.

All my life I had followed with intense interest the work of Christian missions in China. In the spring of 1986 we organized a 14-day tour of that country. We were enthralled with the country and its people. It was more, much more, than we had ever dreamed. We met with Christians and gave them the books they had requested.

In 1987 I retired. We were with our tour group in Jerusalem when I received the message that my brother, Julius, had died suddenly of a heart attack. His death diminished the pleasure of the rest of the trip as I mourned his passing. Another family funeral missed.

Wayne retired in March of 1988. His dream had been to spend a year going across the United States in a motor home just relaxing and exploring the country. Donovan and Robin Davis moved into our home while we fulfilled Wayne's dream. For two months we toured Indiana, Kentucky, Missouri, Kansas, Oklahoma, Texas, New Mexico, and Arizona. Then we parked our wheeled house in California for a few weeks to take a tour group to Australia, New Zealand and Fiji. That summer David and family came home on furlough from Cyprus. We six spent three weeks in our motor home touring the Northwest and Canada.

June 1989 found us enjoying an African Safari in Kenya. The thousands of animals could not be counted. The six boxes of books and Reviews we brought with us were left at the mission office in Nairobi. They were so grateful to have this literature for their churches and schools.

One night, Wayne noticed lumps on his neck. Scott arranged for him to see a head and neck specialist in Kettering the next day. A biopsy confirmed our fears. It was

CANCER treatable but non-curable lymphona. We had looked forward to retirement after 42 years of working for the church. Wayne had only been retired a little more than a year. Now this! He started taking Cytoxin immediately. After six months the cancer went into remission. Optimistically, we hoped that Wayne might have ten more years. His first cousin had survived the same malady for that length of time.

With the introduction of perestroika in 1990, it became easier for people to go Russia. Our good friends, Steven and Esther Tarangle, were interested in visiting there since Steven had relatives living in the Ukraine. Sixteen of us went, taking Bibles, literature, felts for teaching Bible stories, and books for the Seventh-day Adventist believers in Leningrad and Kiev. Many other Russians wanted our Bibles and literature. We had loaded our suitcases with Christian literature, but clearly we had not taken enough. Some of us left money with the churches to buy Bibles from Eastern Europe for the children. The USSR has since been evangelized by Adventists and other Protestant church groups. I would love to visit the same churches there today.

That summer the performance of the once-a-decade Oberammergau Passion Play was on, so we organized a German/Alpine Tour. It was fun to see these countries again and attend the famous Passion Play. However, I believe I enjoyed the Passion Play in the Black Hills of South Dakota more because it didn't last as long and it was in English.

The Berlin Wall came down that year, and we helped chip some of it away. During our ten-day extended European tour, we drove through East Germany seeing many sites of Luther's reformation movement. After visiting the Pergamum Museum, we visited the home towns of my father in Denmark, and my mother in west Germany.

Returning to Battle Creek, Wayne was immersed in numerous Bible studies, a Bible study group, and visitation. But he was tired. The lymphoma was taking its toll. We spent a month in Cancun that fall so he would be completely free and away from everything and everyone. He enjoyed that vacation more than any we ever had. He read books he'd never had time to read before. He returned re-charged and ready to take up new ventures.

Bekki urged us to move to Tillamook, Oregon, where Scott was a surgeon in the County Hospital. We purchased a steep, two-acre slope overlooking the Trask River Valley. Encircling the valley, wooded mountains reach for the sky. The view of God's handiwork is restful and inspirational.

The lymphoma returned. We drove the motor home down to Desert Hot Springs to live in while Wayne got treatments from Dr. Hilliard in Riverside. With a mild drug, the lymphoma went into remission in just a few months. We took another trip to China. But Wayne was too absorbed in making house plans to go on the 1992 summer tour of England, Scotland, Wales, and Ireland.

Our trip back to the Middle East in March 1993 began just as the painting needed to be done in our new house. Moreover, Wayne and I extended our trip a week to go to Germany and Denmark to visit relatives. (I had researched our family roots and discovered we had living relatives there). When we returned to Oregon, Bekki, Scott, and their friends had finished the painting. In May 1993, we moved into our new home.

During the summer, relatives from Denmark came to see us. We drove them down to southern California. It was then that Wayne noticed severe pains in his back. A CT scan showed that swollen lymph nodes were causing the pressure. The lymphoma was back. We went to California again to secure Dr. Hilliard's services. In November, during a two-week respite from treatment, we went to Berrien Springs for Thanksgiving—our last. During that time I was hospitalized with a bowel obstruction, and Wayne's lymphoma returned with a vengeance. As soon as we were physically able, we flew back to Oregon.

Then Wayne started heavy chemotherapy treatments in Portland. Every three weeks he spent three days in the hospital. During those times, they injected into his veins every kind of chemo used for lymphoma treatments. He then came home for 18 days, but on 10 of those days he took shots to raise his white count. Within days the lymphoma flared up again, and he was back in the hospital. It was a vicious three-week cycle. Wayne endured this pain and treatment from November until March I when his case was pronounced hopeless. Charity came to see Grandpa at Christmas, David in February, and Ronnie in March.

The first of April we set up a hospital bed in our bedroom. Ronda came for a week to care for her father. His condition deteriorated until he looked like an inmate released from a prisoner of war camp.

Wayne faced death filled with confidence in God and faith in the resurrection. But he wanted to live. He had been active in God's cause up until February of 1994. Even on our tours he witnessed to many. He got names and addresses of people all over the world to whom he mailed Christian literature.

During the last few months, Wayne's pain was constant. Sometimes it became so severe that only the heaviest of medication could give him relief. I kept praying for a miracle. God had given us so many during the course of our life. For over two months, he needed constant care. I stayed with Wayne night and day. Bekki and Scott were there to help care for his many necessities and his medications. My sister Martena took charge of the household. Sometimes friends took little Jonathan and Lindsay away from the morbid situation. It was hard on the little ones to watch Grandpa gradually fade away. They didn't want him to die because they loved him so much. Wayne's last 27 days were the worst of my life. I was torn between hoping he would be cured miraculously, or that he would die quickly to be relieved of his agony. On April 27, he fell asleep for the last time. That same day I developed a blood clot in my leg and had to be hospitalized.

Our children, most of their spouses, and grandchildren came for the funeral. Relatives and friends came long distances to pay their respects. Joe Warda and Pam flew in from Bakersfield, California; Wayne's 84-year-old brother Virgil and wife drove up from Sacramento; and nephew Jerry and wife came from Walla Walla. Other friends drove in from Washington. Elder Wilcox, ex-president of the Middle East Division, had part in the funeral service. He brought with him a huge wreath donated by people who had served in the Middle East. April 30, 1 was released in a wheel chair to attend the funeral service.

I grieved for my companion of almost 50 years. (He died seven weeks before our 50th wedding anniversary). We shared memories and experiences that few people have. We complimented each other's personalities—Wayne was the serious, businessperson, while I was the optimistic socialite and creative planner. We shared a beautiful life together. During Wayne's illness we talked, remembering we had never had harsh words or serious disagreements.

Then the period of grief recovery continued. Friends and relatives are such a blessing during times of distress. Over 400 cards or letters recounted the way Wayne had blessed their lives. Hundreds of phone calls helped me cope.

Wayne is buried on a hillside facing the setting sun. But when morning comes, he will arise, and we will be together again. I have accepted what I cannot change. God is love. I am grateful for what I had and look forward in faith to what I will have.

I continue to live in the house Wayne built in Tillamook. Sixteen surgeries, seven other hospitalizations, a heart attack, and a few other complications have not kept me from enjoying life. I continue to write, see friends, and work for the church and the school. I enjoy my friends, children, and grandchildren. My life is full; yet there is an empty spot that will always be void. I look forward to heaven when we will no longer remember our days on earth. I will revel in the joys of heaven and the thrill of spending eternity with Jesus, Wayne, my family, and friends.

APPENDIX
MISSIONARY CHILDREN

Sometimes missionary children have been unfairly labeled as "misfits" or "different." In some ways they are different. They grew up in a foreign environment, which was not their choice. They sacrificed along with their parents, whose devotion to God caused them to become missionaries. On the other hand, they have traveled, which has given them a broader vision of the world. They have learned to be adaptable, and appreciate and respect other cultures. A comparative study shows that missionary children are more apt to become professional and/or productive citizens than the average American Adventist child.

The following are the names of missionaries' children whom we knew in the Middle East. They are on my private list of "Who's Who."

Aldrich (Fischer) Sylvia: home cleaning business.
Anderson, Gregg: Intel marketing champion for Anthem Electronics.
Anderson (Sears), Joni: marketing manager for Reply Corporation.

Brauer, Bob: pastor, Maplewood Academy, Minnesota.
Brauer, Jim: pastor, president of Rocky Mountain Conference.
Brauer, Ronald: director of Desktop Publishing Dept. Review & Herald.
Brauer, Marvin: Physician, Woodstock, Virginia.

Chappell, Milton: Attorney, Washington, D.C. area.
Crider (Webb), Sharon: M.A., Southern Utah

Accounting.
Crider (Moser) Dawn: B.A., director of Kids Unlimited.
Crider, Carol: M.S.L., librarian.
Crider, Charles, Jr.: psychologist, supervisor in probation office, Battle Creek, Michigan.

Darnell, Leonard: VP of Systems House Limited.
Darnell, Allan: M.D., resident in family practice and international health, Loma Linda, California.
Darnell, Kenneth: musician, band leader, teaches computer technology and martial arts.
Dinning, Donavan: P.E. teacher. Construction work.
Dinning, Bob: business.

Faimann (Annouza), Isabella: B.S., business management and computer science.
Faimann, Waldemar: B.B.A., CPA, General Conference of SDAs auditor.
Fund, Larry : Toxicology testing at LLU.
Fund (Huston), Nancy: B.S. nursing. Wife of anesthesiologist.

Gemmell, (Wenberg) Sharlyn: occupational therapist, Modesto, California.
Gemmell, (Johnson) Jeannie: OB/GYN physician, Salt Lake City.
Gemmel, David: pastor, Las Vegas, Nevada.
Geraty, Larry: Ph.D., archaeologist, president of La Sierra University.
Geraty, Ron: M.D., Exec. VP, Medco Health Corporation, New Jersey.
Geraty, Kathleen: receptionist, Bellingen, NSW, Australia.
Green, Robert: printer, Hemet, California.
Green, Dan: engineer with Sun Microsystems.
Green, Marvin: computer network analyst, Okinawa.
Gott, Tom: Contractor. Manager GMS, Inc. Built over

200 Adventist churches and other institutions.
Gott, Patsy: M.A. Owns LLT video production company. Makes videos of church history.
Gott, Jacque: Legal secretary, Spokane, Washington

Jensen, Inga: Married, living in Denmark.
Jensen, Glenn: Business, living in Denmark.

Karmy, Bob: M.D., OB/Gyn in Virginia. Hobby is electronics.
Karmy, Jim: M.D., orthopedics, hand reconstruction, pilot.
Karmy, Paul: Owns business making concrete-mixers, stationary & moving concrete plants.
Karmy, Dick: Owns business making concrete-parking lots and other large jobs, Texas.
Keough (Geraty), Jillian: musician, educator, wife of Larry Geraty.
Keough, Graham: Electrical engineer. VP of CONSARC.
Keough (Osborn), Norma: M.A. Assistant pastor, Sligo Church, Maryland.
Keough, Alger: M.A., pastor, Hinsdale, Illinois.
Klein, Richard Arthur: Dentist. Carson City, Nevada.
Klein, Daniel: Real estate. Does evangelism.
Klein, Orville: Pulmonary Lab, LLU. Does evangelism.
Klein, Ronald: M.D., Springboro, OH. Church elder.
Krick, Arleen: B.S., nursing, supervisor in Portland Hospital, Oregon.
Kubrock, Charles: B.A., manages naval chemistry lab.
Kubrock (Natiuk), Martha: M.A., musician and organist.
Kubrock (DuBrosque), Esther: B.A., works in psychiatric hospital, Nashville, Tennessee.
Kubrock, Fred: Contractor, Walla Walla, Washington.
Kubrock (Torossian), Edith: Accomplished water color artist, Napa Valley, California.
Kubrock, Tim: B.S., teaches history, PUC Prep School.

Lesher, Eileen: B.S. nursing. Andrews University, Graduate Admissons.
Lesher (Keough), Martha: B.S. nursing. In-service hospital educator, Chicago, Illinois.

McCulloch (Schwandt), Susan: Likes being a mother/grandmother.
McCulloch, Michael: Executive VP of a real estate investment firm.
McGhee (Koelsch), Annette: interior decorator, real estate salesperson.
McGhee, Eddie: B.S., industrial arts, contractor, musician. Deceased.
McGhee, Fred: M.Div., missionary (Palau), activity director, WWC.
McGhee, Bill: M.D., chief of psychiatric residency, LLU.
McGhee, John: M.Div., minister, missionary (Russia).

Olson (Netteburg), Ronnalee: M.S.N. Andrews University nursing faculty.
Olson, David: M.Div., M.B.A., missionary (Middle East Union).
Olson (Gardner), Bekki: B.S.N., nurse, wife of surgeon in Oregon.
Olson, Ronda: B.S. Office manager Hunter-Douglas Window Dressings, Denver, Colorado.
Osborn, Dick: Ph.D. VP of education, Columbia Union Conference.
Osborn, Ken: M.B.A., missionary (Taiwan & Africa). Undertreasurer, Atlantic Union Conference.
Oster, Don: Business. Salesman for Mercedes Benz, San Jose, California.
Oster, Ellowyn: Nurse in OB/GYN office, Kalamazoo, Michigan.
Oster, Cyrus: Dentist in Santa Cruz, New Mexico.

Rasmussen, Connard, Jr: Medical technologist in charge of Lab, Vandon, Oregon.
Rasmussen, Maynard: Pediatrician, Sharps Hospital, San Diego, California.
Rasmussen, Ronald: Dentist, Sacramento, California.
Rasmussen, Jerry: Teaches science and math, Mt. Ellis Academy, Montana.
Russell, Janet: Medical records transcriptionist, LLU.
Russell, Malcolm: Ph.D., Professor of economics & history, Andrews University.
Russell (Wasdotsky), Ardis: computer instructor at LLU.
Russell, Glenn: M.Div., teaches Bible at Andrews Academy.

Skinner, Larry: B.S., physiotherapist, Portland, Oregon
Skinner, Ron: Manages Safeway stores warehouses, Oregon.
Skinner, Michael: R.N., manages wife's medical practice.

Ubbink, Ann: Para-legal specialist.
Ubbink, Richard (Buster): Computer specialist.

Vine (Fischer), Judy: Supervisor, conventional radiation therapy, LLU.
Vine, Terry: Deceased.

Wagner, Jeannie: Nurse, works for Red Cross.
Wagner, Billy: Chemist. Deceased.
Wagner (Chinnock), Ruth: B.S., married to anesthesiologist.
Waring, Bill: Dentist in Pennsylvania. Active in church work. Organist.
Waring, Randy: Anesthesiologist, Feather River Hospital, Paradise, California.
Waring (Crane), Rebecca: B.S. Missionary (Kenya). Secretary to Giraffe Society for Adventist youth.

Waring (Hammant), Beverly: Physical therapist, Las Cruces, New Mexico.
Williams, Chris: musician, music teacher.
Williams, Larry: Advertising executive.
Wilmot, Rick: M.Div., pastor, Napa, California, chaplain, St. Helena Hospital.
Wilmot, Steve: RPT, physical therapist, Sacramento, CA.
Wilson (Anderson), Shirley: Ed.D., Chair, Department of Nursing, Columbia Union College.
Wilson, Ted: Ph.D., missionary to Africa; president, Euro-Asian Division.

Zytkoske (Lilly), Cherry: Occupational therapist.

I have lost contact with some of the children like Ginerva, Brenda, Marla and Nelda Cowles; Charles and Teresa Jones; Mary Gammon; Bill and Bob Mondics; Jane and Judy Nolen; and Annette, Bobbie and Dale Mole. Therefore, I have no information on what they are doing today. It is also possible that I have omitted some names, for which I apologize.

My prayer for each child I have listed in my book is that their names will be inscribed in God's Book of Life.

Olsons on furlough. Going through England with too much luggage.

Olsons ready for a mission program.

Missionary Children • 267

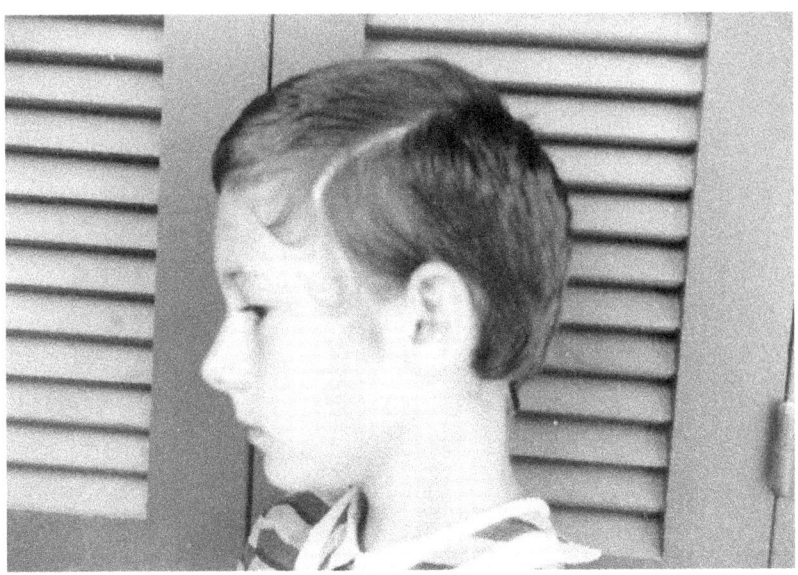

Two months after Ronnalee's skull fracture.
The scar has remained visible.

Week of Prayer, Beirut English Church School. Gordon Zytkoskee, Ien Osborn, Tom Gott, David Olson, Cherry Zytkoskee, Eileen Lesher, Arthur Keough, Midge, David Rice. Desks—back ros: Max Nolte, Norma Keough, Ronnalee, Mike McCulloch, Ardis Russell. Desks—second row: Dick Osborn, Alger Keough, Roger Nolte, Malcolm russell. Front: Ted Wilson and Martha Lesher.

Turtles Macey and Donia were found on this old Roman Imperial Post Road.

Macey and Ronnalee, Donia and David in Lebanon.

Missionary Children • 269

Wayne's first Medical Cadet Corps in dress uniform at the Middle East College campus.

Resting on top of Mt. Herman. Midge is in a fur coat trying to get warm—even though it's August in the Middle East.

Dar Es Salaam Hospital, Baghdad, Iraq.

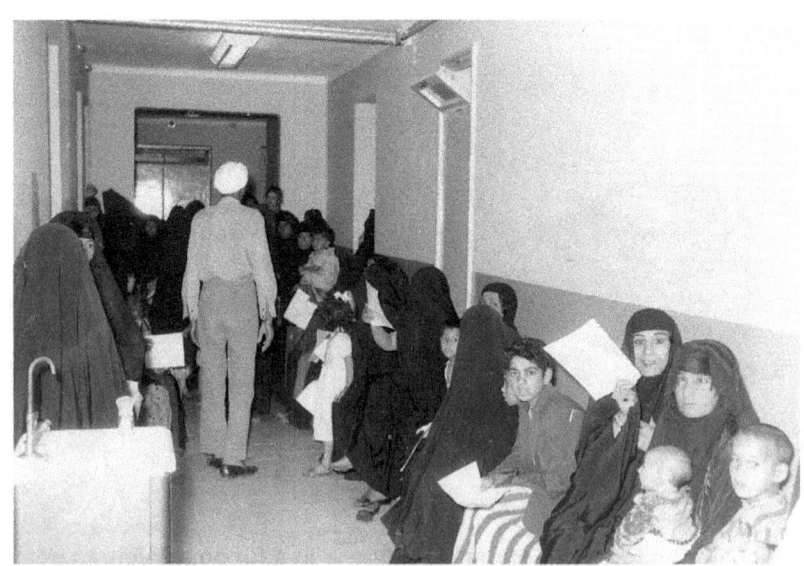

Patients in the free clinic of Dar Es Salaam.

Bringing in the "branch" for our Christmas tree. Dick, Bob, Paul, Jeannie, Ronnalee, Billy, Sylvia, Ann, David, buster, and Jim.

Midge and Wayne with the last graduating class of nurses, in the chapel of Dar Es Salaam Hospital.

The boys' "Dinky Car Road" in back of the school. Bill Waring, Gorm Hansen, Larry Fund, Tom Gott. Eddie McGhee sitting in front of David.

The compound "herd" (Beirut). Elsie anderson with Joanie, Ken Darnell, Bekki Olson, Greg Anderson, Leonard Darnell, and Marvin Brauer.

Missionary Children • 273

Midge, David, and Ronnalee look at Mt. Ararat from the Turkish-Iranian border.

Greet Orthodox boat used for baptizing on the Jordan river.

A street scene during the 1958 Iraq coup.

The day we brought baby Danny home. After 2½ months the new communist government made us leave Iraq and give up Danny. It was a sad, tearful, day.

Missionary Children • 275

Living in the Middle East made Bible stores come alive for Midge and Wayne: Swimming in lukewarm pools at Laodecia (above, right). Baptisms in the Jordan River (above, left). But their greatest thrill was introducing Christ to the people.

TEACH Services, Inc.
PUBLISHING

We invite you to view the complete
selection of titles we publish at:
www.TEACHServices.com

We encourage you to write us
with your thoughts about this,
or any other book we publish at:
info@TEACHServices.com

TEACH Services' titles may be purchased in
bulk quantities for educational, fund-raising,
business, or promotional use.
bulksales@TEACHServices.com

Finally, if you are interested in seeing
your own book in print, please contact us at:
publishing@TEACHServices.com
We are happy to review your manuscript at no charge.

www.ingramcontent.com/pod-product-compliance
Lightning Source LLC
Chambersburg PA
CBHW070543160426
43199CB00014B/2345